Wm L Banks
1 JOHN 3:22

DAILY MANNA II

by

William L. Banks

INFINITY
PUBLISHING

Copyright © 2011 by William L. Banks

ISBN 0-7414-6404-7

Printed in the United States of America

Published January 2011

INFINITY PUBLISHING
1094 New DeHaven Street, Suite 100
West Conshohocken, PA 19428-2713
Toll-free (877) BUY BOOK
Local Phone (610) 941-9999
Fax (610) 941-9959
Info@buybooksontheweb.com
www.buybooksontheweb.com

ACKNOWLEDGMENTS

I am grateful to the following who have granted permission for the privilege of including selections in this volume II of *Daily Manna:*

Abingdon Press, Nashville, TN 37202, for the poem *"The Secret"* by Ralph S. Cushman. Copyright 1932. All rights reserved. Used by permission.

Manna Music, Inc., Pacific City, OR 97135, for the hymn *"Through It All"* by Andraė Crouch. Copyright 1971. All rights reserved. Used by permission.

SpiritQuest Music, Nashville, TN 37203 for the hymn *"The Savior Is Waiting."* by Ralph Carmichael. Copyright assigned 1987. All rights reserved. Used by permission.

Unichappell Music, Inc. Los Angeles, CA 90025 for the hymn *"Lead Me, Guide Me"* by Doris M. Akers. Copyright 1953. All rights reserved. Used by permission.

Word, Inc. Irving, TX 75039 for the hymn *At the End of the Road* by A. H. Ackley. Copyright 1930. All rights reserved. Used by permission.

Word Music, Inc. Nashville, TN 37212 for the hymn *If Jesus Goes with Me* by C. Austin Miles. Copyright renewed 1991. All rights reserved. Used by permission.

THE SECRET – Ralph S. Cushman

I met God in the morning
When my day was at its best,
And His Presence came like sunrise,
Like a glory in my breast.

All day long the Presence lingered,
All day long He stayed with me,
And we sailed with perfect calmness
O'er a very troubled sea.

Other ships were blown and battered,
Other ships were sore distressed,
But the winds that seemed to drive them
Brought to me a peace and rest.

Then I thought of other mornings,
With a keen remorse of mind,
When I too had loosed the moorings,
With the Presence left behind.

So, I think I know the secret,
Learned from many a troubled way:
You must seek Him in the morning
If you want Him through the day!

January 1

Is anything too hard for the LORD? (Genesis 18:14)

Sarah Listened: Genesis 18:10. At the time Abraham was 99 years old and Sarah about 89. She listened in on the conversation and heard that she was to give birth to a child in her old age. **Sarah Laughed**: Genesis 18:12. It was easy to laugh, for at her age who would expect her to have a child? Earlier, Abraham himself had laughed (Genesis 17:17), but there is no record he was reproved. Evidently his heart was right with God and he did not laugh in disbelief.

God shall laugh at the wicked (Psalms 2:4, 37:13, 59:8). A crowd laughed Christ to scorn when He told them that Jairus' daughter was not dead, but sleeping (Matthew 9:24). Laughter can get you into trouble. I gave a loud "horse-laugh" in class at Widener Elementary School and the teacher, Mr. Kessler, impeached me (I was the class vice-president), kept me after school, made me write on the board, "I will not disturb the class again" one hundred times, and gave me a series of long divisions to do.

Sarah Lied: Genesis 18:15. She denied she laughed, but God knows what goes on in our hearts, and there is nothing hid from Him. Under no circumstances is a Christian justified in telling a lie. But because of fear we often do what **we** think is right under the circumstances. Ethical problems (we call them "situational ethics" today) are never solved by that lack of faith we demonstrate when we take matters in our own hands and attempt to solve our troubles.

This is the only contact that is of a personal nature that Sarah had with God. The question "Is anything too hard for the LORD?" was actually a reproof of Sarah. However, it seems from this point on her faith was called out and strengthened (Hebrews 11:11; I Peter 3:6). May we remember this day that we can do all things through Christ who strengthens us (Philippians 4:13). There is no problem He cannot solve.

Abraham called the name of the place, The-LORD-Will-Provide. (Genesis 22:14)

What a wonderful God we serve! He provided a covering for Adam and Eve; an ark for Noah; a ram for Abraham; a bride for Isaac; a new name for Jacob; and a palace instead of a prison for Joseph. Why shouldn't we be faithful to such a Lord? He provided a change for Job; a way through the sea for Moses and Israel; a reason for Miriam to dance for joy; and manna in the wilderness for the Israelites.

He provided for Joshua the crumbling walls of Jericho, and deliverance for Rahab. He gave Deborah a song to sing; and offered Gideon a sign. He renewed strength for Samson; blessed Ruth with a kinsman-redeemer, and Hannah with a son. Five smooth stones were given to David; wisdom to Solomon; a chariot to Elijah and a mantle for Elisha. He provided oil for the widow; a great fish to save Jonah; a vision of divine glory for Isaiah; fifteen more years of life for Hezekiah; rescue from a dungeon for Jeremiah; and a call into the prophetic ministry for Amos.

He provided cooling for the three Hebrew boys and lockjaw for the hungry lions in the den with Daniel; locusts and honey for John the Baptist; and an interview by night for Nicodemus. Our God provided forgiveness for an adulteress; life to the daughter of Jairus; and bread and fish for the hungry multitudes.

He gave salvation to a penitent robber; to Thomas he gave another opportunity; he enlightened the hearts of the disciples from Emmaus. He opened the heavens for Stephen; had mercy on Paul; gave encouragement to Timothy; healing for Epaphroditus; emancipation for Onesimus, and a revelation to John the Apostle. What a wonderful Provider! Rest assured this day that—having been cleansed in the blood of Jesus Christ—He will supply your needs too—just when you need Him most.

And when I see the blood, I will pass over you. (Exodus 12:13)

Men scoff at judgment preaching. It is too negative they say. They complain that it creates guilt complexes which are to be avoided at all cost. Hell is sneered at while maudlin sentimentalists accent God's love and are silent about His holiness. However, it is apparent that on the hearts of all humanity are written the words, "The wages of sin is death."

Everyone has a conscience. Although the conscience is *not* an infallible guide, somehow even the dullest and darkest conscience realizes that it is a terrible thing to fall into the hands of an angry God. Over the clamor of protests there is heard the still small voice reminding us there is a judgment to face after death.

Perhaps one of the most striking illustrations of divine judgment is the series of plagues which befell the Egyptians. It was Jehovah's purpose to demonstrate that the gods of the heathen were nothing, just powerless idols. Each plague was a knockout punch thrown by God and connecting to the jaw of an Egyptian god or goddess, all of whom were unable to protect their worshippers.

Recall that in the tenth plague Moses warned Pharaoh that all the firstborn in the land would die. The Israelites were told to kill a lamb without blemish and smear its blood on the side posts and the upper doorposts of their houses. When the destroyer angel came over and saw the blood, he would pass over them.

The lamb used by the Jews was a type (foreshadowing, representation) of Jesus Christ. His blood is the only thing that delivers us from the penalty, power and presence of sin. This is God's promise: to spare, protect, preserve, and pass over. Do you believe Him? God's unspeakable, inexpressible Gift is Jesus Christ who was judged at Calvary. He is God's Gift to you. Have you received Him? If you have, rest today in the assurance there is therefore now no condemnation!

Now Amalek came and fought with Israel in Rephidim.
(Exodus 17:8)

Such is the nature of the world, the quality of its character, the trend of the times, and the reality of life that no one can truthfully say he or she has no enemies. At various times enemies combine to cause different kinds of warfare. For example, the worst enemy some of us have is ourselves. Some of us fight ourselves. Indeed, we have found the enemy and he (or she) "is us."

There are also secret enemies, hypocrites who grin in our face but curse us when our back is turned. In our presence they wish us well; in our absence they hope we will drop dead. Deceived by the Devil they are automatically the enemies of those genuinely washed in the blood of Christ.

Our attention is drawn to Amalek who fought against Israel in Rephidim. The Amalekites, descendants of Amalek, the grandson of Esau (Genesis 36:12), were a vicious people, fierce, rapacious, and wicked. When the Jews were coming out of Egypt the Amalekites struck at those feeble stragglers in the rear; in a cowardly assault they fell upon the "faint and weary" that were behind (Deuteronomy 25:17-19).

They plundered but their motives went beyond mere looting. Their attack motive was beyond any territorial disputes. The text states that Amalek did not fear God. In their hearts was a hatred for God's people, a desire to destroy Israel. It is still true today; some people hate Christians although we have done them no evil personally. Because we seek to live a Christian life and serve the Lord we find ourselves victims of a godless hatred and hostility.

Here is a picture of the world-system, ever seeking to hinder believers from earthly blessings and holy living. Amalek represents the world's hatred of Christ, and hating Him the world hates us. Though we face tribulation in the world, rejoice; be of good cheer, for we serve Him who has overcome the world.

January 5

So Joshua defeated Amalek and his people with the edge of the sword. (Exodus 17:13)

Understand today that the believer *can* be victorious. But consider this very strong statement concerning the Amalekites that may unsettle you. Deuteronomy 25:19, "Therefore it shall be, when the Lord your God is giving you rest from your enemies all around, in the land which the Lord your God is giving you to possess as an inheritance, that you will blot out the remembrance of Amalek from under heaven. You shall not forget."

How harsh this sounds! However, we learn that God cannot and will not tolerate such active evil as that perpetrated by the Amalekites against the Israelites. In other words, sooner or later, the Devil will get his due.

As Joshua defeated, discomfited, "discombobulated," or wiped out the Amalekites so all the enemies of God shall be destroyed. As God provided for Israel, so shall He also take care of us, His Church which is the body of Christ. Don't be discouraged by what you see happening. For the outcome of the battle is not always determined by the sword. Let the wicked sue, plot, curse, threaten, ostracize, close their fists, brandish knives, throw stones and shoot guns! There is a power that comes from on high.

Lift up your hands in holy prayer, support one another in prayer, and depend upon prayer. Pray for each other. That's the secret of victory. For the Lord Jesus shed His blood on the cruel cross of Calvary in order that we who are cleansed by that blood might enter boldly into the presence of God the Father. God answers prayers and in the midst of conflict there is no greater cooperation than that of prayer warriors who lift up holy hands to a holy God.

January 6

And you shall make holy garments for Aaron your brother, for glory and for beauty. (Exodus 28:2)

Why such fuss about the clothing of the high priest? Did it really matter what he wore when ministering? After all, it is said that what is in the heart is what counts, not what is on our backs. Why should not Aaron wear whatever he pleased, whatever was convenient, in style, fashionable, and practical or even comfortable—you know, "Come as you are!"

God was very particular about what was worn by those who served Him. He selected each article of clothing to be worn by the high priest. Even those who made the garments were filled with Holy Spirit wisdom and skill, for each article of clothing pointed to some truth about the Lord Jesus Christ who is our High Priest.

It is suggested that our clothing glorify God when we come before Him in worship. Interestingly, while much of the heathen world pranced naked around their gods and goddesses, or half-naked in rituals that were obscene, and full of gross sensuality, the priests of Israel were clothed. They obeyed God's demand for worship performed in modesty and with decency.

Fitness for the priesthood was not inherent in Aaron. The special clothes he wore indicated this. His clothing showed he was separated from the common people, for none of the others in that population wore those clothes. He was separated unto Jehovah. This is sanctification. The clothes represented and typified those qualities which resided in the true High Priest, Jesus Christ. Only thus could Aaron minister to Jehovah in the priest's office.

By wearing such garments Aaron indicated that he could not stand before Jehovah in his own merit. But that he had to be clothed as God desired. Today we are not under such a law system. We are to let the Christ living in us be seen on the outside. Rejoice today that you are clothed in the righteousness of the Lord Jesus Christ.

. . . gifted artisans, whom I have filled with the spirit of wisdom . . . may make Aaron's garments, to consecrate him, that he may minister to Me as priest. (Exodus 28:3)

As Aaron was the high priest in Moses' day, Christ is our High Priest today. We Christians are a royal priesthood (1 Peter 2:9); we do not have to wear any special clothing as a sign of consecration. The blood shed at Calvary opened the door, split the veil of the temple so that we may enter boldly into the holy of holies, unto the throne of grace. And we can come just as we are at any time! Washed and cleansed by the blood of the Lamb, we stand before the presence of a Holy God, not in our own merit, but in the name of Jesus Christ, dressed in His righteousness alone.

We have a High Priest superior to Aaron and to all those high priests who came and *died*, who served and *died,* who ministered and *died,* and mediated and *died.* Our High Priest offered Himself not for His sins, for He had none, yet He sacrificed Himself for you and for me. What Aaron performed in type or shadow we are to do in reality. We are to show forth the only Apostle and High Priest, Jesus Christ.

We are to consider Christ, put our minds on Christ, preach Christ, glorify Christ, teach Christ, and show forth the beauty of Him who called us out of darkness into His marvelous light. God does not want our outward appearance to make a lie out of what we really are on the inside.

Kenneth Wuest said, "Don't let the modernism of your appearance make a lie out of the fundamentalism of your beliefs." To masquerade is abhorrent to God. What we say we believe should be supported by what we wear; what we wear should lend dignity to what we believe. I thank God my robe is white. Salvation is my helmet. Gospel shoes are on my feet. The belt of truth is around my waist. Holiness fits me well. The Holy Spirit is my Tailor. Garments of praise hang in my closet. I look good!

January 8

I am the LORD your God, who brought you out of the land of Egypt, that you should not be their slaves; I have broken the bands of your yoke and made you walk upright. (Leviticus 26:13)

True freedom is to become the slave of righteousness. When Christ broke the yoke He made us walk erect, as free people. True freedom is the ability to please the Lord. Self-will looks like liberty, but in reality is slavery. True freedom does not mean the conscience is shut up. One who attempts to silence the conscience runs the risk of enslavement to evil impulses and to the tyranny of Satan.

Sin once committed desires to be committed again. The drunk keeps on drinking; the homosexual continues his life-style; the adulterer goes back again; the liar tells another lie. And so it goes. But true freedom recognizes that sin is a liar, and that sin deceives. Sin makes you think you have gotten away with murder. Even when caught and punished, sin makes some men feel *they* are the ones victimized.

When cut and scarred, sin tries to hide the disfigurement and covers up the mirror of reality. Sin tells you that you have hurt nobody but yourself. Then when you have covered up your dirt, sin works on your guilt and there is no controlling of guilt feelings. And so you are not free.

Redemption from Egypt gives a personal independence and individuality of character no one can buy. True freedom means you can hold your head high. True freedom means you are not a slave to circumstances. Christians are not drift-wood pushed along by the current; we are not tumbleweeds blown about by the wind. God's redemption opens the eyes of the blind. His forgiveness removes guilt.

When He redeems us He frees us from sin's dominion, from serving self, from deception, from the control of evil men, and from slavery to circumstances. The God we serve wants us to be truly free. This is why He brought us out; this is why He is still bringing us in.

January 9

"Stretch out the spear that is in your hand toward Ai, for I will give it into your hand." And Joshua stretched out the spear that was in his hand toward the city. (Joshua 8:18)

God uses a variety of weapons and instruments in the battle against wickedness. Today the only offensive weapon Christians have is the Bible, the sword of the Spirit, and as good soldiers of Christ we must study the Word in order to effectively wield the sword. Surely the Bible is no less effective than the spear in Joshua's hand, the rod in Moses' hand, the jawbone in Samson's hand, the fire at Elijah's command, the slingshot and stone in David's hand, or the trumpet and shout of the priests and people marching around the walls of Jericho.

Recognize that God the Father is our General, and Jesus Christ the Captain of our salvation. He ordains our circumstances, places troops, supplies the whole armor, gives orders, plans strategy, and picks the weapons He wants us to use. In other words, beware going into battle with the same weapons and strategy with which you fought last month or yesterday.

Let God decide that for you. Stay open. Let Him put the armor on you. Let Him decide the strategy; let Him fight the battle. And if He puts a rod, or a spear, or a slingshot, or a jawbone or a Bible in your hands—use it! See each event in your life as a new opportunity to capture a city for Christ, an opportunity to spread light in darkness and for souls to be saved; to be salty salt to slow up corruption. See each event as a campaign to edify saints; to spread joys; to manifest peace; to demonstrate love, and to see God give you the victory. You will discover that for every new challenge, there is new power—Holy Spirit power. Seek God's face through Jesus Christ, and He will lead you to victory today.

January 10

Wherever you go, I will go . . . Your people shall be my people, and your God, my God. (Ruth 1:16-17)

When Naomi heard that famine in Judah had ended, she decided to return to Bethlehem. While traveling back home Naomi sought to release her daughters-in-law from any obligation. She acknowledged the Lord's hand in their lives, and their kind treatment of her. It is evident that these ladies—mother and daughters-in-law—got along well.

Orpah and Ruth protested and said, "Surely we will return with you to your people." However, Naomi persisted in advising them not to continue with her. After all, their husbands had died, and she had no more sons to give them. After more weeping, Orpah kissed Naomi and left. However, Ruth clung to her. Despite Naomi's plea to Ruth to leave, Ruth would not. We have here a beautiful "expression of love, loyalty and devotion."

There was nothing in Moab for Ruth but a graveyard. So she turned to the God of Israel for help, and threw in her lot with her mother-in-law, Naomi. She wanted the same destination, dwelling place, people, God, and burial place. What a step of faith by a Gentile from a pagan nation! What important decisions in your life did you give to the Lord? Did you include moving to where you now live; going to school; your job; the person you married; the church you joined? What kind of a God would anyone have who decided to follow your God? What would you do if the Lord Jesus Christ asked you to emphasize Christ-centeredness in all that you do? What impact would you have on a godless, self-centered, me-first society? Today may your heart-song be:

If Jesus goes with me, I'll go anywhere!
'Tis heaven to me, Where'er I may be, If He is there!
I count it a privilege here His cross to bear;
If Jesus goes with me, I'll go anywhere!
(C. Austin Miles)

January 11

And she said, "Let your maidservant find favor in your sight." So the woman went her way and ate, and her face was no longer sad. (1 Samuel 1:18)

Hannah's Situation. Hannah had to share her husband Elkanah with his second wife, Penninah, who hated Hannah. She repeatedly poked fun at Hannah because she had no children, and the constant pressure caused Hannah to cry, tremble, grieve and stop eating.

Hope at Shiloh. The tabernacle was still stationed at Shiloh, and Elkanah and his family went there to worship the LORD of Hosts. While there Hannah prayed and poured out her soul before the LORD. Her hope was centered upon having a baby boy; the cry of her soul was for this child. And yet her vow was, "If You give him to me I will give him back to You." Whoever heard of asking the Giver for a gift for the Giver? But so it was that Hannah expressed her hope at Shiloh.

Heaven's Solution. So fervent was Hannah's prayer, so totally involved was she, that when the priest Eli saw her lips moving, but heard no sound, he thought she was but one of the women who hung around certain religious centers. "Go away and sleep off your drunk!" he commanded. But Hannah protested. She was no liquor store lush, but someone on speaking terms with the Lord of life. When Eli realized this he spoke comforting words to her, and caused her to be assured God would answer her prayer.

Yea, heaven is a solution for every sorrowful sad situation. We are fortunate today because we don't need to travel to Shiloh to find God in order to talk with Him. When Christ died on Calvary the veil of the Temple was split from top to bottom, making it possible for us to enter into the very presence of God. We have the assurance now that when we pray, Christ in heaven is working on a solution for our every problem.

January 12

Samuel took a stone . . . called its name Ebenezer, saying, "Thus far the LORD has helped us." (1 Samuel 7:12)

Stone of Declaration: After the men of Israel pursued the Philistines and killed them, Samuel took a stone and set it between Mizpah and Shen. He named it Ebenezer which means literally, "The stone of the help," for here was the place God stepped in and set Israel free from her enemy. This memorial was a visible reminder of God's redeeming grace, mercy and power.

We learn that the real victories in life are not won with secret caucuses or changed locks and safe combinations, the deliberations of City Council, new laws, court decrees, cattle prods, sticks, stones, lies, fists, dirty tricks, anonymous notes and phone calls. Nor with guns, tanks and bombs! For Samuel it was not a military battle, but a spiritual battle.

Humbling of the enemy takes place on another plane of life, on an invisible level. God would remind Christians that we wrestle not against flesh and blood. The battle is not really ours but the Lord's. The real victories of life belong not to us, but to our God. He is the Victor; He is the Hero of the Hour, the Man of War (Exodus 15:3).

My, how easily we forget! How quickly it flees from our minds how we got over in His strength. Through the storm. In the night. Up the mountain. Down in the valley. In the waste howling wilderness. Through grief because of the death of a loved one. We forget the slavery we suffered in Egypt before the Lord redeemed us.

And now the Spirit cries out, "Look! There's your stone of help. There's your Redeemer!" And we realize that the God in Christ who helped us hitherto, up to this time, is still our God, who shall preserve our going out and our coming in from henceforth (Psalm 121:8).

January 13

Samuel took a stone . . . called its name Ebenezer, saying, "Thus far the LORD has helped us." (1 Samuel 7:12)

Source of Their Defeat: Israel's situation was bad. The Philistines had captured the ark of God and murdered Eli's two wicked sons, Hophni and Phinehas. However, in time the ark of the Lord became too hot for the Philistines to handle, for God smote them with boils. After several months they returned the ark to the Israelites, and this joyous occasion became a rallying point for revival. The ark remained at Kirjath Jearim, neglected for some twenty years. And during that time the Philistines continued to vex, oppress and harass the Jews; and Israel lived miserably.

With religious slogans printed on their togas; with religious medallions hung around their necks; with religious tale-stickers pinned on their donkeys; bumper stickers stuck on their chariots; and with religious buttons and badges proclaiming: "The Ark Is Ours," and "Smile—Jehovah Is Just," obviously the ark was no more than a good luck charm. They were satisfied with the outward symbol of the presence of God, but there was no inner heart belief.

Failure to honor the true and living God made them physically incapable of withstanding the onslaught of the Philistines. Christians experience defeat for the same reasons that Israel suffered defeat. We depend too much upon externalities and formalities. All too often self is enthroned instead of surrendered to Jesus Christ. Where self reigns the flesh rules; flesh is no match against the principalities, powers, rulers of the darkness of this world, and against spiritual wickedness in high places. Sing this hymn this day:

Here I raise mine Ebenezer; Hither by Thy help I'm come; And I hope, by Thy good pleasure, Safely to arrive at home. Jesus sought me when a stranger, Wand'ring from the fold of God; He, to rescue me from danger, Interposed His precious blood. (Robert Robinson)

January 14

Thus far the Lord has helped us. (1 Samuel 7:12)

Sign of Their Deliverance: Under the leadership of Samuel reformation began to take place. The Jews sought with all their heart to return to the LORD Jehovah. However, the Devil's crowd never likes to see God's people get down to business with and for the LORD. So naturally Satan was agitated and when he is moved he likes to stir up other folks. When the Philistines heard about the revival, they gathered their troops together to fight against the Israelites.

The frightened Israelites then sought Samuel to pray for them. Power in prayer depends upon the life we live. If we are more interested in athletics than in spiritual exercise, we will miss out on the main event. If we love TV more than we love the church, our cry to the Lord in an emergency just may be on the wrong channel, if plugged in at all.

Samuel then took a suckling lamb, presented it for a whole burnt offering to the LORD, and then cried to the LORD for Israel. God answered him. Jehovah stepped in and thundered with a great thunder against the Philistines, throwing them into utter confusion and chaos. Led by the Lord, "the men of Israel went out of Mizpah and pursued the Philistines, and drove them back as far as below Beth Car." Surely God used Samuel to help Israel.

For the rest of Samuel's days the Philistines no longer gave the Jews the invasion jitters. Peace, independence, and freedom were enjoyed for some twenty years more— deliverance gained not by the strength of Israel's arms, not by the prowess of her soldiers, not by the swiftness of any chariots and horses, but by the mighty voice of the God who thunders! May there be no worldly wax in our ears today that would prevent us from hearing the thundering voice of our God, and enjoying divine deliverance.

January 15

Therefore all the elders of Israel came to the king at Hebron, and King David made a covenant with them at Hebron before the LORD. And they anointed David king over Israel. (2 Samuel 5:3)

Three reasons for making David king over all Israel are given: (1) <u>Kinsmen to a King.</u> "Behold, we are your bone and your flesh," declared the representatives of the tribes. This was true, for all the tribes of Israel were descendants of Jacob (Genesis 49:28). (2) <u>Leadership by a Leader.</u> "You were the one who led Israel out and in." David had been their actual leader even when Saul was king (1 Samuel 18:5). (3) <u>Anointed by the Almighty</u>. They knew that the LORD had chosen, called and anointed David.

Is the Lord Jesus King in our lives for the same reasons? Are we His bone and His flesh? Yes. He became one of us, born of a woman, found in fashion as a man, made in the likeness of men, partaker of flesh and blood. He is not ashamed to own us as brothers and sisters (Hebrews 2:11). We are family.

Is He King in our lives because He is our Leader? Yes. We triumph in Christ because He always leads us to victory (2 Corinthians 2:14). He leads us out of Egypt and brings us into the Promised Land. He is our File Leader (*archegos*) who takes the lead and thus affords an example. He is our predecessor, the Author and Captain, and chief leader of our Salvation. (Hebrews 2:10; 12:2).

Can we sing, *Savior, like a Shepherd lead us, Much we need Thy tender care; In Thy pleasant pastures feed us, For our use Thy folds prepare*? (Dorothy A. Thrupp). Can we say He is King in our lives because He is the Apostle of God, the anointed One, Messiah, and the Called, the Sent-One? Yes. Indeed He was sent by the Father, who so loved the world. I tell you Jesus Christ in every way qualifies to be our King, the Blessed King of kings.

"LORD, I pray, open his eyes that he may see." Then the LORD opened the eyes of the young man, and he saw. And behold, the mountain was full of horses and chariots of fire all around Elisha. (2 Kings 6:17)

The God of the Bible specializes in opening blind eyes. He opened Balaam's eyes and he saw the Angel of the LORD standing in the way with sword in hand. Cast out by Sarah, Hagar and Ishmael wandered in the wilderness; then, water gone, prepared to die. But the Angel of the LORD heard her cry, spoke to her and opened her eyes to see a well of water.

When the religious rulers sought to disparage Christ for giving sight to the man born blind, the man said, "Whether He is a sinner or not, I know not; one thing I know, that, whereas I was blind, now I see." The two disciples from Emmaus talked with a stranger they invited into their home. He opened their eyes and they recognized he was the resurrected Savior.

Lord, open our eyes. Help us to see beyond the jealousy that put Joseph in a pit; beyond the sea in front and enemy soldiers in back; beyond the giants in the land, the flames of a fiery furnace, the den of roaring lions, or the mud in the dungeon. Help us to see beyond the betrayal of associates, the denial of friends, the waves of the stormy sea, the circumstances of poverty, the defects of birth, the cruelties of men, and the failures of the past!

Open our eyes that we may see through faith in the shed blood of Christ a rainbow in the sky, guardian angels watching over us, the victory which is already ours, a new robe, a body of glory, a crown of joy, a prepared place, a mansion in the heavens, privileges as Your children, our names written down in the Lamb's book of life! May we see and use for His glory the power given to us by our resurrected Savior. *Come, Holy Spirit, come; Let Thy bright beams arise; Dispel the sorrow from our minds, The darkness from our eyes.* (J. Hart)

January 17

For the eyes of the Lord run to and fro throughout the whole earth, to show Himself strong on behalf of those whose heart is loyal to Him. (2 Chronicles 16:9)

During Thanksgiving Day services we were scheduled to sing, "Count Your Blessings". When I turned to that hymn I was shocked to discover that someone had torn out several pages, including the chorus of that hymn. The thought occurred: This hymnal is no longer at peace, for it is no longer able to do fully what it was manufactured to do, namely, to help the worshiper sing all of the words of all of the hymns listed in the index. Evidently someone not at peace with himself could not help but act belligerently toward a poor, little old helpless red hymnbook. In other words, a perfect hymnal was rendered imperfect; a complete hymnal was made incomplete.

All this came to mind because the word rendered "loyal" means complete, perfect, and comes from a Hebrew word whose root is *shalom* or peace, a concept which involves wholeness, completeness, integration, and safety and therefore, peace. A complete person is one at peace with God, one whose heart is loyal or perfect with the Lord, a person of whom it is said, "His heart is completely God's."

The Holy Spirit looks for folks whose hearts are sincere, single minded, set on pleasing the Lord Jesus. The eyes of God are looking for people who have eyes only for the Lord. He searches for hearts that are loyal, blameless, wholly devoted to Him, completely His. His purpose is not to show us off to demonstrate what *we* can do, but His eyes look everywhere for opportunities to show Himself as the helper of all who are devoted to Him through faith in the shed blood of Jesus Christ. He desires to show *His* great power in helping us. The God we serve wants the world to see how He takes care of His own. Today, let Him show Himself strong in your behalf through a heart made perfect, loyal and complete in Jesus Christ.

January 18

For the eyes of the LORD run to and fro throughout the whole earth, to show Himself strong on behalf of those whose heart is loyal to Him. (2 Chronicles 16:9)

Does God have eyes? Yes, for Noah found grace in His eyes. Moses said, "The eyes of the LORD your God are always upon it [the Promised Land]." We read that, "David did that which was right in the eyes of the LORD." Jehoram wrought that which was evil in the eyes of the Lord. Job said, "For His eyes are on the ways of man, and He sees all his steps . . . He does not withdraw His eyes from the righteous."

The psalmist said, "His eyes behold the nations." Solomon stated, "The eyes of the LORD are in every place, beholding the evil and the good . . . the eyes of the LORD preserve knowledge" (Proverbs 15:3, 22:12). Jehovah spoke to the religious hypocrites through Isaiah: "And when you spread forth your hands I will hide my eyes from you . . . put away the evil of your doings from before my eyes." Jeremiah said, "For your eyes are open upon all the ways of the sons of men, to give everyone according to his ways."

Amos wrote "Behold, the eyes of the Lord God are upon the sinful kingdom." Habakkuk said, "You are of purer eyes than to behold evil, and cannot look on wickedness." Zechariah preached, "The eyes of the LORD run to and fro through the whole earth." Paul preached, "And the times of this ignorance God winked at (overlooked), but now commands all men everywhere to repent" (Acts 17:30). And Simon Peter said, "For the eyes of the Lord are on the righteous" (1 Peter 3:12; Psalm 34:15).

Yes, God has eyes! Thus the symbolism of the seven eyes of the Lamb (Revelation 5:6) is that of omniscience, absolute knowledge and awareness of all things, and consequently a providential care that knows no bounds. Rest assured today that because your heart is surrendered to the Lord Jesus, He will guide you with His eye (Psalm 32:8).

January 19

The king granted him all his request, according to the hand of the LORD his God upon him . . . according to the good hand of his God upon him. (Ezra 7:6, 9)

Ezra returned to Jerusalem to re-establish the proper worship of Jehovah there. He was allowed to appoint magistrates, to offer sacrifices, to teach the word of God, and to beautify the temple. We learn that in order to do restoration work, God's good hand must be upon the believer. That God's hand *is* good is amply taught in the Bible. With a long outstretched hand the Lord smote the Egyptians in judgment, and with a mighty hand He delivered the Israelites from the land of Pharaoh. Job said that in God's "hand is the life of every living thing, and the breath of all mankind" (Job 12:10).

The psalmist said the earth and the heavens are the works of God's hands: "Your hands have made me and fashioned me," and though a good man fall, he shall not be utterly cast down, for the Lord upholds him with His hand (Psalms 8:6; 102:25; 119:73; 37:24). With His healing hands the Lord Jesus gave sight to the blind, cleansed lepers, and straightened out crooked limbs. And thank God, all who believe in the shed blood of Christ are in the Father's hands, and no one is able to snatch or pluck them out of His hands.

Now when God's hand is upon you, people should be able to see it. The phrase means divine favor. In Ezra's case, the Lord touched the heart of king Artaxerxes of Babylon and made him favorably disposed toward the Jews. We see that God's good hand was upon Ezra, and with the official sanction of the king, the 900-mile trip that took four months was accomplished and Ezra's efforts were crowned with success. Be encouraged today. With God's good hand upon you, there can be no failure.

January 20

For Ezra had prepared his heart to seek the Law of the LORD, and to do it, and to teach statutes and ordinances in Israel. (Ezra 7:10)

In order to do restoration work we must set our hearts to study God's word. Restoration work requires dedication to the Bible. Without the study of God's Word, without sharing that Word with others, we will not experience God's good hand in blessing. Restoration work requires preparation. Ezra was a man who believed in laying a foundation first before stepping out.

His heart was prepared: It was prepared to seek God's law, prepared to do what God's law demanded, and prepared to teach Israel the will of God as that will was made known in statutes and ordinances. Such preparation speaks of a commitment that cannot help but produce spiritual success.

There is a supernatural quality about the Bible. When studied it strengthens us. When exalted, God is pleased. When preached souls are saved. When taught saints are edified. When heralded the world is convicted. When wielded as a sword spirits are separated from souls; swung as a hammer, hypocrisy is smashed; held high it is a light shining on the pathway of life; and a fire that burns away sin.

Without the Word of God no restoration work can be done successfully. We contend that like Ezra, Christians who desire to do a restoration work for the Lord must prepare their hearts to study and to teach God's word. We need to be restored in the image of God through faith. Backsliders must be restored to the church fellowship.

The Christ we preach is able to do this. He is God the Restorer, the Regenerator, the Reclaimer, the Recreator, the Redeemer, the Recoverer, the Recuperator, the Reconciler, the Rehabilitator, the Regulator, and the Remedy for all that ails us. The Christ we preach builds up what is torn down, heals what is sick, binds up the broken and wounded, and makes whole what has gone to pieces.

January 21

So we built the wall . . . for the people had a mind to work.
(Nehemiah 4:6)

Often opposition rises to thwart the common good. For
Nehemiah it came in the persons of Sanballat, Tobiah,
Geshem and others who became exceedingly angry when
they heard the work on the walls was progressing. However,
Nehemiah was blessed to have people with a mind to work.
Of course, not everyone works *with* the leader. One minister
was asked what percentage of his members were active, and
he answered, "All of them, 100 percent!" He was asked how
he got them to be so active. The pastor replied, "It's simple.
Fifty percent of them are working for me; and fifty percent
are working against me. So all of them are active and 'have a
mind to work.'"

When you read the remainder of Nehemiah chapter 4
you discover the LORD not only gave Nehemiah people with
a mind to work with him, but He also informed Nehemiah of
the plans of his enemies (vv 7-8); a third help: God answered
prayer (v. 9). In the fourth place, the LORD let the enemy
know that Nehemiah knew what the enemy was doing (v.
15). In the fifth place, note Jehovah supplied Nehemiah's
people with the whole armor—spears, shields, bows, coats of
mail—and everyone had a weapon at hand.

We Christians have been supplied with the whole armor
of God (Ephesians 6:12-17). We have the belt of truth, the
breastplate of righteousness, sandals of preparing to spread
the Gospel of Peace, the shield of faith, the helmet of salvation, and the only offensive weapon, the Sword of the Spirit,
which is the Word of God.

There are those who would prefer not to spiritualize here
and would feel safer if they could bolster God's panoply
with some merchandise from Smith & Wesson. However, it
is best for us who truly love the Lord Jesus to let God fight
our battles His Way! Look what He did for Nehemiah!

Wherever you hear the sound of the trumpet, rally to us there. Our God will fight for us. (Nehemiah 4:20)

God fights our battles by giving us the strength to build walls, and bear burdens, v. 17. God fights our battles also by giving us a trumpet to blow, vv. 18-20. No preacher should ever put down his trumpet. As long as health remains we dare not let politics, secular attractions, racial advancement societies, secret societies, or anything else seduce us in muting our trumpets. We are warned clearly not to get entangled in civilian affairs (2 Timothy 2:4).

We are to preach in season and out of season, warning men, women, boys and girls of the wrath of God, Hell, and the deceit of Satan, and the trickery of evildoers. And at the same time invite them to enjoy the love of God, and the bliss of the blessed. What a joy to have eternal life right now, and know that our names are written down in the Lamb's book of life.

From Ezekiel we learn that it is our solemn duty to blow the trumpet, and warn the people (Ezekiel 33:1-6). And let us make sure that we blow the trumpet in no uncertain sound, for the Gospel message is clear. Stand on the wall; tell the world that Salvation comes only through faith in the shed blood of Jesus Christ. Do this and I declare unto you, God will fight your battles for you, cause you to run through troops and leap over walls. You will be led in victory by Him who rose from the grave and lives forever more.

Purtiest preachin' ever I heard, Way ovah on de hill,
De angels preach an' I preach'd too,
Preachin' wid a sword in ma han', Lord,
Preachin' wid a sword in ma han', Lord.
Preachin' wid a sword in ma han',
In ma han', Lord, Preachin' wid a sword in ma han'.
(*Negro Spiritual*)

January 23

Think not [KJV] in your heart that you will escape in the king's palace any more than all the other Jews. (Esther 4:13)

The Gospels use the phrase "think not" four times. In Matthew 3:9 John the Baptist warns the Pharisees and Sadducees, "Think not to say within yourselves, 'We have Abraham as our father'" Christ uses the phrase three times: (1) Matthew 5:17: "Think not that I am come to destroy the Law, or the prophets" (2) Matthew 10:34: "Think not that I am come to send peace on earth" (3) Matthew 24:44 (Luke 12:40): "Therefore be ye also ready; for in such an hour as ye think not the Son of man comes."

The "think nots" center upon the purpose of our Lord's coming into the world as a Man. The record needs to be set straight, for even today men don't know why He came. *He came* to fulfill the law. *He came* to seek and to save that which was lost. *He came* to die, and through death to destroy him that had the power of death, that is, the Devil.

He came to deliver them who, through fear of death, were all their lifetime subject to bondage. There will be no peace on earth until He returns to set up His headquarters in Jerusalem to reign during the Kingdom age or Millennium.

In the Book of Esther we find that Mordecai is rather blunt. Though her cousin, he is also a foster father (2:15); and he does not hesitate to call upon Esther to risk her life for the Jewish people. Esther is to be delivered from wrong thinking. She is not indifferent to the plight and fate of her fellow countrymen, but must realize that her own life is in danger as well. **Right thinking is always in order.**

Think not more highly of yourself than you ought to think; think soberly (Romans 12:3). *Think not* you are standing lest you fall (1 Corinthians 10:12). *Think not* yourself to be something when you are nothing (Galatians 6:3). Thank God today for ordering our thoughts (2 Corinthians 10:5; Philippians 4:8), even as he ordered the thoughts of Esther.

January 24

Now there was a day when . . . (Job 1:6, 13; 2:1)

I remember when Robert Ralph Young's day came. He was a Wall Street speculator who became a powerful railroad tycoon. Despite all of his power and wealth, he brooded when his stock plans failed. He had expected stock in the New York Central Railroad, of which he was chairman, to go up to $100 a share from $25; instead, it went down to $13.25. Thus Robert Young's day came. All hope of developing an empire slipped away.

One morning, January 25, 1958, he sat down in one of the rooms of his 25-room mansion, took a double-barreled 20-guage shotgun, placed it between his knees and killed himself. His estate was valued at $8,367, 237. What a difference a day makes!

Jacob's day came when he was told that Joseph was dead: "All these things are against me," he lamented. David's day came when he was informed of the death of his son, Absalom. Job's day likewise came. Before it ended he lost seven sons, three daughters, most of his servants, his oxen, donkeys, sheep and camels; and a body stricken with boils.

Things happen so quickly that "Here today, gone tomorrow!" has become "Here today and gone today!" Dreams vanish; hopes are dashed; bank-savings are depleted; children leave you; homes burn down; friends disappoint; jobs are terminated, and health is broken.

Yet see what a difference Christ makes in a life. Just as the gloom of Golgotha was changed when the Lamb of God rose from the grave, so the saint will see midnights of sorrow become mornings of joy; Mondays of despair turn into Tuesdays of rejoicing. May you be a witness today that the Lord Jesus Christ makes the difference that really counts—He will make your day.

And still he holds fast to his integrity. (Job 2:3)

Job was a complete person with an integrated character; he was together, all of a piece, not all in pieces. He was not one thing on Sunday and something else on Monday; he was not terribly holy in the church and a holy terror at home. Integrity means completeness, wholeness of character. Job never claimed sinless perfection. He speaks of the iniquities of his youth; and acknowledges that God watches over his sin; "My transgression is sealed up in a bag, and You cover my iniquity" (Job 13:26, 14:16f).

What Job experienced encourages us to hold fast despite adversity. Satan will insinuate. Skin will be made sore; children may be slain; sheep stolen, servants made slaves, spouse may speak nonsense, and associates show insensitivity to our sad situation. But if we have integrity, completeness or wholeness through faith in Jesus Christ, by the power of the indwelling Holy Spirit we can stand the strain of calamity. We can make it because Christ made it.

He persevered through ridicule, mockery, blasphemy, reviling, attempts to murder Him, traps, spies, testing, legal entanglements, envy, jealousy, denial, betrayal, arrest, perjury, desertion, interrogation, illegal detainment, condemnation, crucifixion and death—but He held fast.

He committed His spirit into the hands of God the Father. And on the third day He got up out of the grave with all power in His hands. Be encouraged. Determine that whatever comes, you will hold fast to Christ, who is able to forgive sin and make you whole. He is your Integrity! Hold fast to Him in whom there is life abundant and fullness of joy. His love will not let you go.

When I fear my faith will fail, Christ will hold me fast;
When the tempter would prevail, He can hold me fast . . .
He will hold me fast, He will hold me fast; For my Savior
loves me so, He will hold me fast. Ada R. Habershon

So are the paths of all who forget God; and the hope of the hypocrite shall perish, whose confidence shall be cut off, and whose trust is a spider's web. (Job 8:13, 14)

In one of the *Peanuts* cartoons the dog Snoopy runs to get under the umbrella Lucy is holding as the rain comes pouring down. She shouts at him, "Get away from me, you hypocrite," adding, "You just pretend to like me because I have an umbrella." Then Snoopy walks away and mutters, "Even hypocrites hate to get wet."

Indeed, hypocrites are in bad shape—all wet—their expectation shall perish (Proverbs 10:28). What they deem security fails them; what they say can be controlled goes haywire; their wealth vanishes; their strength fails, even as Jeremiah (17:5) warns, "Cursed is the man who trusts in man, and makes flesh his strength, whose heart departs from the LORD." To forsake the LORD is folly (Jeremiah 17:13).

To leave the fountain of living waters is to suffer the drought of despair and the dryness of spirit; it is to taste the dust of defeat, and the desperation of dismay. To leave the true and living God for dumb idols is deception and delusion. For the works of idols and all that we put before Christ are nothing; to forsake the Lord is to feed on wind.

To forsake God is like leaving the Garden of Eden in order to live in the City Dump. And worse, to be so deluded that you are not perturbed by the smell of the garbage and gas or the presence of the rats. It is to leave wisdom and become a fool. To forsake the Lord is to walk out of an oasis into the desert with its unbearable heat.

Christian, let the world know by your daily living that you trust Him who loved you and gave Himself for you. Let men and women, boys and girls know today that your hope is built on nothing less than Jesus' blood and His righteousness!

January 27

I put on righteousness, and it clothed me. (Job 29:14)

Should saints be concerned about what they wear? I thought about this and found a long list of Bible characters that were either very clothes-conscious, and desired many changes, or whose clothing affected lives—their own lives and the lives of others. After disobeying the Lord, Adam and Eve had their eyes opened, and they knew that they were naked; they sewed fig leaves together and made themselves coverings (Genesis 3:7).

Unsuccessful in her attempt to seduce Joseph, Potiphar's wife caught the fleeing Joseph by his garment and later lied in using it as evidence that Joseph tried to rape her (Genesis 39:13-15). Achan stole a beautiful Babylonian garment and because of his sin Israel was defeated at Ai (Joshua 7:21).

King Saul sought to arm David with royal armor, but David took them off and entered the fray armed only with a slingshot and five smooth stones (1 Samuel 17:38f). Gehazi, servant of Elisha, ran after Naaman cured of his leprosy, and lied in order to get a talent of silver and two changes of garments (2 Kings 5:22).

When the Roman soldiers crucified the Lord Jesus, they took His garments; each of the four soldiers received one part. Unwilling to tear the seamless robe, they cast lots for it (John 19:23f; Psalm 22:18). The first mention of Saul of Tarsus (Paul) is made at the stoning of Stephen. The men throwing the rocks took off their outer garments and laid them at Saul's feet (Acts 7:58).

You see then the importance of clothing in the Bible. Saints are exhorted to wear the armor of light, put on the breastplate of faith and love, don tender mercies, put on the new man, put on the whole armor of God, including righteousness who is Christ who shed His blood for us at Calvary. Determine that you will be a well-dressed Christian today!

January 28

God thunders marvelously with His voice; He does great things which we cannot comprehend. For He says to the snow, 'Fall on the earth'; likewise to the gentle rain and the heavy rain of His strength. He seals the hand of every man, that all men may know His work. (Job 37:5-7)

Those are the words of Elihu. The other "friends" of Job believed the evil that had befallen Job was God's way of announcing that Job was a bad man pretending to be good. Their attempts to prove Job a hypocrite showed that they did not really understand the ways of God. Elihu, who concludes his argument in chapter 37, deals in a more spiritual manner with the question, "Why do the righteous suffer?"

His view of God is higher; therefore his view of sin is deeper. He recognized a truth many moderns fail to see: namely, the Sovereign God is Lord of nature, and His works are wonderful. He uses rain, snow, cold air, ice, lightning, thunder, clouds, etc, to teach and discipline the children of men. Weather can be quite severe, making men cease their activity, close shop and take refuge.

The paralyzing effect of harsh weather is designed to remind us that we are but creatures. God alone is Creator, and able to seal up our hands so that we cannot work with them. For three nights The Manna Bible Institute was closed because of the snow storm here in Philadelphia. But God was still teaching. And we are glad that the Lord of nature, who calmed the ocean wild, stilled the winds, turned water into wine, cursed a fig tree that drooped and died, and walked upon water—is the same Lord Jesus who shed His blood for us at Calvary. Surely, with such a Lord and Savior, we know that all things are made to work together for our good, even snow storms!

January 29

What is man that You are mindful of him, and the son of man that You visit him? (Psalm 8:4)

Sin makes human beings nobodies. Because of sin he is the very essence of nobodiness—vain, empty, a nebbish. For brute strength he cannot compare with the elephant. He cannot climb a tree with the agility of a squirrel, or swim with the rhythmic cadence of a porpoise or dolphin. He cannot camouflage himself with the skill or quickness of a chameleon. His physical speed finds him choking in the dust kicked up by the feet of the ostrich or the cheetah.

What is man? His beauty does not distinguish him. His paintings and artificial flowers are dull and lifeless in their imitation. He is outnumbered by insects, at the mercy of the weather, destroyed by earthquakes, helpless against hurricanes, and vulnerable to volcanoes. At best man is a vapor, a puff of steam, a hand span, a tale soon told, a sigh uttered, a piece of clay, a blade of grass—here today and gone tomorrow!

Yet, having been made in the image of God, he was put over all creation, to have dominion over the fowls of the air and the beasts of the field. They are to be his servants and his supper. But even here sin has prevailed. For while men have minds to create, invent, adapt and make machines that enable them to far surpass the speeds and strengths of beasts, yet sin in man's heart has so effected him that his superiority over other creatures does not snatch him from nobodiness.

What counts is not man's relationship with creation, but his relationship with his Creator. Sinners resisting God, creatures against the Creator, simply cannot be somebodies! To rectify man's fallen, pitiable condition, to solve his problems, alleviate his misery, God became a Man in order to die on the cross and pay the penalty of our sin. And now we do not have to remain nobodies. We are Somebody in Christ!

January 30

If the foundations are destroyed, what can the righteous do?
(Psalm 11:3)

A little boy had a cat named "Chessy," and one day the cat gave birth to kittens. When the boy saw the newborn kits around the mother cat, he ran screaming into the kitchen to his mother, and cried, "Mommy, mommy, Chessy's gone to pieces!" The thought comes, "How do you react when things go to pieces?"

Note that although David was moved by the Spirit of God to write this Psalm, the words of our text are part of the advice given by evil men. At the time David was surrounded by stealthy hostility, men with treacherous intentions. He was also troubled by King Saul (1 Samuel 18:11, 19:10).

Listen to what David was told: (1) "Be off, like a bird to the hills" (Moffatt). Take refuge there. (2) The wicked bend their bow. (3) The arrow is on the string. (4) They shoot in the dark at night. That is, they hold secret meetings and plan strategy; rumors are spread, lies are told, facts twisted, and slander is spoken. And (5) the pillars of the State are falling!

This is to say that established institutions, community order, social foundations are cracking. Bribes are taken, politicians are perverted, justice is subverted, homes are lost in foreclosures, scales are falsified, the poor and the widows mistreated, the city is about to collapse under the weight of the corruption! What is there you can do about it? Nothing! So flee!

But David would caution, "Be careful about the advice you receive." No matter how bad things appear to be, remember that the Lord Jesus loves righteousness. And there *is* something the righteous *can* do. Let your motto today be: "When things go to pieces I will put my trust in the Lord. He is my Peace, my Completion, my Togetherness, my All in all, and my Deliverance!"

If the foundations are destroyed, what can the righteous do?
(Psalm 11:3)

The lips of the pessimists who do not trust the Lord advised David, "Flee as a bird to your mountain." Their bad advice is akin to that of Job's wife to curse God and die (Job 2:9); or to that of the false priest Amaziah (Amos 7:12) who sarcastically told Amos to go back down South "and there eat bread, and prophesy there!" Or to the advice of the Pharisees to Christ, "Run and hide, for Herod wants to kill You" (Luke 13:31).

David answered, "No. I put my trust in the Lord. And when things go to pieces, I will take refuge in Jehovah." Yes, things certainly can go to pieces: Bills pile up, children get into trouble, health breaks, accidents occur, jobs close down, a stroke cripples, eyesight fails, loved ones die, etc. Still, Christians can respond, "With the Lord Jesus on our side, there *is* something we can do, and we can do it because the Holy Spirit enables us, God's Word teaches us, angels watch over us; our names are written down in the Lamb's book of life; we have access to His throne; we are citizens of heaven, clothed in righteousness. Why should we flee?"

What then shall we do? We are to stay where we are and see the salvation of the Lord! We can suffer gladly, hope blessedly, wait willingly, sing joyfully, fight the good fight, pray fervently, rejoice evermore, wear the whole armor, believe confidently, wrestle with vigor, walk in the light, show ourselves approved, run through troops and leap over walls, love without hypocrisy, set our affections on things above, seek first God's kingdom, and triumph finally.

Yea, we remember Calvary; we have a Savior who knows just how much we can bear; One who loves us, cleanses us; and now will not leave us alone. He's a solid foundation that will not crumble. Say then as David said, "In the Lord I put my trust."

February 1

How long, O LORD? Will You forget me forever? How long will You hide Your face from me? (Psalm 13:1)

A visitor at an insane asylum met the gardener there and very much admired his work. She protested that anyone who could do such beautiful work could not possibly be crazy. So she invited him to work for her, promising to look into the matter. As she left, the man picked up a rock, threw it at her and hit her on the head, and said, "Don't you forget, now!" The God of the Bible cares for you. The fact that you may feel He has turned His face away does not mean He *has* forgotten you. It is a contradiction to even ask "How long, O Lord? Will You forget me forever?" Who dares ask an omniscient all-wise God such questions?

On several occasions when I went to the YMCA to swim I forgot the numbers of my combination lock; often I wasted much time trying to guess the correct numbers. Eventually, I printed the number with indelible ink on the inside of my swimming trunks. Thank God, His memory does not fail! Hear Him say, "Can a woman forget her nursing child, and not have compassion on the son of her womb? Surely they may forget, yet I will not forget you. See, I have inscribed you on the palms of My hands" (Isaiah 49:15f). He has numbered the hairs of our heads; and our names are written down indelibly in the Lamb's book of life in heaven. *How can He forget?*

We have been sealed unto the day of redemption. The Holy Spirit has made our bodies His temple. We have been adopted, placed already as sons and daughters of God. *How can He forget?* Christ has gone to prepare a place for us in Heaven. Right now He is seated at the right hand of God the Father, making intercession for us. And He promised to come back again for us—does any of this sound like we have been forgotten? The God of the Bible knows His sheep by name, and promised never to leave us. He cannot forget us.

February 2

How long, O LORD? Will You forget me forever? How long will You hide Your face from me? (Psalm 13:1)

It is a fact that God has a face. Describing God by using the features of human beings (anthropomorphism) is supported by other Scriptures. For example: He has eyes. Noah found grace in the eyes of the Lord (Genesis 6:8). The eyes of the Lord run to and fro throughout the whole earth (2 Chronicles 16:9). "I will guide you with my eye," is the promise of the Lord (Psalm 32:8).

God also has a mouth. Man shall not live by bread alone, but by every word that proceeds out of the mouth of God (Matthew 4:4). He has lips: "But oh, that God would speak, and open His lips against you," argued Zophar with Job (11:5). He has ears: "Incline Your ear unto me, and hear my speech," said the psalmist (17:6). He has a nose. Concerning Noah's sacrifice we read, "And the Lord smelled a soothing aroma" (Genesis 8:21). Jehovah said in Amos (5:21), "I will not smell in your solemn assemblies" (KJV).

And so because God has eyes, a mouth, lips, ears and a nose, we conclude, He has a face. Indeed, when Moses requested to see God's glory, the Lord answered, "You cannot see My face" (Exodus 33:20).

This brings us to the matter of God hiding His face. It is an expression signifying anger, displeasure, and indifference. This is why the psalmist could plead, "Do not hide Your face from me . . . Do not hide Your face from Your servant, for I am in trouble . . . Do not hide Your face from me, lest I be like those who go down into the pit" (27:9, 69:17, 143:7).

The only hiding of God's face the psalmist desired is expressed in Psalm 51:9, "Hide Your face from my sins." In other words, look the other way. Thank God today our sins have been washed away forever; and in Jesus Christ we see the glory of God's face!

February 3

How long, O LORD? Will You forget me forever? How long will You hide Your face from me? (Psalm 13:1)

All of us have our doubts at times; and we have our questions. We have our "How-long, O-Lords?" There are times we begin to wonder what it is all about. We speculate about the reality of it all. And sometimes at our lowest ebb the Holy Spirit gives us a shot in the arm—not of dope, but of hope. In other words, God's face shines upon us.

Understand then the reason for the request often made in the Psalms: "Lord, lift up the light of Your countenance upon us . . . Make Your face shine upon Your servant . . . God be merciful to us and bless us, and cause His face to shine upon us . . . Restore us, O God; cause Your face to shine, and we shall be saved" (4:6; 31:16; 67:1; 80:3, 7, 19).

All of these requests are based upon Aaron's benediction, Numbers 6:24-26: "The Lord bless you and keep you; the Lord make His face shine upon you, and be gracious to you; the Lord lift up His countenance upon you, and give you peace."

When God's face shines upon you, it means He favors you. Yea, the very source of life is to have His face shine thus. Otherwise darkness and death will be your lot. Christ experienced this at Calvary. There He who knew no sin became sin. And in that awful moment, when the Father's face was hidden from His Son, the Son cried out, "My God, My God, why have You forsaken Me?"

But now through faith in that cleansing blood you and I are in God's favor. In Christ we see His face. In Christ we know that He cannot ever forget us. I trust His mercy. Do you? I rejoice in His salvation. Do you? Thank God today for shining in our hearts to give the light of the knowledge of His glory in the face of Christ (2 Corinthians 4:6).

February 4

How long, O LORD? Will You forget me forever? How long will You hide Your face from me? (Psalm 13:1)

I do not know the specific circumstances or the exact period in David's life that elicited these words, "How long?" He certainly was constantly in trouble with enemies on the outside and at home. Within the soul of the psalmist is an assurance that while affliction may seem to last an eternity, God will put an end to it. And instead of singing, "How long," we can sing, "I'm so glad trouble **don't** last always!"

Thank God the Psalm closes with confidence. Despair is chased into oblivion, despondency is dissipated, doubts are settled, loneliness is dispelled, sadness is turned into joy, restlessness is tranquilized, and shame turned into glory. When you wait on the Lord He will deliver you! A sense of insignificance gives way to a sense of somebodiness. Meager threadbare resources become abundance. The plans of your enemies go awry. Your foes fall flat on their dirty faces. Their upper hand becomes a broken arm.

When you wait on the Lord, He will deliver you! And trusting in God's mercy leads to rejoicing in God's salvation. Faith pierces the darkness of the unknown. And the quickening power of God's face shines forth. The peril of death is removed and your eyes are lightened. Surely this deliverance is the right of every believer. Delay is a test. He may not come when **you** want Him, but whenever He does come you will discover He is on time.

God has not forsaken us. Indeed, the resurrected Savior said, "Lo, I am with you always, even unto the end of the age" (Matthew 28:20). Do you believe Him? It is recorded in the Book of Hebrews that He said, "I will never leave you nor forsake you" (13:5). Do you believe Him? I do.

February 5

You enlarged my path under me, so my feet did not slip.
(Psalm 18:36)

I have trouble getting a hat in my size. You see, the 7¾ size of hats is not stocked in the variety of colors and styles as are the smaller sizes. When you have a big head it makes a difference. But I am glad my feet stopped growing at 12D, for whereas I can often go without a hat, I believe in wearing shoes. And so 12D is not too bad.

While pondering this verse, I wondered what David meant by "You have enlarged my path under me." We learn it is a song of deliverance (see 2 Samuel 22). David praises God for snatching him out of the hands of his enemies and from the hand of King Saul.

Elsewhere the verb "to enlarge" is used of borders or coasts of a country. To enlarge your border is to increase your land holdings, usually in the context of victory in war and conquering the enemy. Incidentally, in Isaiah 5:14 the Bible speaks of Hell enlarging itself to accommodate the unfaithful of Israel. Indeed, Hell and destruction are never full (Proverbs 27:20).

Now to make broad or wide your steps signifies God gives you ample room for standing. He secures you; prevents you from falling or slipping as you would do if you had to walk on a narrow piece of ground or if straitened by hard times. When God prepares your way He enlightens, encourages and leads you, so that there is plenty of good room for exercise, growth and development. In short, God gives the victory. He alone enables us to stand. This is the significance of having our path enlarged. Feel free today to take giant steps for Jesus Christ.

February 6

The law of the LORD is perfect, converting the soul; the testimony of the LORD is sure, making wise the simple. (Psalm 19:7)

More beneficial to man than the rays of the sun are the words of the Son. The sun gives light for the physical, but the Word is light for the soul. While there are those who value more highly the *works* of God than they value the *Word* of God, it is a fact that nothing in this wide world compares with the value of the Bible.

The Bible is: the seed of the sower; the fire from the Father; the hammer from Heaven; the sword of the Spirit; the Good Book for bad people; the expression of the mind of God; the revelation of His will and the description of His Son. It is the story of His love, the saga of man's ruin in sin; the uncovering of the deeds and devices of the Devil; and the manifestation of God's grace.

It is the mystery of God's plan of the ages; the prescripttion of God's perfect remedy; the mirror of man's moral make-up; the universal heart fixer and mind regulator; the primer on prayer, the road map to glory; the light for living, the power in preaching and the world's best seller!

Hear then the message of David. The Law or Torah represents the commandments, statutes, words, precepts, ways, judgments, testimonies and ordinances of God. The Law is the revelation of God's will. Going beyond the Ten Commandments, the Law is the whole teaching of the Scriptures. And the revelation made by His Word is far superior to that revealed in His works. Thank God for His Word.

Sing them over again to me, Wonderful words of life;
Let me more of their beauty see, Wonderful words of life;
Words of life and beauty, Teach me faith and duty:
Beautiful words, wonderful words, Wonderful words of life.
(Philip P. Bliss)

February 7

Lift up your heads, O you gates! Lift up, you everlasting doors! And the King of glory shall come in. (Psalm 24:9)

The city gates are now silent. They had been opened wide and the LORD Jehovah, seated enthroned above the cherubim of the sacred Ark, entered into Zion, the city of God. That historical day and dispensation has long passed. God now dwells within the hearts of all who believe in Jesus Christ.

Tell me, are the gates of your heart closed to God? Some doors are closed by poor values, by shackling habits, crippling fears, twisted thinking, and immoral deeds. Some doors are closed by our indifference to the things of God. Some are closed by our insistence upon having our own way in life. Some doors are closed by covetousness and greed; closed because we have hard heads.

You see, if you turn your back upon the sunshine of love you will walk in the darkness of hatred. If you refuse the Prince of Peace, you will have fighting inside and wars outside. Reject the Light of the World, and you will stumble in the blindness of sin. When all you have to do is open up, yea, lift up your heads, open the gates of your hearts, and let the supreme Sovereign of the universe come in.

I ask again: Are the gates of your heart closed to God? If they are, you have made a bad mistake. For the tenant living in your house and running your life is ruining your life. Paint up the outside if you please; get your teeth fixed; purchase those new eyeglasses; bathe and perfume your body; put on a new suit or dress—but if the old man [equal opportunity: the old woman] in you is still the boss, your house will soon become a slum.

Let the King of glory in and He will break the lease of your present tenant; He will put a new spirit in the office of your heart and begin an inner recreation which includes clean hands, a pure heart, a soul not chasing after emptiness and vanity, and He will give you lips without guile or deceit.

February 8

The earth is the LORD's and all its fullness, the world and those who dwell therein . . . The LORD of hosts, He is the King of glory. (Psalm 24:1, 10)

He who demands admission to the city is the One who commands countless visible and invisible powers. He makes rivers to slow up, dry up, stand still, overflow, divide or change their courses. The creatures in the waters do His bidding: fish swim where He directs them; frogs hop out and cover the land. Recall that a great fish arrived on time to swallow Jonah the runaway prophet. An IRS fish came along with a coin in its mouth to help pay the temple tax.

He used Samson to tie torches to the tails of foxes to burn up the crops of the Philistines. He enabled a donkey to talk and save Balaam's life. God ordered lions in the den to keep their jaws shut; He turned their growls into contented purrs, and Daniel made a pillow out of a lion's mane.

The Lord of hosts moves mountains; He levels hills, fills up valleys, causes volcanoes to belch fire and smoke; from heaven He rains quail, manna, fire and brimstone, hurls thunderbolts and flashes lightning. He controls the wind, gathers it in His fists (Proverbs 30:4). He multiplies loaves and fishes. He increased the widow's oil; cursed a fig tree causing it to droop and die; opened up the earth to swallow rebellious men, sent snakes to bite murmuring Israelites, and bears to tear in pieces the young people who mocked the prophet Elisha. Yea, He has illimitable resources at His command, visible and invisible, material and immaterial.

May we today lift up our heads, stretch out our arms, unclench our fists so God can fill our hands; let go vanity and serve reality; let go lies and receive the truth; open up our hearts and see the Lord supply our every need. Whatever is missing He can supply. It is in His storehouse. Lift up your head and let the Lord of hosts give you what you need.

February 9

Vindicate me, O LORD, for I have walked in my integrity.
(Psalm 26:1)

To walk in your integrity means you do not get upset when folks slander you because you know what they say is not true. To walk in your integrity is to have peace of soul while all around you the winds of adversity blow and blustering storms of lies howl and scream. Integrity says, "Why should I steal when God has promised to supply all my needs?" Integrity says, "Why should I seek revenge when God has stated vengeance belongs to Him?"

Integrity says, "Why should I feel abandoned when the LORD said, 'Lo, I am with you always'"? Integrity says, "Why should I fear death when Christ pulled death's sting?"

There is no claim here of sinless perfection. That David was a man after God's own heart means deep within he desired to please the Lord. David wanted for Israel what God wanted.

Despite the lust, adultery, murder and bloodshed; despite his fears, faults and faltering, when confronted with his sins, when convicted, he repented. David was not hard, conscienceless or bitter. Way down in his soul he desired what God desired. His inner man sought after the Lord.

To walk in your integrity is to live without any known, unconfessed sin in your life. It is to have your inside disposition parallel, consistent with your outside conduct. It is to trust God so that faith and works unite. So David is saying, "God knows my heart." He had the confidence that God knows those who belong to Him, and will deliver them. Wholeness is what integrity is all about.

And we are complete, whole, in Jesus Christ. All we need is in Him. We are judged and vindicated because in Him there is no condemnation. By His blood we are made whole, integrated. Do you believe that? Then walk in your integrity. Trust Him and do not doubt His Word. And walk on until walking days are over.

February 10

Though an army may encamp against me, my heart shall not fear; though war may rise against me, in this I will be confident. (Psalm 27:3)

One of the ladies in our church suffered several strokes, a bout with diabetes and became an amputee. Yet seldom in my pastoral ministry had I met anyone with the pluck and determination of this beautiful woman. Though faced with such affliction, she insisted upon coming to the house of the Lord. Her efforts to attend church put to shame many who were well, but had no push to attend, and no compunction about missing church services and the fellowship of believers.

When you have spiritual stamina, the inability to speak won't stop you from praying; blindness won't stop you from seeing Christ; crippled hands won't prevent you from holding the hand of the Lord Jesus; and amputations won't hinder you from walking with the Lord. But it takes a courage born out of the belief that when the wicked, even your enemies and your foes come upon you to eat up your flesh, they will stumble and fall. This is a courage based upon the fact that the Lord is your light and your salvation; yea, He is the strength of your life.

The foes of the Christian are many: self, sin, sinners, Satan, sickness—all combine and appear as formidable as the Goliath appeared to the Israelites. Remember how confident David was: "The Lord will deliver me out of the hand of this Philistine!" and as he confronted this man over nine feet tall, David said, "This day will the Lord deliver you into my hand." With Jehovah at his side David slew the giant.

With the Lord as your light, your foes will stumble in darkness; with the Lord as your salvation, there is the peace of knowing it is well with your soul. With the Lord as the strength of your life, you can go out and do battle with the forces of evil, knowing that since Christ rose from the grave with all power in His hands the victory is yours!

February 11

Be of good courage, and He shall strengthen your heart, all you who hope in the LORD. (Psalm 31:24)

Christians are people who wait on the Lord. The meaning of the word "hope" in this verse is to wait, to expect. It is as if we should have an attitude when we wake up in the morning that says, "I wonder what the Lord is going to work out in my life today?" But now only believers dare to think like that. Unbelievers are not concerned with Jesus Christ, but seek to run their own lives. And because those who compose the world-system have their own individual particular wills there is a clashing, a confusion and chaos. Every man does that which is right in his own eyes. And so there is conflict.

Waiting on the Lord is easily said. However, the natural tendency for us is to go on and do what we want to do; to do as we please as quickly as we can. Once our minds are made up to do something, there is no stopping us. And shame on anybody who gets in our way. But what a mess we make of things. For often such self-reliance is an expression of pride. We ignore the advice of others. We seem to go through a period in life when we say, "I don't need anybody to tell me what to do. I can run my own life!" And the run becomes ruin because of the "I".

There are those who put their trust in astrology or horoscopes (Deuteronomy 18:9-14). David would say to them who hope in their "lucky stars", why not thank Him who made the moon and the stars, who ordained them, the work of His fingers? For all of us were born under the sign of sin, but God the Father sent His Son to pay the wages of sin which is death. When you wait on the Lord, the heart becomes a castle where the courage of Christ controls. When you hope in God, crooked places are made straight, rough roads are smoothed, mountains of despair are leveled to the ground, and the weeping of the midnight hours becomes shouts of joy in the morning.

February 12

I will instruct you and teach you in the way you should go; I will guide you with My eye. Do not be like the horse or like the mule, which have no understanding. (Psalm 32:8-9)

I have watched people grow under a Bible teaching ministry. Their secret is a desire to become like Jesus Christ, a willingness to submit to the searching, piercing scrutiny of God's Word. Other folks come Sunday after Sunday and the Bible bounces off their heads, giving them a spiritual headache. They then criticize the preacher, but have only themselves to blame; they become like the horse or the mule that has no spiritual understanding. Obstinate hardheadedness, resisting God's Word leads to sorrow and destruction.

The Bible resisted becomes a hammer that smashes! God chastens those whom He loves and spanks every son whom He receives (Hebrews 12:6), so that at times the instruction and teaching involve pain. When we want to have our own way God may let us have it until we learn that His way is better. The God of the Bible, states Paul, is He who would not have us to be ignorant.

He is a Teacher who loves His students, a Father who adores His children. An ignorant Christian is a contradiction, an anomaly. God *illumines;* we have no business groping in darkness. God *reveals;* we have no business wallowing in ignorance. God *empowers;* we have no business being weak. God *commands* we endure hardness as good soldiers of Jesus Christ; we have no excuse for getting entangled in civilian affairs. God *supplies* what we need to wage a good warfare; we have no valid reason for not wearing the whole armor. God *teaches;* we have no excuse for not learning. God *guides;* we have no business losing our way.

Precious promise God hath given, To the weary passerby, On the way from earth to heaven, I will guide thee with Mine eye. (Nathan Niles)

February 13

The angel of the LORD encamps all around those who fear Him, and delivers them. (Psalm 34:7)

When I read this verse for the umpteenth time, the thought came, how can *one* angel encamp round about *them*? Imagine one angel surrounding all believers! And so I thought, if it were plural, angels, I could better see it. Well, **the** Angel of the Lord is none other than Jesus Christ, God the Son, the Second Person of the Trinity, a member of the Godhead. He was the invisible Lord God who appeared to men in the Old Testament, the only Person of the Godhead who is ever visible to humans.

Those who reverence God, who realize His greatness, who stand in awe of Him, and whose fear produces a hatred of evil as well as a love of God, give evidence of their honor for the Lord. Men who do not fear God have no Deliverer. The lack of godly fear makes them hard, callous, and brutal. They are ignorant, no matter how brilliant their scientific achievements; for the fear of God is the beginning or foundation of all of man's learning. Without such fear men may make material progress, but their characters deteriorate.

Man *must* fear. He was made that way. If he does not fear God he will soon fear the gods of his own making. Any man who does not fear the true and living God opens himself up to the fears and phobias of all that is false and unreal, and when those fears run out, man begins to fear Fear itself. He becomes afraid of being afraid.

But Christians serve the true and living God, and our lot is one of joy. Because of the Bible our eyes are open and we see the heavens filled with the angels of God. We know for a certainty that we are surrounded by an invisible host. Thank God there are tremendous forces working for our good, directed by the Captain of the Host, the Lord Jesus Christ. Praise God today for the awareness that the angels in Heaven, *under His command* are watching over you.

February 14

The steps of a good man are ordered by the LORD, *and He delights in his way. Though he fall, he shall not be utterly cast down; for the* LORD *upholds him with His hand.* (Psalm 37:23-24)

Steps: Unfortunately most people do not know their steps are numbered or counted by God (Job 14:16; 31:4). Furthermore, while we make plans and devise our own way—so we think—the Lord directs our steps (Proverbs 16:9). It is not in man that walks to direct his steps (Jeremiah 10:23). Surely in present times, in today's environment, our steps need to be established, set firm, made steadfast, settled, secured and fixed.

Satisfaction: According to the Bible there are many things which please or satisfy God. For one, He delights in, is satisfied by, and is pleased with the steps and way of the believer. Like a father and mother are pleased with the first tottering steps of their child, so our heavenly Father is pleased as we walk in the way. He delights in seeing us walk not by sight, but by faith.

Support: I hope I have said nothing that gives you the idea that the Christian life is a flowery bed of ease. Having your steps established by God does not mean life for you will be "peaches and cream." Rather, it means you are solidly grounded no matter what comes. Yes, you may even fall down along the way. This is not denied.

Most of us know by experience what it means to fall. "For a righteous man may fall seven times, and rise again" (Proverbs 24:16). He rises because his fall is not his final ruin. He is not utterly, finally prostrated. He does not fall so as not to rise again. When the wicked fall, that's it! But when the godly fall they have a holy bounce. God is able to keep you from falling fatally and finally (Jude 24). As Paul said, "We are hard pressed on every side, yet not crushed; we are perplexed, but not in despair; persecuted, but not forsaken; struck down, but not destroyed" (2 Corinthians 4:8-9).

February 15

For my iniquities have gone over my head; like a heavy burden they are too heavy for me. (Psalm 38:4)

We learn from David that our sins can weigh us down. Failure to confess and forsake known sins can indeed cause depression and weight us. But the Christ who paid the penalty for our sins wants also to mediate the present affects of such sins; He wants to break the power of sin in our lives. We are commanded to throw our burden on the Lord (Psalm 55:22). To disobey is sin. And such disobedience may actually constitute the trouble itself. Failure to cast our burden upon the Lord may serve to make the burden heavier.

Furthermore, we should put our burdens on Christ in order to be of service to others. If you are burdened your ministry of service to others is hindered. Some saints are so oppressed they are not used of God to pray for others. Have you ever gone to visit a sick person who cheered you up, so that when you left you felt better than when you entered? Well, then have you ever prayed for other people, and discovered that your own burdens were lifted?

How can the Lord give you something else to do if your hands are loaded with frustration, worry, anxiety, or self-pity? If weighed down with what the Lord *has* committed, what more can He commit to your hands? Free your hands so God can use you! Free them not only from sin so you will have clean hands, but free them from burdens, so you will have hands available for God's service. Be reminded today that if you are a burden-bearer you have a Burden-Sharer, Jesus Christ who said, "Come to Me, all you who labor and are heavy laden, and I will give you rest" (Matthew 11:28). Cast all your care upon Him (1 Peter 5:7).

Take your burden to the Lord and leave it there;
If you trust and never doubt, He will surely bring you out.
Take your burden to the Lord and leave it there.
(C.A. Tindley)

February 16

LORD, make me to know my end, and what is the measure of my days, that I may know how frail I am. (Psalm 39:4)

The first word in this text is LORD, indicating that David did not turn to man, but to God. He did not turn to the scientist who would freeze the body, hoping later to restore it to life; nor to the politician who dreams of a united world through human efforts; nor to Hollywood with its make-believe celluloid world; nor to the preacher who would, without the King, build a kingdom on earth. He went to the Lord, for God alone knows the answer to the mysteries of life.

It is precisely because our days are measured, our steps numbered, the months established, and the years appointed that we realize that against the backdrop of eternity we are but frail, feeble creatures of time. Awareness of my mortality makes me more humble, more diligent while I am able to serve actively; more dependent upon divine strength; more patient and submissive to the divine will.

As I grow older, I am increasingly aware that my salvation is nearer than when I first believed. God alone lets me know that the hell of Hell is that there is no end to its misery; however, the joy of Heaven is indeed a hope beyond the grave. Yes, life is short—a handbreadth, a vapor or puff of steam, a sigh, a tale soon told—so that David is not asking "Lord, how much longer do I have to live?" No. he desires to realize in a better way that he did not come here to stay. For life is short.

But thank God, trouble cannot last always. There is an end to affliction. There is an end to suffering. There is an end to misery. There is an end to disease, to aches and pains. There is an end to death. So we need not despair because of life's brevity. In Jesus Christ there is a better life, a longer life, an abundant life, indeed, an eternal life!

Why are you cast down, O my soul? And why are you disquieted within me? Hope in God, for I shall yet praise Him for the help of His countenance. (Psalm 42:5)

What did the psalmist do about his depression? What effect did his disquietude or disturbance have upon him? The answer is *introspection*, defined as turning one's thoughts inward, examining one's own feelings, or contemplating one's private perceptions. This is what the psalmist did. An interesting reaction, isn't it?

How many of us when depressed search ourselves for the reasons, or contemplate within our own minds what attitudes and actions we should take. I am afraid that our initial reaction is to find someone else to blame, especially someone close, like a husband or wife, child or parent, or preacher! What are your reactions to sorrow and depression? Do you question your feelings?

J. Sidlow Baxter said, "Should we not make our feelings give an account of our behavior before the united board of reason, judgment and conscience?" Have you ever awakened feeling depressed? I have, and knew it was because of a bad dream. I wake up, unable to recall exactly what I dreamed, but able to pin my despondency on the dream. Depression has many roots: sometimes friends disappoint us. Sometimes relatives really upset us. Ingratitude hits hard; and a cold, careless callousness cuts deep.

See here a believer who sought the source of his sorrow, who stopped and said to himself, "What's going on here? Why am I so down in the dumps? What's the matter with me? Why am I so blue? Why am I acting as if the world stopped spinning and then kicked me off?" What a reaction! Imagine having the Holy-Spirit presence of mind to stop in the midst of disappointments, doubts, despair, depression, sadness and sorrow—and questioning your soul, interrogating your inner being, making inquiry of your spirit—and then thanking God for the help of His presence.

February 18

Why are you cast down, O my soul? And why are you disquieted within me? Hope in God, for I shall yet praise Him for the help of His countenance. (Psalm 42:5)

Note the formula that dispels despondency: Hope in God. Biblical hope is not a perhaps, maybe thing like in the expression, "I hope so." Bible hope is the expectation of good. This is the way we use it when we sing, "My hope is built on nothing less, than Jesus' blood and righteousness." The psalmist said, "In your moments of despair, repeat these words and see whether an inner peace takes hold of your heart." Jeremiah said, "The LORD is my portion, says my soul; therefore I hope in Him" (Lamentations 3:24). And again, "Blessed is the man who trusts in the LORD and whose hope is the LORD" (Jeremiah 17:7).

The apostle Paul wrote, "Hope does not disappoint" (Romans 5:5). Furthermore, Christ in us is the hope of glory (Colossians 1:27). Simon declared, God "has begotten us again to a living hope through the resurrection of Jesus Christ from the dead," and exhorted that we be ready always to give an answer (a defense) to every man that asks us a reason of the hope that is in us (1 Peter 1:3; 3:15). The apostle John said that Christ is coming back again, and when He comes we shall be like Him, for we shall see Him as He is. This is our purifying hope (1 John 3:3). Spurgeon said, "In the garden of hope grows the laurels for future victories, the roses of coming joy, and the lilies of approaching peace."

Irrepressible faith challenges us—not to seek to change circumstances, alter environment, overcome unemployment, eliminate slums, eradicate racism or ban the nuclear bomb—but rather seek to change our attitudes, values, and hearts, and improve our spiritual health in Christ. Hope in God. Don't stay down in the dumps. Look up! The God of the Bible will interpose Himself; He will step in on your behalf. He is on your side, at your side and on the inside to handle all of life's adversities.

February 19

Oh, send out Your light and Your truth! Let them lead me; let them bring me to Your holy hill, and to Your tabernacle.
(Psalm 43:3)

I am lost, if You take Your hand from me,
I am blind without Thy light to see,
Lord, just always let me Thy servant be,
Lead me, oh Lord, lead me.

Lead me, guide me, along the way,
For if You lead me, I cannot stray.
Lord, let me walk each day with Thee.
Lead me, oh Lord, lead me. *Doris Akers*

Because we come into this world intent upon doing our own thing, we do not want God to lead us. It takes a new spirit in us for us to be willing to surrender our wills to God's will. To say, "Lord, send out Your light and truth and let them lead me" takes a miracle. For at times, even when we have been led astray by others, we still are not willing to follow God. Without Holy Spirit guidance we are gullible, open to the trickery of the Devil and the hypocrisy of men.

We need both light and truth to lead us. So the psalmist does not cry out for one and ignore the other. Truth without light may be no more than head knowledge or mental assent; and experiences will be misinterpreted. Truth without light is but doctrine to be talked about and not lived.

Light without truth is also dangerous. That which shines but has no truth is but a false light, a mirage in the desert. Light without truth is like a purse with a hole in the bottom, untrustworthy. So both light and truth are needed. The psalmist recognized he needed help along life's journey—and so do we. If this text expresses the desire of our heart, God in Christ will be the delight and source of all our joy. And our fellowship with Him will be more than satisfactory.

February 20

Oh, send out Your light and Your truth! Let them lead me; let them bring me to Your holy hill, and to Your tabernacle. (Psalm 43:3)

We noted yesterday that the two ingredients of God's leadership are light and truth. Those two leadership agents are used to guide us through life. Light symbolizes knowledge and intelligence; it speaks of the brilliance, radiance, and majesty of God, for an omniscient God dwells in that light whereunto no man can approach. Truth, the second thing the psalmist desired to lead him is fact, reality, that which can be substantiated, to which "amen" can be said. Truth is steadfastness, genuineness, stability, certainty, honesty, and it is eternal.

Truth is combined with a number of other virtues and attributes. For example: Moses said that the Lord God was abundant in *goodness* and truth (Exodus 34:6). Joshua exhorted the Israelites to serve the Lord in *sincerity* and in truth (Joshua 24:14). David promised to praise God's name for God's *lovingkindness* and for His truth (Psalm 138:2). Jeremiah (33:6) prophesied God will reveal to Israel the abundance of *peace* and truth. And John said that *grace* and truth came through Jesus Christ (John 1:17).

The combination found most frequently is *mercy* and truth. All the paths of the Lord are mercy and truth to the obedient (Psalm 25:10); God is plenteous in mercy and truth (86:15); mercy and truth are to be bound about the neck, written upon the tablet of the heart (Proverbs 3:3); and by mercy and truth iniquity is purged (Proverbs 16:6).

Let us thank God for His light. It dispels darkness, illumines the pathway of life, opens minds, uncovers wickedness, gives wisdom, enables us to work while it is day, and reflects the glory of the Lord. Thank God for His truth. His Word is Truth. Christ is **the** Truth. And truth will stand the test of time. When we follow the Truth we will be successful in life's journey.

February 21

There they are in great fear where no fear was. (Psalm 53:5)

At times the wicked in their illogical sense of security boast of their superior armies, tanks, planes and bombs. From their point of view they have it made and need fear no one. But then suddenly they are seized with a seemingly causeless, terrifying panic. This happened to the Philistines after Jonathan and his armor-bearer killed twenty of them. God then caused an earthquake in the midst of the host of Israel's enemies (1 Samuel 14:15).

Subsequently, the Philistine soldiers panicked, fought and killed each other. Such is the lot of the wicked, the inevitable outcome for all who dare match their strength with God's strength. The Lord scatters their bones; they are left unburied, their skeletons picked clean by the buzzards, hyenas and bugs of the field.

On another occasion Jehovah made the Syrian army hear a noise of chariots and horses, the noise of a great army (2 Kings 7:6) and this caused the Syrians to flee for their lives. Again, in Hezekiah's day, during the ministry of Isaiah, the LORD heard the blasphemous speech of the servants of the king of Syria. Jehovah said, "Surely I will send a spirit upon him, and he shall hear a rumor and return to his own land; and I will cause him to fall by the sword in his own land" (2 Kings 19:6f; Isaiah 37:36).

Clearly the Lord causes the wicked to fear in the midst of their vaunted fearlessness; He makes them tremble in their security; He makes them terrified within their own castles. Surrounded by their own soldiers they shake themselves to pieces. Where there is defiance of Deity there is divine discomfiture. We learn that to fail to fear the Lord is to stand in fear of them who are really no cause to fear. Sinners are scared of their own shadows, for evil scrambles the conscience. Thank God, the genuine Christian has not been given such a coward spirit of fear (2 Timothy 1:7). May it be ours today to say, "I will fear no evil." (Psalm 23:4)

February 22

Cast your burden on the Lord, and He shall sustain you.
(Psalm 55:22)

Simon Peter, using the Greek Old Testament, renders *burden* as *care* (1 Peter 5:7). The word means anxiety, that which draws us in different directions or distractions. Different words rendered burden mean such things as pressure, oppression, depression, load, weight, bundle, moral faults, or something to be lifted. In Isaiah 13:1 burden has the meaning of divine judgment. Translated into everyday language, burden means trouble: poor health, mounting bills, leaking roof, disobedient children, unemployment, etc.

There are also burdens of a spiritual nature: Are your children saved? Is your husband a Christian? What can be done to strengthen the spiritual life of your church? When will you be delivered from the shackling sin that so easily besets you? And so it goes (Job 14:1).

What shall we do with these burdens? The Bible says put them on the Lord. There is no adequate substitute for casting your burdens on Christ. Escapism, Hollywood, regret or remorse, indignation, revenge, recreation and pleasure, bitterness, alcohol, dope, money, job advancement, material goods, trips, etc. may lift some burdens only temporarily. But in time the burden is felt heavier.

Only the unburdening of the heart and placing all on the shoulders of the Lord Jesus will satisfy the aching heart. The sensible thing to do is not let burdens accumulate, but seek relief in prayer immediately. Do not let burdens crush you into do-nothing. Take them to the Lord and leave them there.

For we have a Friend in the Lord Jesus: All our sins and griefs to bear. What a privilege to carry Everything to God in prayer. Have we trials and temptations? Is there trouble anywhere? We should never be discouraged, Take it to the Lord in prayer. (Joseph Scriven)

February 23

Cast your burden on the LORD, and He shall sustain you; He shall never permit the righteous to be moved. (Psalm 55:22)

There is no escape from the deep impact sin has upon life, for all of us are sinners by birth and by choice. However, what we do with our life's assignment is very important. What we do with our burden tells a lot about us.

A wonderful Savior is Jesus my Lord,
He taketh my burden away;
He holdeth me up, and I shall not be moved,
He giveth me strength as my day. (Fanny Crosby)

Never a trial that He is not there,
Never a burden that He doth not bear,
Never a sorrow that He doth not share,
Moment by moment, I'm under His care. (Dan Whittle)

Because we differ in our make-up, with varying temperament, intellect, background, personality, character, spiritual health and physical condition, our reactions to burdens differ. Some of us make shortcuts, cover up, tell lies, sham or pretend, put on a front, and become defensive and offensive. We act as if we have no burdens, but we are only acting. Others become bitter and verbalize their feelings that they have had more than their share of misery. One young man told me that he did not believe in God. I asked him why. He replied, "Because He let my father die, and my father was a good man." David would suggest instead of criticizing the Lord that we cast our burdens upon Him. Remember today:

Just when I need Him Jesus is strong,
Bearing my burdens all the day long;
For all my sorrow giving a song,
Just when I need Him most. (Wm. C. Poole)

February 24

He shall never permit the righteous to be moved. (Psalm 55:22)

Christians are new creations. As such we have new names signifying we are new persons. Can you imagine then finding the following people in our churches: Jittery John, Sad Sue, Nervous Nellie, Ailing Alice, Troubled Tillie, Doubting David, Pitiful Paul, Woe-is-Me-William, Climbing Up-the-Rough-Side-of-the-Mountain Moses, et al? Sunday after Sunday they come to church all burdened down, and in spite of the messages of hope in Christ, they still complain, whine, wring their hands, and bite their fingernails!

"Boomerang-Baptists" cast their burdens on the Lord, and then snatch them back. Sometimes it is because they put the Lord on **their** own time schedule. When He does not work as fast as they think He ought, they step back in and pick up the burden. This should not be, for the Lord is more than capable of keeping us. He is faithful.

Perhaps you are retired and on a limited fixed income; or you suffer badly from all kinds of physical ailments. Those of you with gray hair, whose steps have slowed down, whose hands tremble, legs are bowed, the grinders cease because they are few, and eyes are clouded with cataracts; and you have watched old friends and family members one by one depart from these mundane shores—remember, the Lord will not allow you to be moved outside of His tender loving care. Distress may come. Stumbling, faltering, mistakes, backslidings, adversities, trouble—yea, these all may be our lot, but in the end we are unmoved.

When my burden's heavy, I shall not be moved,
When my burden's heavy, I shall not be moved,
Like a tree planted by the water, I shall not be moved.
(Edward Boatner)

February 25

They mark my steps. (Psalm 56:6)

How true this was of the Lord Jesus Christ. Though He came to do the will of the Father, and the Father was well pleased, yet His foes kept their eyes upon Him. His steps were marked. He was tested by the Devil, laughed to scorn, and murmured against. Stones were picked up to kill Him. He was plotted against; derided by the religious leaders, reviled by hypocrites, and told to His face that His witness was false. He was called crazy, possessed by a demon, a Samaritan, in league with Beelzebub, and labeled a deceiver.

His own brothers did not believe in Him. Many would-be disciples turned their backs on Him and went away. Enemies tried to trap Him in His talk. He was spied on, lied on and made unwelcome. Accused of breaking the Law of Moses, he was limited by unbelief and pursued by sign-seekers. His authority was challenged. He was betrayed, denied, arrested, deserted, mocked and spat upon.

His beard was plucked. He was smitten with closed fists and slapped with open palms. He was whipped, cursed, illegally tried and accused of blasphemy. A crown of thorns was mashed down upon His brow. Spikes were driven into His hands and feet. And He was lifted up upon a cruel cross. Shedding His blood for you and for me, He gave up the ghost.

See, from His head, His hands, His feet,
Sorrow and love flow mingled down;
Did e'er such love and sorrow meet,
Or thorns compose so rich a crown?
(Isaac Watts)

February 26

Lead me to the rock that is higher than I. (Psalm 61:2)

Rock is one of the many names of God. In the Psalms we read: "The Lord is my rock . . . who is a rock, except our God? Blessed be my Rock . . . My God the rock of my refuge" (Psalms 18:31, 46; 94:22). The prophet Isaiah also calls Jehovah the rock of strength . . . the Rock, the Mighty One of Israel. The question is asked, "Is there a God besides Me? Indeed, there is no other Rock; I know not one" (Isaiah 17:10; 44:8).

Moses declared, "He is the Rock . . . Jeshurun (Israel) grew fat and scornfully esteemed the Rock of his salvation . . . the Rock who begot you . . . their rock is not like our Rock" (Deuteronomy 32:4, 15, 18, 31). It is a rock, said Isaiah, that is "a strength to the needy in his distress, a refuge from the storm, a shade from the heat . . . as the shadow of a great rock in a weary land" (25:4; 32:2).

Now this Rock, this asylum, haven, succor, impregnable place of safety, shelter, refuge and deliverance, unattainable in man's strength is Jesus Christ. Indeed, the Rock that supplied water to the Israelites in the wilderness is none other than the Lord Jesus (1 Corinthians 10:4), the ever present Lord sustaining and nurturing His people.

And we too have a Rock following us in this wilderness below. We too are a privileged people. In the Lord Jesus Christ we are secure. He is our Rock, higher than we are— God who came down from the highest in order to die, who rose again, ascended and sat down at the right hand of the Father. It is mighty good to have a God in heaven. When things happen to remind you of your weaknesses: when arthritis cripples, when a husband walks out and you're helpless to make him stay, when pain wracks the body, when Death moves in the family and his cold hand touches loved ones—at just such a time it is good to be reminded that there is a Rock, strong, steady, impregnable, solid, a shelter that is higher than we.

February 27

Lead me to the rock that is higher than I. (Psalm 61:2)

The psalmist recognized his inability to help himself. Some of us go quite far in life, self-reliant, independent, sure of ourselves, before we come to the point we realize we cannot make the journey by ourselves successfully. There are times when strength fails us, thoughts are blocked, pain is unbearable, money is gone, friends betray, hope vanishes, dreams are deferred, and fears shatter our fragile minds.

David lived long enough to discover this, and the Psalms are replete with his requests for divine help, leading, guidance, direction, hearing, deliverance, and salvation. So you and I must learn that it is not in man that walks to direct his steps. We need help and we cry, "Lord, lead us."

Now not everybody *can* help us. Human help is of no value when it comes too late or too little. Reuben, the oldest brother, wanted to help Joseph, but when he returned to the pit he discovered his brothers had sold Joseph into slavery for 20 pieces of silver. Sometimes motives are bad. Abraham refused the spoil offered him lest the king of Sodom should say, "I have made Abraham rich."

Forgetfulness is a factor also. Joseph was forgotten in prison by the chief butler for two full years. We don't know enough, and so ignorance limits our usefulness. Illness incapacitates. Ingratitude also restricts our ability to help, because a man who is not thankful for what he has becomes unable to use what he has to help others; ingratitude does not foster a desire to help others.

The self-righteousness of Job's friends detracted from any ability to really help Job. And so it goes. We mortals can go only so far in our ability to aid one another or to help ourselves. David knew all of this and so sought help from the Rock on high. Remember this today: The help you need is not in you, but in Jesus Christ enabling you to do all things according to His will.

February 28

Lead me to the rock that is higher than I. (Psalm 61:2)

There is a help that requires certain moral attributes to be evident. When *truth* is needed, man is bankrupt, for the Word says that all men are liars. When *righteousness* is required, man is useless, for all sinned and are falling short of God's glory. There is none righteous, no, not one. When *peace* is needed, man has little to offer if he himself is not at peace with God. And so it goes. No matter who you are, outside help is needed.

As a king David had at his disposal great wealth and power. Yet there came times when even the mighty monarch cried for help. The rock must be higher than the king; so high that even astronauts cannot fly over it. This rock is too high for men and their arms of flesh; too high for the Devil and his fiery darts; and too high for demons who seek to possess humans. However ambitious men may be they cannot climb this rock. Mad bombers cannot blow it up; political and military leaders cannot topple it; abortionists cannot cut it out; legislators cannot veto it; Hollywood cannot commercialize this rock; and musicians cannot play this rock.

Hear David's impassioned plea for help, his heart faint, overwhelmed, burdened down by a sense of having been left all alone, isolated, weak and insecure. He needs a sense of God's presence and protection. Men are impressed with the granite strength of rocks, symbols of eternal strength, enduring, unassailable, of illimitable power and immutable stability, attributes found only in God. How reassuring to know our God is the unchanging Lord of heaven, stronger than the Rock of Gibraltar, which He created.

The Lord's our Rock, in Him we hide; A shelter in the time of storm; Secure whatever ill betide, A shelter in the time of storm. O, Jesus is a Rock in a weary land, a weary land, a weary land; O, Jesus is a Rock in a weary land, A shelter in the time of storm. (V. J. Charlesworth)

February 29

Come and hear, all you who fear God, and I will declare what He has done for my soul. (Psalm 66:16)

It is my custom to talk with church members who are sick in the hospital about their souls, and about their personal relationship with Jesus Christ. Even for long-time members I do this, for you never know what will happen, and I want the satisfaction of hearing their profession of faith in the shed blood of Jesus Christ. Of course, you can only take their word for what they say they believe.

There is no X-ray machine or electronic scanning device with which to look into their hearts and discover what people believe. This is God's prerogative; He alone knows the thoughts and intents of every human heart. As the Negro spiritual says, "Oh, He sees all you do, and hears all you say, My Lord's a-writing all the time."

All this came to mind as I visited one of our members, a badly burned patient at the St. Agnes Burn Center in Philadelphia. He would not have recognized me by sight, for I had on a gown, mask and cap. But he could hear. And when I told him who I was and he recognized my voice, he moved, tried to raise his bandaged right hand, and the excitement showed up on the heart monitor, causing the nurses to rush to his bedside. I left with tears in my eyes, feeling absolutely helpless, and wondering if the patient could survive. I marveled too at the dedication and skill of the nurses who worked there. However, the next day, he died.

Today, think about the opportunities that may come your way to testify of Calvary. Take advantage of them. Tell others what the Lord Jesus has done for your soul. For the time may well come when you would like to speak but no sound will come forth.

March 1

Whom have I in heaven but You? And there is none upon earth that I desire besides You. (Psalm 73:25)

Observation of the wicked can be discouraging: Watching the wicked may affect us negatively. For one thing, seemingly, they die easy. Their eyes bulge from fatness. They seem not to be in trouble as other men; rather they are at ease, prosperous, increased in riches, even though they mock God, and poke out their mouths against heaven.

For believers to observe such goings on, to see things break thus for the ungodly can have an adverse effect. If we are not careful, bitterness may set in and produce reactions resulting in ignorance and folly.

Emphasis upon things leads to despair: Note the text does not state "**what** have I in heaven?" We do not read "and there is **nothing** upon earth that I desire beside **it**." In other words, the emphasis is not upon things, for things cannot permanently satisfy the longings of our heart. They cannot fill the aching void.

True prosperity is found only in God: It is found in Him who lives in heaven. The human soul finds its portion not in things but in a Person; and that Person is Jesus Christ. This is the message of the psalmist, Asaph. Let your song this morning be,

Thou the Spring of all my comfort,
More than life to me,
Whom have I on earth beside Thee?
Whom in heav'n but Thee?
Savior, Savior, Hear my humble cry;
While on others Thou art calling,
Do not pass me by!
(Fanny J. Crosby)

March 2

Remember Your congregation, which You have purchased of old, the tribe of Your inheritance, which You have redeemed—this Mount Zion where You have dwelt. (Psalm 74:2)

The light is not focused upon the psalmist but upon God: "Lord, *You* remember *Your* people whom *You* purchased—*Your* inheritance, which *You* redeemed—Mount Zion where *You* have dwelt." Here is a clue to solving our situation. It requires knowledge of what *God* has done for us. Only a knowledgeable Jew could appreciate this verse.

We Christians should not be one whit behind them. We too were purchased; the blood of Christ shed at Calvary for us was more precious than silver or gold. We too were redeemed, brought out of slavery from Egypt's land and old Pharaoh's hand. Instead of dwelling within sticks and stones, the Holy Spirit lives within us. We are walking Mount Zions! So Lord, come and see about us! Remember us!

It is true that Jehovah purchased Israel. He redeemed her from slavery in Egypt, and brought her to the Promised Land. God had a peculiar right and title to her, as the rod of His inheritance (Jeremiah 10:16). It is likewise true that Jehovah selected Mount Zion as His dwelling place. "And I will dwell among the children of Israel, and will not forsake My people Israel" (1 Kings 6:13). "For the Lord has chosen Zion; He has desired it for His dwelling place. This is My resting place forever; here I will dwell, for I have desired it" (Psalm 132:13f). Whatever you do today, don't let your life on earth give a lie to the life you shall live in Heaven. Show the world what God in Christ has done for you already!

Savior, since of Zion's city, I through grace a member am;
Let the world deride or pity, I will glory in Thy name;
Fading is the world's best pleasure, All its boasted pomp and show; Solid joys and lasting treasure None but Zion's children know. (John Newton)

March 3

Remember Your congregation, which You have purchased of old, the tribe of Your inheritance, which You have redeemed—this Mount Zion where You have dwelt. (Psalm 74:2)

Does the exhortation to God to remember mean it is possible for God to forget? No. Here we talk *about* God and talk *to* God in terms that we use with other human beings. Such language (*anthropomorphism*: man-form) is heard often: "God remembered Noah . . . God remembered Abraham . . . God remembered Rachel . . .God remembered His covenant" (Genesis 8:1; 19:29; 30:22; Exodus 2:24).

The fact that something happened, some action was taken, some event occurred, is a phenomenon explained by saying "God remembered." By this we mean God did something, He performed some act. We explain God as He chose to reveal Himself; He is described in human language through the book He gave us. So telling God to remember something or someone is a common biblical exhortation.

Sometimes He is called upon to remember people with kindness, or to grant requests, protect, deliver, punish, intercede in mercy, extenuating circumstances, their sins, etc. During the Good Friday services the well-known words are heard, "Lord remember me when You come into Your kingdom" (Luke 23:42). We find in the text what theologians call expostulation, literally, demand entirely or strongly, and so to reason earnestly with someone in an effort to dissuade or correct, to remonstrate; it is objection in the form of earnest reasoning. So we find the psalmist *expostulating* with God.

Do you talk to the Lord this way? When you think things go wrong, do you tell Him you don't like it, or why you don't like it? Or do you pout in a private pity party, or stop going to church? Perhaps the first thing to do this morning then is to determine that you will be more open with God, more frank, aboveboard, as you speak to Him today, and walk where He dwells.

March 4

Remember Your congregation, which You have purchased of old, the tribe of Your inheritance, which You have redeemed—this Mount Zion where You have dwelt. (Psalm 74:2)

Regardless of your circumstances, or how bad things look, you must not ever feel that God has utterly forsaken you. He has not and will not, for He has promised in His Word, "Lo, I am with you always, even to the end of the age. Amen" (Matthew 28:20). "I will never leave you, nor forsake you" (Hebrews 13:5). Situations may seem impossible to understand, but God knows and He cares. He knew what was going on there at Calvary—the anguish, consternation, the pain, and broken heartedness—all that made up the cry from the cross, "My God, My God! Why have You forsaken Me?"

Make no mistake, God the Father knew what He was doing. He knew that His Son, Jesus Christ who had not sinned, became sin there on the cross. So that whatever you experience, if you belong to Him, rest assured He has a purpose for your life; He knows and He cares. You may be moved to cry out like the psalmist, "Lord, remember me!" Remember You bought me and redeemed me—remember You cleansed and made me whole—remember You snatched me from the burning jaws of Hell!

Remember You changed my name and wrote it down in Heaven—remember You melted my heart of stone—remember I am your child—remember I am part of Your inheritance—remember I am in Your body, the Church—remember I am the sheep of Your pasture—and remember Your Holy Spirit lives in me! Because God's honor is at stake, because of His relationship to you and with you, He cannot desert you; He cannot forget. Whether He comes with swift steps of solution for your sad situation or not, be it known your Heavenly Father does remember. And He cares.

March 5

I will hear what God the LORD will speak, for He will speak peace to His people and to His saints; but let them not turn back to folly. (Psalm 85:8)

When Isaiah was commissioned Jehovah sent him to a people who "hear indeed but understand not" because their ears were *heavy* (Isaiah 6:9f). The apostle Paul, in announcing his ministry to the Gentiles cited the Isaiah Scripture and described the ears of the Jews as *dull* of hearing (Acts 28:27). Jeremiah's language too is strong. Concerning Israel's inability to hear and obey the word of the Lord, the prophet said their ear was *uncircumcised*; this means unreceptive.

Paul warned that the time would come when folks would turn their ears from the truth and with *itching* ears burning with curiosity would desire to hear something pleasant, tickly, "spicy and nicy" (2 Timothy 4:3f). And so, heavy, dull, uncircumcised and itching ears are figures of speech describing causes for disobedience and sin.

Then there are *stopped up* ears. Proverbs 21:13 warns, "Whoever shuts his ears to the cry of the poor will also cry himself and not be heard." Such are the kinds of ears whereby hearers turn again to folly. There are also *bored* ears, that is, pierced ears. If a servant desires to remain with his master when he could be free, then the master would bore the servant's ear with an awl. This meant as long as the servant lived he would serve him. A pierced or bored ear signified an open ear, ready to do the will of the master (Exodus 21:5-6 Psalm 40:6).

We have no trouble understanding that the open ear means obedience. Job 36:10: "He also opens their ear to instruction." Isaiah 50:5: "The LORD GOD has opened my ear, and I was not rebellious" This is what the psalmist had in mind when he wrote, "I will hear what God the LORD will speak." What kind of ears will we have today?

March 6

Bless the LORD, O my soul, and forget not all His benefits.
(Psalm 103:2)

I can still remember the times when I had no ark of safety in the time of flood--no city of refuge to flee to--no manna from heaven to feed upon--no friend to stick closer than a brother--no peace in the valley--no beauty to behold, and no deliverer from Egypt.

I can still remember when I had no desire to go on living--no shield to quench the fiery darts of the Evil one--no escape in the night--no angel to shake my dungeon, break my shackles or cool my fiery furnace--no High Tower to run into and no Shield or Buckler to protect me from my foes.

Yea, I still remember when I had no Captain to lead me in victory--no balm in Gilead, no physician to heal me--no heaven in my view--no bright morning star in my sky--no Comforter to strengthen me--no Holy Spirit to fill me--no Good Shepherd to call me by name--no oasis in the desert, and no well of water to quench my thirst.

I can still remember when there was no Promised Land in my sight--no love in my heart--no bright mansion above--no song in my soul--no melody in my mouth--no praise on my lips--no eternity on my mind--no lawyer to plead my case—and no crown on my head.

I can still remember when I had no robe for my back--no spring in my steps--no God in my thoughts--no hope for tomorrow and no help for today--no joy in my spirit and no blood to cleanse away my sins!

But now I can thank God for all His blessings and benefits! For Jesus Christ shed His blood for my sins, and bought me out of the slave market. And from Him all blessings flow!

March 7

He sent a man before them—Joseph—who was sold as a slave. They hurt his feet with fetters, he was laid in irons. (Psalm 105:17, 18)

Analysis of Joseph's pilgrimage from his father's protection to a pit to Potiphar to prison to the palace of Pharaoh reveals the father's favoritism, divine dreams, the brothers' envy, a woman's wrath, and a friend's forgetfulness. Consequently Joseph suffered terribly, sensitive soul that he was. Often circumstances seem to contradict the promises of God; and our patience runs short, for we put God on our own time schedule. So we must marvel at the patience of Joseph here. The story starts when he was but 17 years old. When he stood before Pharaoh, king of Egypt, he was 30 years old (Genesis 37:2, 41:46).

Within this time frame of approximately 13 years he suffered immensely. He faced the jealousy of his brothers, whose cruelty degenerated into a murderous hatred. Indeed, he would have been killed were it not for his oldest brother, Reuben, and later for his brother, Judah, who suggested they sell him into slavery. He faced the humiliation and degradation of enslavement. Treated as a piece of baggage, a thing, in horror his feet were chained as he endured slavery. He faced the false accusation of Potiphar's wife. Staring injustice in the face, he was imprisoned as a common criminal among cutthroats. For nearly ten years he suffered this unjust imprisonment.

Some modern day Christians, looking at Joseph, would say, "Man, you *must* be out of God's will. God wants you to be free, happy, well, and rich." Such a thought is based upon misinterpretation of the Scriptures, promulgated by presumptuous ecclesiastical quacks and unholy charlatans driven by a feeling of spiritual superiority. There are those who would look at Joseph in his affliction and suggest he was a hypocrite. But our Sovereign Lord was working something out in Joseph's life!

March 8

*He sent a man before them—Joseph—who was sold as a
slave. They hurt his feet with fetters, he was laid in irons.*
(Psalm 105:17, 18)

It was a long time before Joseph's dreams were fulfilled.
And perhaps some things that have happened in your life
make it appear God has forgotten you. All too often we
believers are adversely influenced by the world. But the
child of God should look behind the scenes and see God's
grace that enables us to suffer the scorn of the skeptics, put
up with the contempt of the uncouth, deal with the indifference of those we serve, suffer the lack of sympathy from
supposed friends; and endure the neglect of neighbors, the
lies of hypocrites, and the tensions within the family.

Through it all Joseph believed the Lord God was with
him. Somehow he reckoned that his troubles were stepping
stones. Though his faith was sorely tested he prevailed. He
graduated from the school of hard knocks with high honors.
Experience taught him that it pays to serve the Lord. The
dreamer saw what others could not see; and the vision stayed
with him through the evil vicissitudes of life.

When you have a foretaste of Heaven, a walk and a talk
with the Lord, the experience prepares you for all the
troubles that lie ahead. Don't give up. The Lord is working
out something special in you, for you, and with you. He has a
plan for you. He wants to use you. Joseph believed what God
said and though he went through bitter experiences over a
period of years, he did not give up or give in.

In the end, the Lord fulfilled His plan not only for
Joseph's life, but the life of Israel, His chosen people. So
much so that, years later, Joseph could say to his brothers,
"God sent me before you to preserve a posterity for you in
the earth, and to save your lives by a great deliverance. . .
You meant evil against me, but God meant it for good"
(Genesis 45:7-8; 50:20).

March 9

This is the day which the LORD has made; we will rejoice and be glad in it. (Psalm 118:24)

How often when I awake on Sunday mornings and discover it is raining or snowing outside I feel despondent. I am saddened to know that church attendance will be down, and so will finances. And so I am down. But then God speaks to my heart through this text and gives consolation. I rejoice in knowing that our Lord is Creator; it is He who makes both the rain and the day, thus He is the Creator of rainy Sundays. So rejoice and be glad in them.

James Stalker was a minister who constantly gave God thanks for everything. Some members of his congregation were becoming irritated at such constant rejoicing, so one Sunday when it was bitterly cold outside, and not too warm inside the church, they were anxious to see what the pastor would thank God for this time. There was no large furnace to warm the room, just a small pot-bellied stove woefully inadequate for the piercing, biting wind. "Aha, we caught him this time! There's nothing to rejoice over on a day like this!" said one of the parishioners. But the grateful minister began the service and prayed, "O Lord, we thank Thee that it is not always like this!"

Today we live in troubled, perilous times. Cursing, crime and corruption are common; deluded dope dealers deceive; and murderers stalk the streets as blood touches blood. Fears paralyze the bravest of souls; and apostasy is at home in too many churches. But thank God it will not always be like this. Today is used by the Ancient of Days to accomplish His plan and to bring about the close of his dispensation. Praise God we are able to rejoice in the day of trouble, sing a song while sojourning in a strange, sorrowful, sin-sick land. And we are to understand that the Lord knows the situation we are in. He knows every step we will take today.

March 10

This is the day which the LORD has made; we will rejoice and be glad in it. (Psalm 118:24)

There is no suggestion here that the Christian should walk around like a Cheshire cat with a frozen grin on his or her face. That would be phony. There are times when we are sad and it shows in our countenances. We are pained, disappointed or discouraged. But still we have a hope, an expectation of good. We know a better day is coming; weeping may endure for a night, but joy comes in the morning.

In this prophetic or Messianic psalm, we see first the rejection of the Lord Jesus as the Stone, and then we see His final exaltation as the Head of the corner. Here is described a festive, gala occasion, a day of celebration based upon Jehovah's victory. It is time to celebrate the many deliverances of the Lord. At such a time there is to be no sadness, for such an emotion would be like treason.

It is almost as if to be sad at such a time were an expression of ingratitude. So the command comes, rejoice! Be glad! This is the day of our Lord's victory! See then joy as a duty. No regenerated heart has any business being unduly burdened down; we should not be crying the blues, habitually climbing the rough side of the mountain. Try going around it some time; or by faith casting the mountain into yonder Schuylkill River.

No soul should be too heavy to leap up for gladness. Somehow all that is wearisome and sad in your life takes a back seat when you see Jesus Christ. Something about Him banishes pain, makes you forget the rain, calms the angry waves, hushes the boisterous winds and tells your soul, "Peace, be still." And you are reminded that every day is a day He has made.

March 11

The LORD will perfect that which concerns me. (Psalm 138:8)

The word rendered *to perfect* means to accomplish, end, come to an end, or complete. God will bring to an end that which concerns us. Intervening on our behalf, He will do what He promised; He will fulfill His purpose and work out His plan for our lives. He is the God who accomplishes, performs all things for us (Psalm 57:2).

The God of the Bible is not a Giant Watchmaker who wound up the earth's clock, then went about His business while letting the earth tick-tock down all on its own. No! As Creator He is also Sustainer, Director, Maintainer, Preserver, Provider, Ecologist, Chief Engineer, and Perfecter. It is His role as Perfecter that presently claims our attention.

Bible perfection for believers does not mean sinlessness. It involves growth. And whatever we need, when we need it, God provides. His aim is to make us more like His Son, the Lord Jesus. What a joy to know that the God of History, the Most High God, the Father of our Lord and Savior Jesus Christ is concerned about us. And that He works on and works with that which concerns, pertains to and involves us. Yea, He makes all things work together for our good, because we love Him because He first loved us.

What a joy to know that He who bought us with His own blood is not an absentee landlord, but an ever present loving Lord, indwelling, molding, shaping, instructing, guiding, leading, edifying, improving, warning, exhorting, pleading, commanding, opening doors, removing stumbling blocks, putting down enemies, raising up friends, springing traps, thwarting the Devil, healing and providing—yea, whatever effects your life, my life—He perfects, brings to an end. Thank God today for the assurance that what the Lord started in you, He will accomplish, perform, perfect, bring to an end, and complete it until the Day of Christ Jesus (Philippians 1:6).

March 12

The LORD will perfect that which concerns me. (Psalm 138:8)

This text speaks of things that concern me and not things that give me concern. The things that give me concern are only a small part of the things that concern me. Yes, there *are* things that worry me. And it is good for us to worry, for after all, some of the things we worry about never happen! Note the subjective element in the Psalms. For example, in Psalm 23: "The Lord is *my* Shepherd; *I* shall not want. He makes *me* to lie down . . . He leads *me*." Of course, someone may say, "David does not speak just for himself as one individual person. He speaks for the nation Israel, the chosen people of God." This is true.

Even in Psalm 138 David's thanksgiving is an expression of Israel's gratitude. David's voice of assurance is Israel's term of confidence as well. We have no quarrel with this. But the personal element is not thereby eliminated. So that our fore parents, imprisoned in slavery, had no choice but to consider what the Lord meant to them personally. Call it subjectivism, compensatory, or whatever, they knew that the God of the Bible was concerned about the believer's personal welfare.

We hear these words of the Negro spirituals: "It's *me*, O Lord, standing in the need of prayer," "Sometimes *I* feel like a motherless child," "Swing low, sweet chariot, coming for to carry *me* home," "*I* ain't got long to stay here," "Give *me* Jesus," and "Every time *I* feel de Spirit."

I am not unmindful of the corporate nature of the Church. But everybody in the church is not in the Church. For you who sure enough are cleansed by the precious blood of Christ, the Lord will perfect that which concerns you. Rejoice today that He is also going to finish what He started in you.

March 13

Where can I go from Your Spirit? Or where can I flee from Your presence? (Psalm 139:7)

God Is Beneath Us. Omnipresence is a word distinctively peculiar to Deity. An eternally active attribute, it speaks of a God who always has been, is now, and ever shall be everywhere present at the same time. A God who is not omnipresent is an absurdity. However, man's finite mind cannot grasp the concept of the infinite. We say the words, we verbalize the ideas, but we are creatures of time, limited to being in one place at one time, and even then our stay is unsteady. But God's perfection demands that He be everywhere present, and that He be wholly present in every place.

Moses said that God is beneath us (Deuteronomy 33:27). As he was soon to die, his body buried by an angel, and Joshua to take his place, he reminded Israel of Jehovah's unfailing support in bearing and sustaining them. In their prosperity and in their poverty, He supports them. His Almighty arms are beneath them.

God asked Job, "Have you an arm like God?" (40:9). Of course not, for God's arm strengthens; it is a mighty arm that scatters the enemy. He has made bare His righteous arm in the eyes of all the nations; He swears by the arm of His strength. Yea, His arms shall judge the peoples, and on His arm shall they trust. With an outstretched arm He redeemed Israel, and brought them out of the land of Egypt, and led them to the Promised Land.

He is our arm every morning, our salvation in the time of trouble. He's coming back again with strong hand, and His arm shall rule for Him. He shall gather the lambs with His arms and carry them in His bosom. Let us sing unto the Lord a new song, for His holy arm has gotten Him the victory. Thank God He is beneath us, enabling us to say, "We are secure, leaning on the everlasting arms!"

March 14

Where can I go from Your Spirit? Or where can I flee from Your presence? (Psalm 139:7)

<u>God Is Around Us.</u> Here is another reason we cannot escape His Presence: "The Lord surrounds His people" even "as the mountains surround Jerusalem" (Psalm 125:2). Mountains are symbols of permanence, steadfastness and strength. For Jerusalem to be surrounded by mountains or high hills signifies her security, guardianship, and Jehovah's care of the inhabitants. Now like those mountains in which Jerusalem sits enthroned, so the Lord surrounds His own faithful people; those who trust in the Lord are immovable.

Sometimes we believers fail to realize our Lord is all around us, encircling us. Peer pressure moves us to seek to break through the protecting circle. We feel hemmed in, and that biblical Christianity is too restrictive. But true freedom is to be limited by God; the slave of Christ is the person who is most free. Men who seek to break through the encircling mountains soon find themselves full of anxiety, fears, distrust and suffering from symptoms of stress. Outside the circle of God's presence are darkness and all kinds of things that seek to shake us from our foundation.

We discover we cannot live *in* Jerusalem and *outside* of Jerusalem at the same time. To be happy in this life, stay within the circle of God's all-encompassing protection. Stay in His will. As the mountains round about Jerusalem signify restful strength, stability, and a protecting wall, so the Christian is encircled by the power of God. As you are faithful to His Word you will come to realize in a very practical way that your God is all around you.

Zion stands with hills surrounded, Zion, kept by pow'r divine; All her foes shall be confounded, Tho' the world in arms combine; Happy Zion, what a favor'd lot is thine!
(Thomas Kelly)

March 15

Where can I go from Your Spirit? Or where can I flee from Your presence? (Psalm 139:7)

God Is In Front Of Us. We learn today that our omnipresent Lord is before us, even as the Lord went before the Israelites "By day in a pillar of cloud to lead the way, and by night in a pillar of fire to give them light" (Exodus 13:21). It took the slaying of their firstborn to force the Egyptians to free the children of Israel. And there was not a house where there was not one dead, from the lavish palace of the Pharaoh to the pitiful shack of the peasant to the poor prisoners in the dungeon—God had moved!

Now see the Jews on their way out of Egypt by way of the wilderness of the Red Sea. They took their journey from Rameses to Succoth—some 600,000 men, beside women and children. From Succoth they encamped in Etham, on the edge of the wilderness.

We do not always understand why God leads us by way of the wilderness. It seems He takes us round about, and as far as we can see a straight line is not only the shortest but the best route. However, the Lord may have other plans. His way may be circuitous, rambling, perilous, time-consuming, rocky, desert-like, dark and shadowy, beset with traps, enemies lurking everywhere, a road full of pain and heartaches—in order that we might realize God is there.

At this point the Lord gave an outward sign to the Israelites that He was present there with them. He had not delivered them to desert them. No, God does not work that way. When He gives you victory in one area, expect Him to stick with you all the way. That's encouraging, isn't it? Note now that there is but one pillar. By day it was a pillar of cloud; by night a pillar of fire to give them light. God's folks have no business walking in the darkness. The one pillar is the one symbol of the presence of the Lord Jehovah going *before* His people.

March 16

Where can I go from Your Spirit? Or where can I flee from Your presence? (Psalm 139:7)

<u>God Is Behind Us.</u> The omnipresent God of the Bible speaks and our ears hear a word behind us, saying, "This is the way, walk in it" (Isaiah 30:21). Israel was exhorted to trust the Lord; however, the Jews were not willing. "In returning and rest you shall be saved; in quietness and confidence shall be your strength," said the Lord (Isaiah 30:15). But Israel would not have it thus. They chose to flee upon horses, to ride upon the swift; and so they did, only to flee pursued by the swifter.

Many there be who propose *their* ways, their blessing plans, their lawyers, their expertise, their know-how, who plot, plan, scheme and dream; but compared to God they all are but blind leaders of the blind. There is a way that seems right unto a man but the end thereof are the ways of death. You see, an omnipresent God is too big for folks to manipulate. Some people are so mean and little in mind that they have a little god, one they can carry around in their handbag or back pocket. Ignorant of an omnipresent God, they do not hear the Lord who stands behind them and says, "This is the way! Walk in it!"

Now the prophet comes and says the LORD wants to show them mercy. "Blessed are all those who wait for Him" (v.18). Here is comfort for God's chastened and repentant people. Through affliction and trial the Christian learns to appreciate the presence of God. Through suffering Israel learned to despise false gods, who could not rescue them from danger. And when your way appears dark, and the weary traveler on life's highway is lost, having eaten the bread of adversity, having drunk the water of affliction— then may your ears hear a word behind you, and the Master Teacher saying, "This is the way, walk in it!"

March 17

Where can I go from Your Spirit? Or where can I flee from Your presence? (Psalm 139:7)

<u>God Is Above Us.</u> Hear David request of an omnipresent God, "Stretch out your hand from above," send Your hand from on high (Psalm 144:7). David spoke here of his troubles. He sought deliverance out of the deep or great waters, a symbol of overwhelming danger like a flood, or the attacks of alien soldiers or the tyranny of foreign kings. He was in trouble because their mouths speak deceit and vanity. He was in trouble because their right hand is a right hand of falsehood. Furthermore, says the psalmist, they make false charges and they break treaties and covenants.

This is why we need an omnipresent God. If He were just in one place at one time, He might not be able to reach Philadelphia in time to help me when an emergency arises. Or some other Christian might be calling on Him at the same time. Who would He answer first? So that in such a condition believers need a God who is not only beneath, in front of, and behind us, but also who is above us.

And what a marvel it is when we realize that so much is above us already—bullets fly over our heads, radio waves are there, airplanes, missiles, and spy satellites. And of course the Devil is the prince of the power of the air. No wonder we need a God above us!

"Come down, Lord," cried David. Bend the heavens and come down! Touch the mountains that they may smoke! Flash forth lightning! Scatter the stars! Ride the wind! Push through the clouds! Stretch forth Your hand from on high. And pluck me out of the hand of the enemy. Such is the plea for heavenly intervention. Hear the words of the Negro spiritual: "Over my head, I see trouble in the air. There must be a God somewhere."

March 18

Where can I go from Your Spirit? Or where can I flee from Your presence? (Psalm 139:7)

Thank God that He is omnipresent, for it means that everywhere you go you have a Friend, Protector and a Savior. You can bet He's there. You cannot see Him, but it does not mean He is not there. You cannot see the wind but you know when it's there. You cannot see electricity but if you touch a live wire, you will know it's there.

At times the Lord makes His presence known by the lightning and thunder, or He speaks in a still small voice. The hoot of the owl, the sad tone of the mourning dove, the trill of the mocking bird, the cry of the brand new baby lets you know God is there. The roar of the lion, the trumpeting of the elephant, the splendor of the giant sequoia trees, the soaring flight of the giant condor over the Andes!

It may be the fury of a hurricane, or two feet of snow or a half inch of ice paralyzing the city, or earthquakes, tsunamis and tidal waves announcing His presence. When the crocuses push their way up through the ground; when metamorphosis takes place and cocooned caterpillars become beautiful moths or butterflies—whether the scene is one of calamity or one of tranquility, He is there. Sun rise and breaking daylight are proof God is present.

The soul genuinely saved through faith in the finished work of Jesus Christ cannot help but rejoice that the true and living God takes great joy in making His presence known to His own. To know that God is beneath, around, in front of, behind and above is refreshing like an oasis in the desert. It is satisfying like water for the thirsty traveler; comforting like warm clothing to the naked cold.

To know He is near to turn bitterness into sweetness; to make springs of joy burst forth in a dry land, and rain to fall in time of drought. To know Christ is near lightens the pressure of poverty, eases the pain of sickness, dissipates the fear of failure and fills the vacuum created by loneliness.

March 19

Search me, O God, and know my heart. (Psalm 139:23)

From time to time I hear talk about a religion that calls for introspection, turning one's thoughts inward, examining one's own feelings and thoughts. Folks sit cross-legged, arms folded, eyes closed, and by deep concentration and meditation look within themselves. From a Bible point of view no man can ever improve himself by contemplation of himself. Nothing from nothing leaves nothing. Introspection is like looking at muddy water.

According to the Bible evil thoughts proceed from the hearts of men (Mark 7:21). Man's heart is "deceitful above all things and desperately wicked, [incurably sick]; who can know it? I, the LORD, search the heart, I test the mind, even to give every man according to his ways, according to the fruit of his doings" (Jeremiah 17:9f).

True knowledge of self comes first of all from an outside source. By himself a man does not realize the condition he is in. Drunk, he thinks he is sober; mad, he believes he is sane; weak, he feels strong; foolish, he considers himself a philosopher; carnal and worldly, he claims to be spiritual; and on his way to Hell, he seeks to build his own heaven on earth.

Man tends to see what he wants to see. The ego is deceived. Sin in the heart loves darkness and refuses to let in the light of God's Word. Measuring himself by himself man is not wise. He fails to understand that God must come in and search. Then whatever report that God gives, that's the way it really is. This text does not encourage us to search ourselves. Rather, God is invited to investigate. David welcomes the continuance of such divine, piercing scrutiny. The psalmist could truthfully sing,

Have Thine own way, LORD; Have Thine own way!
Search me and try me, Master, today! (A. A. Pollard)

Bring my soul out of prison, that I may praise Your name.
(Psalm 142:7)

David fled from the jealous wrath of King Saul at least
twice. On one occasion he and his men hid in the cave of
Adullam. At another time they hid in a cave at En Gedi.
There Saul with 3,000 chosen soldiers went looking for
David. As providence would have it, the very cave Saul
entered to relieve himself was the one in which David hid.
David arose, and stealthily cut off the edge of Saul's robe (1
Samuel 24:4). Later he called Saul and showed him the piece
of the robe; the hunted had spared the life of the hunter.

Hiding in the caves from Saul moved David to regard
his distress as a prison. Thus, "Bring my soul out of prison,"
while taken literally, also figuratively means bring my soul
out of distress, save me from the trouble I am in. He sees his
trouble as imprisonment, and cries, "Lead me out, Lord!"
Have you ever felt like that—locked in and locked up?

Surely sin, self, and Satan desire to put you behind bars.
And lock the doors. And throw away the keys. Men may
offer the keys of humanism, communism, luck, racism, sex,
dope and alcohol—all kinds of gimmicks, philosophies and
escapes, but all to no avail. Deliverance comes only from the
Lord Jesus Christ. Put your faith in Him.

Once the foul fetters of falsehood and foolishness are
fractured; and the doors of despair and disappointment in the
dark, dank dungeon of doom are opened wide, you see that
God leads His children out into the sunshine of freedom.
Who wouldn't praise a God like that? Surely an escaped
prisoner is willing to speak well of his liberator. So ought we
to magnify the name of our Redeemer.

*Christ breaks the pow'r of canceled sin, He sets the prisoner
free; His blood can make the foulest clean, His blood availed
for me.* (Charles Wesley)

March 21

Teach me to do Your will, for You are my God. (Psalm 143:10)

Desire: Christians should desire God's will, even as David did. Christ said, "If anyone wills to do His will, he shall know concerning the doctrine" (John 7:17). Paul said, "Therefore do not be unwise, but understand what the will of the Lord is" (Ephesians 5:17).

Delight: Saints should delight in God's will. The psalmist said, "I delight to do Your will, O my God; and Your law is within my heart" (Psalm 40:8).

Doers: Christians should also be doers of God's will. Our best example for this is Jesus Christ. Prior to coming to the earth, He said, "I have come to do Your will, O God" (Hebrews 10:7). Once on earth He said, "For I have come down from heaven, not to do My own will, but the will of Him who sent Me" (John 6:38; 4:34, 5:30).

Just before going to die on the old rugged cross, hear Him say, "Father, if it is Your will, take [hasten] this cup away from Me; nevertheless not My will, but Yours, be done" (Luke 22:42). A new relationship is pointed out in the words of Christ when He said, "For whoever does the will of My Father in heaven is My brother and sister and mother" (Matthew 12:50). Finally, John reminds us that "he who does the will of God abides forever" (I John 2:17).

Discover: Christians who desire, delight in and do the will of God will discover that His will is the best thing that could happen to them (Romans 12:1-2). God's will for your life is good, acceptable and perfect. There is joy unspeakable in discovering God's will for your life. There is no greater sense of fulfillment in the world than to know God's will and to do it!

March 22

Take firm hold of instruction . . . hold fast the pattern of sound words . . . holding fast the faithful word. (Proverbs 4:13; 2 Timothy 1:13; Titus 1:9)

The exhortation assumes we are teachable. God who commands we hold fast to instruction, to His Word, also makes it possible for us to obey. Teachableness is one of the gifts of the Holy Spirit who lives in the bodies of all who have faith in the shed blood of Jesus Christ. The God of the Bible is He who would have us not to be ignorant, the God who bids us come, learn of Him. Thank God for the Spirit, our Teacher, who patiently works within us.

The exhortation *alerts* us to spiritual thieves. There are those who do not want us to receive or retain any kind of divine wisdom, holy discipline, moral education, Holy Spirit instruction, or rightly-divided Word of God. The command to hold fast should make us aware of the value of our soul. Hold fast what you are taught.

Yea, keep it for life. Don't let anyone steal it. It is predicted that in these last days there will be an increase in false teachers, phony prophets, and spiritual thieves; so that we must develop strong grips on the truth taught and not allow false doctrine to slip in on us.

The exhortation *assures* us that we are on the right track. Whatever the word, the pattern or model of sound, healthy words, we are to hold fast. Whatever the confession of faith, the creed, the basic outline of doctrine, thank God and obey it from the heart.

You will have to depend upon the Holy Spirit in you to determine the truth when you hear it. God will let you know so that you will know and you will know that you know. If God tells you to hold fast, then it means what you have is good. He wants you to keep it. Such a command indicates then that it is possible to know; it is possible to have assurance. You *can* know that God is real. Hold fast!

March 23

Do not enter the path of the wicked, and do not walk in the way of evil. (Proverbs 4:14)

When I was a boy I never joined a gang, for the Lord used Proverbs 1:10 in my life: "My son, if sinners entice you, do not consent." I have since learned that the Bible often warns of bad company (Proverbs 13:20; 1 Corinthians 5:11; 15:33), and the need for alertness and watching where we walk. Christians should be careful, for there is a snake in every Garden of Eden.

Wherever you go you will find a Cain who hates his brother; an Esau who despises spiritual things; a Balaam for hire if the price is right; a Pharaoh who does not want God's people to be free; a Sanballat to discourage those building the wall; and a greedy Gehazi telling lies in order to line his own pockets. There is in every group a Demas in love with this present world; a Goliath who depends upon his physical size and strength, and loses his head.

Yes, even in the church may be those who actively seek to hinder progress. Paul called them wolves. You will find a Judas who is disloyal; a Sapphira and Ananias cheating on God; and a Diotrephes who seeks to have the pre-eminence. All kinds of folks are in our churches. There are self-righteous Pharisees who ignore those in need and cross over to the other side. There are fearful folks who bury their talents.

There are rich folks who count their money but do not count on God; unwise people in church with lamps but no oil. There are those who have been cleansed of their leprosy but fail to give God thanks; and there are foolish folks who build their houses on sand. Today, as the Spirit leads, watch the company you keep; walk circumspectly (Ephesians 5:15). Do not proceed in the path of the perverse, but walk with Christ who alone is the Way, the Truth and the Life.

March 24

But the path of the just is like the shining sun, that shines ever brighter unto the perfect day. (Proverbs 4:18)

I have had much experience driving in the wee hours of the morning, then watching the darkness break up under the relentless but quiet force of the dawn, as the faint rays of the sun push their way through the ceiling of the night to uncover what for man is a new day. What a wonderful welcome relief, for the breaking of the dawn lessens eyestrain, and brings with it thoughts of eating breakfast soon.

David spoke of the light of the morning when the sun rises, a morning without clouds (2 Samuel 23:4), and we are reminded that the road upon which the righteous travel is like the light of dawn, the sunrise that shines bright and clear, an ever-brightening light, until that light comes with the morning splendor of a full and perfect day. If you are on that path, give Christ the glory!

As we get older we tend to be more conservative, and we think more about the end of the journey. God has built within us a thermostat-like device, sensitive not to heat and cold, but to age and the roughness of the road of life. Like a timer it turns on the lights of a darkened hope.

I am saddened when I see senior citizens mistreated; elderly parents abandoned, crippled physically, impoverished economically or helpless in many ways. I see their days of pioneering unappreciated, the ingratitude of others having scarred their hearts, and their life-savings swindled by unscrupulous lawyers, callous businessmen, and wicked relatives.

Yet there are those who see a bright light ahead. And their faith astounds me, for despite bad environment and meager possessions, there are those whose hope is built on nothing less than Jesus' blood and righteousness. A long time ago they became citizens of heaven and never turned back. It is as if they heard the apostle Paul say, "For now our salvation is nearer than when we first believed" (Romans 13:11). *When the long day is ended, the journey is o'er, I shall enter that blessed abode, For the Savior I love will be waiting for me, When I come to the end of the road* (Alfred H. Ackley).

*A talebearer reveals secrets, but he who is of a faithful spirit
conceals a matter.* (Proverbs 11:13)

There are two different Hebrew words rendered "talebearer";
they mean (1) whisperer or busybody and (2) slanderer,
tattler, or gossip. Believers are warned to stay away from
such folks, for the talebearer's words are but a means to an
evil end. His goal may be to get revenge, weaken authority,
destroy reputations, and cause chaos and conflict.

In contrast to the talebearer, the verse goes on to say that
"he that is of a faithful spirit conceals the matter." The
faithful, reliable spirit is the one God commends. He who is
trusting of mind keeps silence with regards to that which is
confided in him. Confidentiality is essential. Such a person is
trustworthy, and can be confided in, for he will keep hidden
whatever you tell him in secret. He will keep it back from the
knowledge and power of others.

In other words, a faithful spirit is a firm, dependable,
reliable, steadfast spirit; it is a person who is established,
proven to be firm, true, and well-grounded. Such faithfulness
is proof of the presence of the Holy Spirit dwelling within.
The Lord is looking for Christians in this Church Age who
can be trusted—trusted not only with money, time, and
talent, but also with confidences. For it is the desire of the
Lord that His Church be a true fellowship.

Trustworthy Christians strengthen the Church. Pastors
and members help one another because they know what is
spoken in private will not be broadcast in the streets. From
the Hebrew verb *aman*, meaning to confirm or support, we
have derived the word "amen". And from this verb *aman*
comes the word "faithful". Are we able today to say *amen* to
being Christians, possessing a faithful spirit?

March 26

The generous soul will be made rich [fat: KJV], and he who waters will also be watered himself. (Proverbs 11:25)

At prayer meeting I announced Sunday's sermon topic: "How to Be a Fat Christian." Later, my wife informed me she was going to stay home that Sunday morning. But she came; and she had plenty of company. Perhaps *your* mind will be put at ease if you realize that in the Old Testament "to be made fat" means to be enriched, to be made prosperous. The metaphor or figure of speech is derived from the condition of well-nourished animals or good-sized vegetables. A fat olive tree, for example, is loaded with olives and will produce much oil.

So fatness is abundance, luxuriance, productivity, fertility, or increase (not in grease). We learn: "Don't be stingy or you'll be skinny; a stingy saint is a skinny, string-bean sad sack sight!" People who are tight-fisted or miserly not only harm the cause of Christ, but they hurt themselves. After all, every beast of the forest is His, and the cattle upon a thousand hills, and all of the hills are His; the silver and the gold are His (Psalm 50:10; Haggai 2:8).

Now liberality includes not only how *much* you give, but *how* you give. The generous soul is literally the "soul of blessing." A soul of blessing is one from whom blessings go out to others. Your liberal giving to the local assembly makes you a blessing to all of the members. When you do not give out you do not take in.

Thus the text is saying, "Stingy out, stingy in" or "Fat out, fat in." "He that waters shall be watered also himself." The blessing you give out comes back to you. Paul, led by the Holy Spirit put it this way, "He who sows sparingly will also reap sparingly; and he who sows bountifully will also reap bountifully" (2 Corinthians 9:6).

The soul of a lazy man [sluggard, KJV] desires, and has nothing; but the soul of the diligent shall be made rich [KJV: fat]. (Proverbs 13:4)

Note the contrast between the sluggard and the diligent. A sluggard is a lazy person, an idler. As used in Proverbs the word usually has the connotation of a ne'er-do-well, a pan-handler, a sponger, a parasite, or a failure. He has longings but acquires nothing; he craves and gets zilch; he wants much but obtains little; and dreams of wealth but despises work.

In antithesis to the sluggard is the diligent person. Here *diligent* means sharp-pointed, determined. Figuratively it means strict decision; no fooling around, but efficient, getting the job done. Used elsewhere in Proverbs: He becomes poor who deals with a slack hand, but the hand of the diligent makes rich (10:4). The hand of the diligent shall bear rule, but the slothful or lazy shall be put to forced labor (12:24).

Thus we see the diligent, the persevering, the efficient, the sharp, the decisive business person shall be made fat, abundantly or richly supplied and prosperous. This is startling news these days! For there are those who have been brainwashed into believing the world owes them something. Inoculated with the poison of public welfare, they have lost self-respect, dignity and the desire to work. Sure, there are societal structures that work against the poor in general. But where there is a will there is a way.

The Christian must recognize that industry is superior to idleness. Diligent hands are kept busy by acts or decisions of the will, and what escapes others, what is vanity to others, is captured by the diligent. Dreams become reality. Stay busy for the Lord. Offer your hands to Him whose hands were pierced for you.

March 28

There is a way that seems right to a man, but its end is the way of death. (Proverbs 14:12; 16:25)

Both deception and delusion are on the increase. However, there is a slight difference between the two. To deceive involves falsehood, deliberate misrepresentation of truth, concealment, in order to lead into error. To delude refers to deceiving or misleading to the point of rendering a person unable to detect falsehood or make sound judgment.

Some people can recognize a bald-face lie immediately. A dollar coin made out of lead is an absurdity. Years ago when I was a boy, I remember receiving counterfeit half-dollars. They would clunk rather than clank or clink. Counterfeiters know that the closer their work is to the real thing, the better it is, and the more successful they are.

The Devil knows this too. And more and more he works from within Christendom. Second Peter and Jude are two New Testament Books which predict an increase in false doctrine within the visible church. Satan cares nothing for human beings, except to use them to perpetrate his nefarious schemes. He experiences diabolical delight when he can bring shame upon the Christian community.

If you want to hold out to the end, and not be scammed or flimflammed of your spiritual rewards, then there are some things you must do. You must read your Bible, stay in prayer, ask the Holy Spirit to guide you, instruct you, and interpret the Bible for you. There are no special rituals to observe, no laws to be kept, no ceremonies to be performed. There are no tongues to speak in, no beads to count, no trips to take, no need to establish a religious compound, or migrate to another country.

Our job is to follow Jesus Christ, the only Mediator between God and man. All others who claim that right are phonies, antichrists, and wolves in sheepskins! So keep your eyes upon the Lord Jesus, and let the Holy Spirit protect you from every deceiver. He can and He will!

March 29

A man's heart plans [KJV: *devises*] *his way, but the* LORD *directs his steps.* (Proverbs 16:9)

We make our plans and think things out. Sometimes the plans are evil, so that Proverbs 24:8 states, "He who plots to do evil will be called a schemer" (mischievous person, KJV). Examples of such planning are plentiful in the Bible. Cain found occasion to kill Abel; Joseph's brothers plotted against him; Absalom conspired to overthrow David his father; Haman schemed against Mordecai; and there are others who devised evil and at times succeeded in their goals.

Isn't it good that men cannot read minds? Oh, some of us are very clever because we have studied voice inflections, body language, Freudian slips, etc. But still secret thoughts are secret still, except to God. Perhaps we have forgotten about Him. So the text reminds us: Man proposes; God disposes. The Lord directs our steps. To effectively do so He must know what we are thinking. What we think in our hearts determines our real character.

Some of us have graduated from the carnal level to the spiritual level. Once upon a time on the carnal level we had to deal with nicotine and alcohol addiction, stealing, cursing, illicit sex, gambling and other forms of junk. Having won the victory over such, now we have a problem with what goes on in our minds. Often I dismiss my evil thoughts with a verbal pat on the shoulders, "Well, Banks, old buddy at least you didn't *do* what you thought. You ought to feel good about that!" What a dangerous game to play!

Give the Old Man an inch and he will take a mile; and somewhere during that mile's journey the Devil might step in and offer you a ride in his Rolls Royce (Roast?). To indulge in lustful thoughts of power, sex, money, whatever, is still sin. God's holy eyes detect uncleanness even in the deep recesses of our brains, and the hidden closets of our hearts. Thank God for His cleansing direction!

March 30

A man's heart plans his way, but the LORD directs his steps.
(Proverbs 16:9)

It may be God's will to veto or overrule our plans, a matter that really should not bother us. Having bought us with His own blood, He owns us. The gold in our teeth, the money in our bank account, the ring on our finger, the house we live in, the shoes on our feet, the air in our lungs, the electricity in our nerves, the beat of our heart—all are His! He has the right to direct our steps, enlarge them, number or count them, and keep them from sliding. If He tells you take your shoes off as He commanded Moses, or go barefoot as He commanded Isaiah, that's His business.

He does not command, "Do *not* make plans!" Rather the message is "Don't leave Me out! Boast not of tomorrow, for you don't know what a day may bring forth." James warned us to say, "If God wills." If we do not let the sin of pride and presumption becloud our minds and benumb our brains, we realize that there are many things in life over which we have no control. The unknown, unforeseen exigencies, hidden traps, the demonic, the Satanic, our own short- sightedness and unholy ambitions, lusts, ulterior motives—all may combine and produce a destructive arrogance and self-confidence.

I dare not choose my lot; I would not if I might;
Choose Thou for me, my God, So shall I walk aright.
Take Thou my cup, and it With joy or sorrow fill,
As best to Thee may seem, Choose Thou my good and ill.
Choose Thou for me my friends, My sickness or my health;
Choose Thou my cares for me My poverty or wealth.
The kingdom that I seek Is Thine: so let the way
That leads to it be Thine, Else I must surely stray.
Not mine—not mine the choice In things or great or small;
Be Thou my Guide, my Strength, My Wisdom and my All!
(Horatius Bonar)

March 31

A man's heart plans his way, but the LORD directs his steps.
(Proverbs 16:9)

The old nature in all of us ever devises and thinks its own way; we are short-sighted and cannot see what God sees. Our pride, self-confidence, arrogance, and lack of spirituality all blind us to the will of God, so that God's all-ordering providence must overrule our plans.

Indeed, man plans but God "disaplans". Man devises but God revises. Jeremiah said, "O LORD, I know the way of man is not in himself; it is not in man that walks to direct his own steps (Jeremiah 10:23). "A man's steps are of the LORD; how then can a man understand his own way? (Proverbs 20:24).

Why we don't even know the right time of day. One morning I woke up late and wondered why it was so light outside. Usually when I get up during the winter, it is dark outside. When I went to my study and looked at my watch, it said 7:15 a.m. But the electric clock said 6:05 a.m. Believing I had awakened at the usual time, I reset the watch, synchronizing it with the electric clock.

To my chagrin, after turning on the radio to hear the news, I learned that my watch had been correct before I reset it. What happened? Simple: There had been an electrical outage during the night. I had accepted what was incorrect to be correct. It is easy for us to make mistakes, isn't it?

Well, the realization of our frailty ought to drive us all the more to depend upon Him who loved us and shed His own blood for us. And the thrust of this text is to have us include God in the course of our lives; acknowledge Him in all of our ways, so that the Lord Jesus might direct our steps. Our desire is expressed by the psalmist: "Direct my steps by Your word (promise), and let no iniquity have dominion over me" (Psalm 119:133).

April 1

A man's heart plans his way, but the LORD directs his steps.
(Proverbs 16:9)

God orders the Christian's life through the Bible. The psalmist said, "Direct my steps by your word, and let no iniquity have dominion over me" (Psalm 119:133). Man should live and walk by every word that comes out of God's mouth. Life is an integral unit. Although we often split man up for the purpose of analysis, man is a whole being. We cannot therefore compartmentalize man's actions and divorce morality from his deeds.

We cannot talk about that which is purely civic, legal, psychological, political, etc. without touching the moral issue. To talk about the civil rights of a homosexual without talking about the implications of his behavior upon society is nonsense. In essence, what we have is man's sinful attempt to live as he pleases.

He tells God, "Keep Your hands off! I don't need You to tell me how to live." But the man or woman who loves Jesus Christ cries out, "Uphold my steps in Your paths, that my footsteps may not slip" (Psalm 17:5).Christians can truly testify, "He also brought me up out of a horrible pit, out of the miry clay, and set my feet upon a rock, and established my steps" (Psalm 40:2).

Wherever you walk today you will not walk alone. Whether this day finds you tracking through a desert place or a waste, howling wilderness; or climbing up the rough side of the mountain; or painfully and wearily dragging your feet to the hospital; or going to the mortician to make arrangements for the funeral of a loved one; or going to the cold, bleak cemetery to see a body lowered in the grave—yea, even if your steps take you through the valley of the shadow of death, fear no evil. Jesus Christ is with you and He orders your feet, establishes your goings, and directs your paths every step of the way.

April 2

He who is slow to anger is better than the mighty, and he who rules his spirit than he who takes a city. (Proverbs 16:32)

This is called a synonymous proverb because being slow to anger is to rule oneself; and the warrior is also one who takes a city. A true hero first wins the battle within, that is, the battle with himself. It is folly to claim to be a Christian, yet not partake of the power to keep your life from going to pieces. One aspect of Christianity is Christlikeness. This is important because we live in an undisciplined society.

Witness the crime, corruption, strikes, mobs, picketing, screaming, rebellion, etc. And unfortunately the prevailing attitude in our society influences the church, leading some church members to do that which is right in their own eyes. Such folks have not learned yet to let the Holy Spirit keep them cool, calm and collected.

God's Spirit is able to cool hot tempers, immobilize tongues, clean up dirty speech, straighten out crooked values, pull in wandering feet, purify thoughts, direct our eyes to proper objects, and humble proud spirits. He enables us to weather ill-treatment, to withstand being scandalized and maligned without retaliating or seeking revenge. Power to pray for enemies and overcome evil with good is a gift from God available to each of us.

Why don't we take advantage of this power? Is it because we are not truly committed to Christ? Have we let the world influence us, making us afraid to buck the trend, go against the tide, or afraid of the criticisms of our peers? A true hero is one who has self-control. He is greater than a much decorated war hero. A true hero is one who masters his own spirit; he is greater than he who conquers a city. Alexander the Great conquered city after city and established a great empire. But he died an alcoholic while in the prime of life. Surely he who rules his spirit is greater, mightier than he who conquers a city.

April 3

He who is slow to anger is better than the mighty, and he who rules his spirit than he who takes a city. (Proverbs 16:32)

To rule is to reign or have dominion over. Christians must understand that God did not make human beings to be primarily bodily or fleshly. Nor did He make us to be primarily soulish or natural. His will is that we be spiritual. Spiritual Christians let their Holy-Spirit-supervised-human spirits lead them in their daily living. This is the new principle of life, the Holy Spirit living in us so that we walk not after the flesh but after the Holy Spirit who superintends our human spirit.

Self-control is an excellent virtue; it is Christlike, and the Lord Jesus is our Example. When Mary and Joseph were stirred up because they could not find Him, He said, "I was about My Father's business." When Satan tested Him three times, Christ answered each thrust with the words, "It is written." When clever religionists sought to entrap Him with their tricky questions, He answered them all calmly and with great authority.

When folks picked up stones to kill Him, He just passed through their midst. On another occasion when they tried to throw Him over a cliff, He simply walked away. When the disciples caught in a storm were scared to death, He was found asleep in the same boat. When the soldiers replied they had come to take Christ, He calmly replied, "I am He."

When enemies beat Him, plucked His beard, smote Him in the face, He said nothing. He stood before Pilate without complaint. Hanging on the cross, He put Himself into the care of the Father. He was in complete charge until the very last. May we too live today in such a way that our lives will show the Holy Spirit is in control and there are no cracks in the city walls.

April 4

He who is slow to anger is better than the mighty, and he who rules his spirit than he who takes a city. (Proverbs 16:32)

Christ is the best example of One who controls His spirit. In a storm at sea He fell asleep. In a synagogue full of seasoned professional rabbis, He taught. When the wild demoniac came running up to Christ there was no panic. Before a faded, looking-for-a-miracle Herod Antipas, He answered him nothing (Luke 23:9).

Judas was at the same table with Him, and about to betray Him, but He had no harsh words for the traitor. When a mob came after Him with sticks and torches and swords, and Simon Peter cut off the right ear of Malchus, servant of the high priest, the Lord Jesus touched his ear and healed him, preventing any further violence.

Examined by Pilate He answered him never a word, causing the governor to marvel greatly (Matthew 27:14). He was in charge of His own spirit. When beaten, smacked and spat upon, "When he was reviled, reviled not again; when He suffered, He threatened not," when cursed, He blessed; and hanging on the cross, He forgave. And proof of the discipline is to be heard in these dying words, "Father into Your hands I commit my spirit" (Luke 23:46)

Having ruled His spirit, Christ accomplished His goal. He let nothing deter Him—no, not the testing by Satan, nor the fickleness of the crowd, the scoffing at His miracles, the scorn of His home town, His followers' fearfulness, the ignorance of His disciples, the perjury of the corrupt, the antagonism of the Sadducees, the hypocrisy of the Pharisees, the possession activity of demons, the shouts of the mob, the cruelty of the Gentile soldiers, the blindness of the Jews, the unbelief of His own brothers, the attempts to stone Him, the rashness of Simon Peter or the treachery of Judas—none of these things overruled His spirit. Keep in mind this day what a wonderful Savior we have!

April 5

A merry heart does good, like medicine, but a broken spirit dries the bones. (Proverbs 17:22)

The Bible speaks of different kinds of bones: vexed, out of joint, waxed old, rotten, fat and dry. Whatever condition your bones are in, **you** are in. Because your bones reflect your inner attitude, or your inner spirit affects your bones, it is obvious that the subject is the inner person. We learn that to be broken in spirit, cast down, down in the dumps, dejected, sad or melancholic can affect our health. A broken spirit can make us ill, sap our vitality and enervate us.

Surely gloomy times will come. Man that is born of woman is of few days and full of trouble. But Christians do not have to stay down at the mouth, looking like unholy hoboes and sad-sack saints in the sanctuary! We **can** have a good day, for in our hearts we know that our Lord is able to make all things work together for our good.

On the other hand, being cheerful keeps you healthy, causes good healing. With our downs we have ups, and as we wait on the Lord a bright ray of sunshine begins to break through. After the tears of the midnight hour joy comes in the morning. And somehow our minds turn to Jesus Christ. Just to know that God loves us, that Christ shed His blood for us, washed away our sins, rose from the grave, ascended, makes intercession for us, and is coming back again for us thrills our souls.

Think about it—the Holy Spirit restores the joy of our salvation and the dry bones become fat, the broken spirit is made whole. And we are one day closer to Heaven, one day closer to seeing Him who saved us by His grace.

Trusting only in Thy merit, Would I seek Thy face;
Heal my wounded, broken spirit, Save me by Thy grace.
(Fanny Crosby)

April 6

And do not despise your mother when she is old. (Proverbs 23:22)

As the Lord Jesus tarries in His coming, wickedness increases. One sign of growing evil is the disintegration of family life, specifically, the bad relationship between parents and children. This very morning the news came of a 13-year-old daughter of a police officer setting fire to their home and killing him because he "disciplined her." Paul warned of murderers of fathers and mothers (1 Timothy 1:9), and of men disobedient to parents (2 Timothy 3:2). Parents are despised, abandoned, abused, cursed, and robbed; the commandment to honor is disobeyed.

To despise in the original language is to show contempt, to tread upon. In English "despise" means to look down upon (with contempt), to regard as negligible, worthless or distasteful; it is the opposite of to appreciate. Despising is connected with the infirmities of old age: the feebleness and frailty of frame, dimness of sight, hardness of hearing, bent limbs, slowness of steps, trembling keepers of the house, grinders (molars) missing, and economic hardship.

I watched my 86-year-old mother deteriorate, struck speechless by a series of strokes, responsive only to pain, eyelids closed, her left side paralyzed. She spent nearly four months in the hospital before the Lord took her. Later as I daily visited her home, saw the pictures, her favorite chair, my thoughts moved me to tears. The memories were there, hovering about as I prepared to clean the house and ready it for settlement.

How glad I am that Christ enabled me to be a blessing to mom, to see to it that she wanted for nothing in her sunset years. As I grow older my anticipation of the joy of Heaven includes not only seeing the Lord Jesus, but uniting once again with my mother and all the other saints who have outrun me in the race of this earthly life.

April 7

Whoever has no rule over his own spirit is like a city broken down, without walls. (Proverbs 25:28)

It seems that God has made us so that there are built-in safeguards of the human spirit. There are, so to speak, walls around our spirits calculated to preserve, defend and protect us. God's desire is that we exercise restraint, control, or "rule". The lack of self-control tears down the defenses of the spirit and opens up a person to all kinds of evils. Anger has a way of punching holes through the wall.

When you fail to restrain your spirit you create breaches in the wall of your spirit, and thus make it possible for all kinds of enemy soldiers to enter. God cannot at this point lead you as He desires. He may let you go your way until you knock your head against the wall. Some people become so angry that they are implacable. Attempts at reconciliation are impossible because of their vindictiveness and determination to destroy.

Not genuine in their peace talks, they have ulterior motives. Thus an unrestrained spirit, a person without self-control is a person in turmoil. When the wall is broken down it becomes difficult to distinguish right from wrong; darkness becomes light, evil begins to look good, and bitterness begins to taste sweet.

When the wall is broken down mistakes are readily made. And the conscience is rendered unreliable, for the light of the Word of God is blocked out. An uncontrolled spirit is an indication that God is not taken at His Word. Decisions are made that later are regretted. Words are spoken we wish we could call back. When the wall is broken down understanding is deceived. You can see why the Christian is exhorted: Cultivate a calm spirit; be a "cool-cat" Christian.

April 8

The wicked flee when no one pursues, but the righteous are bold as a lion. (Proverbs 28:1)

Despising God's Word and law brings dire consequences. One such evil result is distress. God said, "I will set My face against you, and you shall be defeated by your enemies; those who hate you shall reign over you, and you shall flee when no one pursues you . . . they shall fall when no one pursues" (Leviticus 26:17, 36). Disobedience to the known will and written Word of God causes men to run away from a non-existent enemy.

Folks with bad consciences see accusers and enemies everywhere. They run the risk of faintheartedness, of being chased by the sound of a shaken leaf on a tree, as if running from a man with a sword in his hand. Wicked consciences conjure up terrible images; they see the unseen and hear the soundless and feel the unfelt. Those who do not fear God but fight Him are foes soon forced to fail, flee and fall.

On the other hand, while the godless flee, the righteous are bold as a lion. We may not roar or be as fierce, but an unfettered conscience makes us free. Christ broke the fetters of an unsanctified conscience and Christians are exhorted to be fearless as lions, daringly witnessing, brave to speak the word, courageously standing up for righteousness and confidently entering through the veil into the holiest by the blood of Jesus Christ.

And zealously come into the very presence of a Holy God unto the throne of grace. Yes, we may boldly say, "The Lord is my helper; I will not fear. What can man do to me?" (Hebrews 13:6). Today, let a good conscience give you assurance that in the Day of Judgment you shall have great boldness, liberty and freedom (1 John 4:17).

April 9

He who is of a proud heart stirs up strife, but he who trusts in the LORD will be prospered [made fat: KJV]. (Proverbs 28:25)

Plainly put, a man or woman who stirs up strife among the saints is sickly skinny spiritually. You know, of course, that strife is stirred up by spreading rumors, telling lies, seeking revenge, taking Christians to court, lack of discipline and rebellion against authority, by disregard of the Bible, by selfishness and prayerlessness.

Does it come as a surprise to you to learn that the antidote for strife is to trust? Is it true that people who stir up strife do so because they do not trust the Lord? To better understand this, consider the meaning of the words "a proud heart." The phrase means selfishness, arrogance, a greedy spirit and a grasping nature.

Literally, "proud heart" is wide of soul, large of appetite (soul). The point is, there are many causes for strife, but at the root is the failure to trust God. And so when you see a trouble maker you see one who has not yet learned he or she is better off trusting the Lord. When I trust myself—in my own heart or intellect or experience or emotions—I follow the unhallowed, untrained thoughts and suggestions of the mind. I rely upon my own thinking.

Trust in self puffs me up; but never really satisfies. Thus people who do anything for power, recognition, and acceptance, or the desire to be wanted or well-liked seek such in their own strength, revealing they are not fat, but skinny, and in sad, sorrowful shape.

On the other hand, he who trusts in the Lord, leans on the Lord, rolls on the Lord, takes refuge in the Lord, waits for the Lord, thrives, is enriched, is better off and is richly comforted, blessed, and prosperous. Be a fat Christian today—trust in the Lord!

April 10

Where there is no revelation, the people cast off restraint; but happy is he who keeps the law. (Proverbs 29:18)

This popular verse is often interpreted to mean if you cannot see beyond your nose you are headed for trouble. Basically this thought is true: We do need to think ahead as much as that is possible for finite man. We should make plans for the future, God willing. But a better interpretation of this text, understanding that the Hebrew noun rendered "revelation" is derived from the verb to see, to behold, speaks of vision in the usual sense concerning the ecstatic state.

The word "revelation" means vision from God; it is a prophecy, divine guidance or communication whether in a vision, oracle (utterance) or prophecy. Vision here is that which is revealed by God to men and women. And this is the Bible, the Scriptures, the Lord's revealed Word. Without this the people perish (go to pieces)!

Further proof that "vision" here refers to the revealed mind of God is seen in the second half of the verse: "But happy is he who keeps the law." Note the word "but". It helps us to see that this is what is called an antithetic proverb. The word "but" introduces a statement in opposition to what precedes it. It is an adversative, a word expressing antithesis or opposition. For examples, read Proverbs 29:2-4, 23, and 25, and note the word "but". Thus in contrast to "no revelation" or "no vision" is "keeping the law."

Vision or revelation is parallel with the law. And the law is the revealed mind of God. The Lord God expressed Himself in His Word. When we write or speak we tell what is on our minds. So God spoke. So God revealed what was on His mind. And we have that divine communication today; it is the Bible. Happiness today is ours if we submit to God's Word and let it work effectively in our lives.

April 11

Where there is no revelation, the people cast off restraint; but happy is he who keeps the law. (Proverbs 29:18)

We are blessed. We are made happy in keeping the Word of God, the law. We ought to keep it because the time approaches when God will send a famine in the land, not a famine of bread, nor a thirst for water, but of hearing the words of the Lord (Amos 8:11). Or as we read in 1 Samuel 3:1, "And the word of the LORD was rare in those days; there was no widespread revelation."

Christians who obey the Bible discover that the Word gives them stability. Disobedience leads to instability. The Bible helps Christians keep themselves together. This is integration. This is peace. This is wholeness. People who go to pieces are people who don't have inner peace. The Bible believer has no business going bankrupt personally. When read and kept the Bible acts like glue, a divine cohesive.

Note it is to be kept and obeyed. Some folks read without believing what they read. True belief is in the heart. In other words, we practice what we truly believe. Failure here is one of the causes of disintegration. Both hypocrisy and phoniness cause disintegration and instability. A double-minded man is unstable in all his ways (James 1:8).

Without the Bible the Holy Spirit is limited in the sense that He has nothing much to work with inside the professed believer. And so some of us are naked, stripped, uncovered, without discipline, unrestrained, and hanging in there real loose! And the old nature in us, hating all kinds of restraints anyway, seeks to convince us that we enjoy our freedom.

However, the freedom of sin is slavery. In the kingdom of wickedness the subjects are free but their freedom is to do evil, to do that which does not please the Lord. The wicked man relishes his freedom to do his thing, but the end result of his freedom is Hell, destruction and the grave. Thank God today for that restraint that produces joy in Christ.

April 12

Where there is no revelation, the people cast off restraint; but happy is he who keeps the law. (Proverbs 29:18)

In the KJV the word "perish" is not the usual one meaning to be exterminated, annihilated, destroyed or killed. Rather "perish" or "unrestrained" comes from a verb meaning to let go, let alone, or let loose. It is used to describe unbinding (uncovering) the head by removing a turban (Leviticus 10:6; 21:10). So the basic meaning of to "perish" or to be "unrestrained" is to strip, break up into pieces, break loose, cast off restraint, be without order and be disorderly.

Exodus 32:25 helps us to better understand this word. Recall that Moses went up to Mount Sinai to talk with Jehovah. While he was gone, the people became restless, put pressure on Aaron and he gave in to the majority rule. In Exodus 32:6 we read that the people sat down to eat and to drink, and rose up to play or dance!

In the absence of Moses they cast off all restraint; "they let their hair down," they let loose; indeed, they took off their clothing, uncovered themselves, danced and pranced around the golden cow they had made their idol god. When Moses saw they were stripped, naked, perishing, without restraint, indecent and gone to pieces, he commanded those on the Lord's side to take their swords and kill these partying, wild, frenzied, unrestrained idolaters! And so the perishing perished; those who had gone to pieces were cut to pieces!

Unless the Bible is believed, lived, kept constantly in our view, and in our minds, we break out and break loose from all allegiance to God's Word. The result is: We become ungovernable, disorderly, raucous, and unmanageable. We need spiritual preaching, preaching that comes out of spiritual experiences, preaching that is based upon the Word of God to enlighten us. Fidelity to God's Word is of the utmost importance. His Word is to be praised. Thank Him for His Word today.

April 13

Do you see a man hasty in his words? There is more hope for a fool than for him. (Proverbs 29:20)

"Hasty" here means pressed, pushed, made to hurry, just as the angels *urged* Lot to get out of Sodom before the city was destroyed (Genesis 19:15). The taskmasters of Egypt *hastened* the Jews (Exodus 5:13); they *forced* them, urgently demanded, compelled, pressed them to work without straw in the making of bricks. In Proverbs 21:5, the admonition comes to plan ahead, carefully, diligently and receive plenty, and abundance; for if you act too quickly, presumptuously, you will never have enough, indeed you will come to poverty. Proverbs 28:20 speaks of making haste to be rich. Desire for a quick dollar is destructive. We see how the careers of politicians have gone down the drain in various scandals in our country.

Now take what we have learned from the use of the word rendered "hasty" and put it into our devotional text. We find that a hasty tongue is one that feels compelled, pressed, urged to speak. It is a tongue in a hurry; a quick tongue! There is the suggestion that we could substitute deeds for words here. Words include acts as well. Behind both word and deed is the thought. The idea is that haste—whether in words or deeds—is destructive of reflection.

Strongly put, there is more hope for a stupid person than for a person who speaks without thinking. Such a man cuts his throat with his own tongue. The path to wisdom stands open, but the fool blocks the entrance thereto by his quick tongue. In contrast, all the words of Christ were truth, well thought out, successful in accomplishing what He sent them out to do. Pray today that the indwelling Lord will slow down our quick tongues so that we may please Him.

April 14

For God is in heaven, and you on earth. (Ecclesiastes 5:2)

Heaven is a place created by God, for He is the God of heaven, its possessor. It is His dwelling place. Heaven is where there is joy over one sinner coming to repentance. My Father is there, so that I pray, "My Father in heaven." It is God's throne, earth His footstool. Heaven is where God sits high and looks low. His Word is settled there.

Enoch was translated there; Jacob's ladder ascended to heaven. And Elijah was transported there in a sweet chariot that swung low. Heaven is the place from which Christ came, and after shedding His blood, rose from the grave, stepped on a cloud, ascended and returned there. Now there, He makes intercession for us.

Stephen, full of the Holy Spirit saw Him there. Our hope is laid up there. An inheritance incorruptible is reserved up there. And that is where our affections are set. Yea, the believer's name is written in heaven. We are the firstborn written in heaven. Our citizenship is there. All is holy there. It is a beautiful place, with jasper walls, gates of pearl, and streets of gold; no curse is there, no darkness, and no night.

From thence we shall hear a trumpet sound and be caught up to meet the Lord Jesus. In heaven we shall live as a prepared people in a prepared place, where there's a crown of righteousness waiting for us. In heaven is our mansion with plenty good room. There we shall rest from our labors.

Some glad morning when this life is o'er, I'll fly away;
To a home on God's celestial shore, I'll fly away.
Just a few more weary days and then, I'll fly away.
To a land where joys shall never end, I'll fly away.
I'll fly away, O glory, I'll fly away (in the morning).
When I die, Hallelujah, by and by, I'll fly away.
(Albert E. Brumley)

April 15

Do not marvel at the matter (NKJV); *Do not be shocked* (KJV). Ecclesiastes 5:8

Don't be shocked at the perverting of righteousness: Don't be amazed when you see governmental corruption. In Solomon's day each official made sure he got his share of the spoils by watching the official beneath him in rank. So the text exhorts: Where you have graft and corruption, do not marvel at oppression and injustice.

Because there is hanky-panky at each level, at each stage of the political hierarchy, even the highest ranking officer may not be free from sin. Thoroughly investigate your own society, warns Solomon, and you will no longer wonder at what's happening to the masses. He cautions: Such corruption leads to oppression and injustice. For at the bottom of the pile is the poor man, whose toes are stomped so hard that even the great American middle class is beginning to holler.

Don't be shocked at the necessity of regeneration: Do not even be shocked at our Lord's statement, "You must be born again" (John 3:7). God wanted Nicodemus to understand that flesh can only beget flesh. Skin cannot save from sin. The old man does not evolve into the new man. Works cannot produce grace. A dead man cannot raise himself.

Don't be shocked at the voice of the resurrection: "Do not marvel at this; for the hour is coming in which all who are in the graves will hear His voice and come forth" (John 5:28-29). Christ forbids His hearers to continue expressing an unintelligent wonderment or astonishment, and a critical attitude at His teaching. Don't be shocked that Jesus Christ has the authority to execute judgment; when He speaks all the dead will rise (at different times), for they shall hear His voice and come forth. Surely here is a divine realism with which to begin your day—a day of calmness.

April 16

Do not hasten in your spirit to be angry, for anger rests in the bosom of fools. (Ecclesiastes 7:9) *But he who is impulsive exalts folly.* (Proverbs 14:29)

The writer in Ecclesiastes exhorts us not to be quick-tempered, but to keep our tempers under control, because it is foolish to let anger lodge within the soul, to cherish wrath, to harbor a grudge, or to be vexed into doing something rash. Note also Proverbs 14:29 deals with the quick-tempered, the short-fused, or the short of spirit. What a commandment, what an exhortation for this day and age!

We live in a time when people smoke on public transportation despite signs telling them not to smoke; radios are turned up to deafen all who hear, graffiti goons spray their names on private property, neighbors' dogs run loose, trash is thrown into the streets, immorality increases, racism thrives, and anti-Semitism reappears.

Advertisements misrepresent; relatives disappoint; friends turn their backs upon us; aches and pains course freely through our feeble frames; and the death angel takes away loved ones. We are caught up with crippling labor strikes; we are flimflammed, cursed, swindled, defrauded and professed Christians take each other to court. These are days when the fear of energy shortages plagues us; and murderers stalk the streets.

Surely there seems to be great cause to scream in anguish, to strike out in bitterness, to lose our equilibrium, to give in to "road rage," to become passionately excited and to express anger at all these things. Yet God says, "Don't be a fool; play it cool!" Follow in the footsteps of the Lord Jesus. Through plots and testing, false accusations, mockery and cruelty, He maintained control. Thank God for the cool, calm control available to us in Christ.

April 17

Like an apple tree among the trees of the woods, so is my beloved among the sons. I sat down in his shade with great delight, and his fruit was sweet to my taste. (Song of Solomon 2:3)

I am satisfied with Jesus; He has done so much for me,
He has suffered to redeem me; He has died to set me free.
McKinney

When satisfied with the Savior you do not get upset over what people say about you. Satisfaction with Him gives a peace of mind that passes all understanding; and enables you to hold on a little longer. Yes, I am satisfied with the sacrifice of His life; with the sameness of His attributes, the saving power of His blood, the scintillation of His star, the scepter of His righteousness, the scrumptiousness of His table, the security of His everlasting arms, the sensitivity of His Spirit, and the shadow of His protection.

I am satisfied with the sharpness of His sword; the shield of His faith, the signs of His coming, the simplicity of His message, the skill of His hand, the smell of His perfume, the smoothness of His operations, the solace of His fellowship, the solidity of His foundation, and the solutions He offers to my problems. I am satisfied with the splendor of His beauty, the stability of His ways, the stamp of His approval, the strategy of His warfare, the strength of His character, the success of His Word, the suffering of His love, the sufficiency of His salvation, the superiority of His priesthood and the sweetness of His fruit.

Hallelujah! I have found Him
Whom my soul so long has craved!
Jesus satisfies my longings;
Through His blood I now am saved!
(Clara T. Williams)

April 18

Do not say, "A conspiracy," concerning all that this people call a conspiracy, nor be afraid of their threats, nor be troubled. The LORD of hosts, Him you shall hallow; let Him be your fear, and let Him be your dread. (Isaiah 8:12-13)

Fearing a Conspiracy. About 735 BC, Syria under king Rezin, and Israel under king Pekah formed an alliance against Assyria. They were determined to bring Judah under king Ahaz into the coalition. However, the Lord Jehovah opposed the alliance. So He sent Isaiah to tell Ahaz, "Don't be upset, don't be perturbed. There's nothing to these two stubs of smoldering firebrands. What they plan shall not come to pass. Trust in the Lord; He will surely deliver you!"

Ahaz disobeyed. Shaking like a leaf in the wind, Ahaz sent gifts to king Tiglath Pileser of Assyria, asking him to come and help him fight Rezin and Pekah. Thus Judah defied God. Surely we need to hear the words of Martin Luther:

And though this world, with devils filled,
Should threaten to undo us,
We will not fear, for God hath willed
His truth to triumph through us.

Just because others form coalitions, councils, cliques, committees, clubs, confederations and conspiracies—don't you fear what they fear! For the very gates of Hell, the plots of the wicked working behind the scenes shall not prevail. Just leave the conspirators in the hands of the Lord Jesus Christ. Don't panic, just pray.

Fear the Lord of hosts and you will not fear enemies who join together against you. Trust in Him who loved you, gave Himself for you, and loves you still. Surely Proverbs 29:25 speaks to our hearts today: "The fear of man brings a snare, but whoever trusts in the LORD shall be safe."

April 19

Do not say, "A conspiracy," concerning all that this people call a conspiracy, nor be afraid of their threats, nor be troubled. The LORD of hosts, Him you shall hallow; let Him be your fear, and let Him be your dread. (Isaiah 8:12-13)

Forceful Communication. He speaks effectively; "For He spoke and it was done, he commanded, and it stood fast" (Psalm 33:9). He speaks in dreams with healing words and with cleansing words. He speaks incomparably, for of Him it is written, "Never man spoke like this man." He speaks in His jealousy (zeal), in His holiness, mouth to mouth, from a burning mountain, in parables and in the cloudy pillar; openly, and not secretly in a dark place.

God speaks in plagues; by His prophets; and in His Son. He speaks suddenly, by visions, in the fire of His wrath and in His zeal. Note how Isaiah says God speaks; see how forcefully this message is communicated. He speaks with a strong hand. This is partly because we are hardheaded. But it is also a matter of grace, for God wants us to know. He desires that we understand; He wants to get His point over, and insists upon making it clear to us what He wills.

God spoke with Isaiah with a strong hand (with strength of hand), an interesting expression meaning with great and mighty power, and an overwhelming force; yea, He spoke in the strongest terms. When the Lord lays this hand upon you it is an experience that overpowers you. I am glad He works this way, aren't you? He did not timidly knock on the door of my heart, and then walk away because He got no immediate response. He knew what I needed, and dogged my steps, intent upon changing my walk.

He pleaded with me, begged, strapped, warned and cautioned me. He slammed doors in my face and spoke to my heart in love. And once I submitted to His tender pleading, He took away my fears. Hear Him today saying to you, "Don't fear what they fear!"

April 20

Do not say, "A conspiracy," concerning all that this people call a conspiracy, nor be afraid of their threats, nor be troubled. The LORD of hosts, Him you shall hallow; let Him be your fear, and let Him be your dread. (Isaiah 8:12-13)

Following the Crowd. Fear will make you do almost anything. Fear of your enemies banding together may cause you to give in and to follow the crowd, believing there is security in numbers. This is a false security akin to that of folks who sneer and say they will have plenty of company in Hell. They are not willing to apply this idea when they are sick, and say, "Well, I'm in the hospital and it's all right because I've got plenty of company."

Isaiah and his disciples were exhorted not to walk in the way of this people. Don't follow the crowd; don't walk in the way of a people fearful of a conspiracy. Without God your walk will be in craftiness, in darkness, disorderly, and headed back to Egypt. It will be after the flesh, as a fool goes in a way that is not good; after your own thoughts, after other gods, after all the host of heaven, in the imagination of the heart, in lasciviousness, in lies, and after ungodly lusts.

Without the leading of the Holy Spirit your walk is with a perverse mouth, naked, in the night and stumbling about, after your own plans and devices, in pride, after unprofitable things, with slanders, by sight and not by faith, with necks stretched forth, wanton eyes, mincing steps, tinkling feet, after vanity, and with wicked men.

You can see why the prophet and his followers were instructed not to walk in the way of a people fearful of conspiracy. Don't fear their fears; don't follow in their folly; don't dread their dread; don't walk in their ways! The Christ who died for you desires that you personally know that your salvation is not in a crowd or in the way of the world, but in Him.

April 21

Do not say, "A conspiracy," concerning all that this people call a conspiracy, nor be afraid of their threats, nor be troubled. The LORD of hosts, Him you shall hallow; let Him be your fear, and let Him be your dread. (Isaiah 8:12-13)

Forming a Conclusion. Isaiah knew that the failure to fear God leads to reliance upon men. Such dependence is condemned (Isaiah 31:1-3). The prophet is especially concerned about believers who fear what unbelievers fear, who let the irreverent attitudes of the hell-bound influence them to the point that they too begin to show lack of respect for God and for that which is holy. From the prophet's point of view much of mankind's fears are the results of failure to fear God. So that Christians must be careful not to be brainwashed by the society in which they live.

We have an obligation to be different. Not eccentric, but distinctive. Perhaps "outstanding" is a better word. Pressure is such these days that we feel we must dress, talk, walk and act like the majority. Yet, who but a minority starts these fads and establishes clothing styles?

Is God your Fear? (Genesis 31:42, 53) Is God your dread? Evidently the masses have no fear of the Lord. His name is taken in vain; His church vandalized and its music plagiarized. His Book is Hollywoodized and popularized; His commandments are disobeyed. His saints are sued by the self-centered. Among professed believers there is little fear of God. Instead, fearing what the world fears leads us to seek worldly solutions to our problems. We look for help from the same sources the world seeks it, and there is no help there! To lean on Egypt is to lean on a broken cane and pierce the hand. To ask help from Assyria is to lean upon a shattered crutch. To cry on the Devil's shoulder is to invite him into our house. What should we do? Cast our fears upon Jesus Christ. Let Him be our fear today!

April 22

And His name will be called Wonderful Counselor. (Isaiah 9:6)

Note that I did not split the name as is done in the KJV and in other versions, translations and paraphrases. I take the position suggested by those scholars who omit the comma, and combine the title. In other words, it is **not** Wonderful, Counselor but Wonderful Counselor. This combination does not prevent us from studying each word separately before bringing them together again as one of the four double-titles of the Messiah-King.

We recognize the need for counseling; however, human counsel is faulty, shot through with dangers. Divine counsel is sound, safe, and eternally secure. You can go to this Counselor anytime, free of charge; no referral or letters of introduction are needed, no nominal fee to pay, and no long distance to travel.

To tell Him what is on your mind is better than giving other folks a piece of your mind. You talk to some people and the next thing you know you hear it in church meetings, on the job, over the phone, and sometimes even out of town. You never need fear He will blabbermouth and put your business in the streets. He is a Counselor who keeps complete confidentiality.

Failure to confide in the Lord opens us up to wrong concepts of friendship, loyalty, and fraternal organizations. We follow carnal, worldly, bad advice and stick together in wrongness, afraid to break with folks who use us for their own selfish gains, and to satisfy their own twisted needs and warped personalities. To whom then shall we go?

But this Counselor has the words of eternal life. There is none other like Him. His advice is excellent, exceptional; His understanding of our needs all-comprehending. Furthermore, unlike mere human counselors, this Counselor can do something about what He determines is best for us.

April 23

And His name will be called Wonderful Counselor. (Isaiah 9:6)

The word *Wonderful* is used in the Bible only of God, never of mere man or of man's works. The fact is it requires superhuman wisdom to sit upon the throne of David as King Messiah. No mere mortal man could fulfill the requirements, not even Solomon, for despite his great wisdom, the proverbs that he wrote, the temple that he built, the writing of Ecclesiastes, his fame, his tremendous wealth—morally, spiritually, because of his many wives and concubines, the foolish political alliances he made, his flirtation with idolatry—he does not compare favorably with the Messiah.

To have this government upon His shoulder, to order it, and to establish it with justice and with righteousness, to rule this kingdom with a rod of iron requires more than mere man can give. Upon this Counselor the Spirit of wisdom is to rest (Isaiah 11:2). He is the Ancient of Days (Daniel 7:22). In Him are hid all the treasures of wisdom and knowledge (Colossians 2:3). He is made the wisdom from God (1 Corinthians 1:30). As such this Counselor has no need for a cabinet or council. He does not need to be surrounded by experts hired to share their knowledge and experience, give advice, solve problems or help administrate. This Counselor is God all by Himself. As Creator, He knows what to do for the creature; He is well equipped to rule and to reign.

As is said of Jehovah, He is wonderful in counsel (Isaiah 28:29). Such then is the incomparable title given to this unique Person, the Child born, the Son given. If you believe this, rest assured that His plan for your life is a good one. And because His plan for your life is good, it is imperative that you seek His will, ask His counsel, take His advice and do His Word. Stick with Him who said, "I will instruct you and teach you in the way you should go; I will guide you with My eye" (Psalm 32:8).

April 24

And His name will be called Wonderful Counselor. (Isaiah 9:6)

Mankind needs consultation, counsel, advice, and guidance. He that hearkens to counsel is wise, for where there is no counsel the people fall; but there is safety, victory, and deliverance in the multitude of counselors. Without guidance purposes are disappointed, but in the multitude of counselors they are established, for frustration there is success (Proverbs 11:14, 12:15, 15:22).

While the principle of counsel is accepted some advice is good and some advice is bad. According to the Bible, man's counsel may be shrewd, crafty, ungodly, rebellious, provoking God (Psalms 1:1, 83:3, 106:13, 43), and producing shame (Hosea 10:6). Human counsel may bring woe (Isaiah 30:1), be wicked (Proverbs 12:5), froward or cunningly perverse (Job 5:13), cause weariness of soul with its hopelessness and attempts to hide (Isaiah 29:15, 47:13).

It is clear too that human counsel, whether of an entire nation or of an individual may be brought to naught, reduced to nothing by God (Nehemiah 4:15; Psalm 2:2). As men set at naught all of God's counsel, and would have none of His reproof, so *their* counsel is reduced to folly (Proverbs 1:25, 30). And those who disapprove *of* God may be disapproved *by* God (Romans 1:28).

Examples of bad counsel are seen in the lives of Balaam (Numbers 31:16), Ahithophel (2 Samuel 16:21), Rehoboam (2 Chronicles 10:13), and religious leaders (Matthew 22:15, 27:1). When you need advice today, call on the Lord Jesus Christ, a Wonderful Counselor. And read His Word. Wisdom declares, "Counsel is mine, and sound wisdom" (Proverbs 8:14; Job 12:13). God's counsels are great (Jeremiah 32:19), are faithfully carried out (Isaiah 25:1), are immutable (Hebrews 6:17), and shall stand forever (Psalm 33:11; Proverbs 19:21; and Isaiah 46:10).

April 25

And His name will be called Wonderful Counselor. (Isaiah 9:6)

Discernment is required in order to give good advice. A good counselor must be able to see through the devices and deceit of the Devil and demons, the hypocrisy of the Hell-bound, the chicanery of carnal church members, the suddenness of events, and the tragedies of life. A Wonderful Counselor sees through sham, camouflage, make-believe, foolishness, two-facedness, and deception. All we need is in Christ; His advice, guidance, point of view, ideas, consultation, plan, purpose, recommendation, leading, directions, example and management are invaluable.

Note the word rendered "wonderful" is translated "marvelous" in Psalm 78:12: "Marvelous things He did in the sight of their fathers." The Psalm goes on to describe the miracles performed in the deliverance from Egypt: the plagues, the dividing of the Red Sea, crossing over on dry land, the pillar of cloud by day and fire by night, the rock that provided water, the quail, and the manna—all seen as wonders!

In Judges 13:18, Manoah entertained the Angel of the Lord and asked, "What is Your name?" The Angel replied, "Why do you ask My name, seeing it is Wonderful?" This was God the Son appearing as an Angel, who in His very Person and being is a Wonder, incomprehensible to man, with ways and thoughts far above ours.

Today men are lulled to sleep because evil committed seems to escape with impunity. Evil committed without punishment encourages the commission of more evil. So in our society there is a growing hardihood of wickedness, a lack of the fear of God. Having created our own gods and goddesses, there is felt no wonderment or awe at this Child born, this Son given. May *our* experiences today increase our wonderment of Christ our Wonderful Counselor.

April 26

And His name will be called Wonderful Counselor. (Isaiah 9:6)

Wonderful because of who He is: Omnipotent, omniscient, omnipresent, incomprehensible, immutable, mysterious, eternal, sovereign, full of love, grace, mercy, peace and truth. Wonderful in His birth: the place predicted, born of a virgin in the fullness of time, unique, supernatural, and having escaped the plots of men to abort His birth. Wonderful in all that He said: His word is creative, enlightening, unlimited, cutting, smashing, destructive of evil, penetrative, divisive, sweet, regenerating, pure, life-giving, operative, successful, judging and condemning. Wonderful in all that He has done: seeking, searching, blessing, healing, delivering, raising the dead, teaching, exhorting, warning and encouraging.

Wonderful in all that He suffered: the pain of Calvary, shedding His blood, becoming our sin and paying the penalty. Wonderful in death and wonderful in resurrection: After three days and three nights He got up out of the grave with all power in His hands. Though slain by men, He voluntarily laid down His life. His body did not rot; it saw no corruption. He rose from the grave as predicted; before the stone was rolled away He was gone! And the grave clothes were all in place, neatly and tightly wrapped up.

Wonderful in His counsel: He speaks the truth where men tell lies. His enlightens where man's words darken. Men make promises and break them because of hypocrisy, accidents, ignorance, events unforeseen and over which they have no control. God's advice is not limited, restricted or adversely affected by circumstances. In short,

A wonderful Savior is Jesus my Lord, He taketh my burden away; He holdeth me up, and I shall not be moved; He giveth me strength as my day. (Fanny J. Crosby)

April 27

*Therefore the L*ORD *will wait, that He may be gracious to you; and therefore He will be exalted, that He may have mercy on you. For the L*ORD *is a God of justice; blessed are all those who wait for Him.* (Isaiah 30:18)

God said, "Since you put your trust in Egypt and not in Me; since you prefer to lean on that broken cane; since you are hooked up with that gang, I'll wait to see how you make out. It's not that I am not interested in justice; I am concerned. Yea, I yearn to bless you, to fight your battles for you, to defend, protect and deliver you, for I love you. You're the apple of My eye. I desire to have pity on you and show you mercy, for I am the righteous Judge, the God of justice. But I must wait."

The Jews were disobedient, rebellious, lying children who paid no attention to the law of the Lord. Disobedience to God breeds fear; and fears drive us to do all kinds of dumb things. Listen to what the people told their preachers: "You seers, stop seeing visions. You prophets, stop preaching to us what is right. Speak unto us smooth, pleasant words, prophesy illusions, and declare deceits. Let us hear no more about the Holy One of Israel!"

Thus they despised the Word of God, the very Word that warns, "He who despises the Word will be destroyed" (Proverbs 13:13). When folks no longer want to hear the Word of God there is a vacuum in their lives. They seek to fill in what is missing but sin distorts their thinking. Judah was in trouble and went to Egypt for help.

It did so without God's advice, for the Lord would have said, "Clean up your act. Trust Me; don't trust Egypt, for her help is vain and to no purpose. Trusting unreliable Egypt brings shame, she will fail you in the time of greatest need. Furthermore, I will break Pharaoh's arms (Ezekiel 30:22). What you need to do Judah is wait for Me. Will you wait on Him today?

April 28

Therefore the LORD will wait, that He may be gracious to you; and therefore He will be exalted, that He may have mercy on you. For the LORD is a God of justice; blessed are all those who wait for Him. (Isaiah 30:18)

Our God has His own schedule. Early in history He said, "My Spirit shall not strive with man forever" (Genesis 6:3). Eventually He opened the flood gates. Recall that the Angel of the Lord waited until Jacob could wrestle no longer and then blessed him. God waited a long time for the folks in the Book of Job to stop talking. Joseph spent two full years in prison before the chief butler remembered him. And see how the Lord Jesus waited for Lazarus to die!

Divine delays however are not necessarily denials. God's "wait" does not mean "won't." It is just that He has a time schedule. When He does move, He moves swiftly, and in His own good time brings justice. His waiting then should not be adjudged by us as a do-nothing passivity. God is not asleep. Waiting is not slumbering.

When He deems the time ripe, whether on the international scene or in the life of an individual, He moves, involving justice, peace, mercy and salvation through Jesus Christ. Why should we become upset by the injustices in this present world? The Prince of Peace will establish peace. Yea, the lion will eat straw with the ox; children will play unharmed with snakes no longer poisonous; spears will be made into pruning hooks and swords fashioned into plowshares; and nations will study war no more.

Such are the promises of God. When you believe peace will come at the hands of God—not by the wisdom of man—you can live with frustrated purposes, shattered dreams, deferred hopes, and what appear to be unanswered prayers. God is waiting, for He has His own time schedule. And it is His desire that we learn to wait on Him.

April 29

Therefore the LORD will wait, that He may be gracious to you; and therefore He will be exalted, that He may have mercy on you. For the LORD is a God of justice; blessed are all those who wait for Him. (Isaiah 30:18)

Don't try to hurry God! Some people who march and demonstrate for justice act like they are more concerned than God is. Their feeble attempts to force God's hands are doomed to failure. Remember Moses? He sought to take matters into his own hands, and killed the Egyptian who was smiting a Hebrew. The murder became known; Moses was rejected and fled to Midian. Forty years later when it was God's time, he returned to Egypt to deliver Israel.

An omniscient, loving, compassionate God finds it at times appropriate to wait. And we must learn we cannot drive Him! Wait *on* the Lord; wait *for* the Lord. Pushing the Lord, jumping ahead of Him gets us into trouble. Because the Lord waits, we often think it means He wants us to go on our own way; considering His ways restrictive, we rebel, we break loose.

Later, when we wake up, come to our senses, our hearts cry out, "Oh, if only I had waited." There is a blessing in waiting for the God who waits. The psalmist said that folks who wait on the Lord would not be made ashamed (25:3), and Jeremiah said the Lord is good unto those who wait for Him (Lamentations 3:25). Sometimes there is delay because we need the experience. It is as if waiting gives God an opportunity to work a miracle He could not do before, give a bigger blessing, or teach a deeper lesson. He waits for the ideal time to show His mercy and favor, and blesses those who wait on His waiting.

Time after time He has waited before, And now He is waiting again, To see if you're willing to open the door, O, how He wants to come in. (Ralph Carmichael)

April 30

Your eyes will see the King in His beauty. (Isaiah 33:17)

This verse deals with the millennial kingdom on earth; its purpose was to encourage the hearts of the Israelites. Distressed Jerusalem eventually will be delivered; her enemies destroyed. Terror will end. Invasions will cease. Foreigners will no longer confuse others with their strange speech. Fire will no longer ravage homes. Sickness and disease will vanish. The land will be healed. The temple will be safe. The walls of the city no longer breached.

Divine forgiveness will chase away feelings of guilt. The joy of salvation will ring out! Once again the far reaches of the land beyond what the eye can see, beyond the distant horizon, will be open and free to travel in safety. And the city will be defended by God. What a picture of the results of redemption! The King whom the world needs, the King promised by God the Father, the King whom every eye shall behold—see Him dressed in royal splendor, head-quartered in Jerusalem but ruling over the entire world.

Christ our beautiful King is eternal: "The Lord is King forever and ever." He is a universal King: "For He is a great King over all the earth." He is a holy King: "The holy One of Israel is our King." And He is supreme (Psalms 10:16, 47:2, 89:18, 95:3). This beautiful King is righteous: "Behold, a King shall reign in righteousness." He is a Savior: "The Lord is our king; He will save us." He is Creator: "I am . . . the Creator of Israel, your King" (Isaiah 32:1, 33:22, 43:15). He is just (Jeremiah 23:5), eternal, immortal, invisible, and the only wise God (1 Timothy 1:17). He is the King of glory (Psalm 24:7-10), the King of kings. Open up the gates of your heart and let Him in!

O brighter than that glorious morn Shall this fair morning be, When Christ our King in beauty comes And we His face shall see! Early Greek Hymn

May 1

Your eyes will see the King in His beauty. (Isaiah 33:17)

The word rendered "will see" is used of visions which the prophets saw. It implies that something more is to be seen than that which the outer eye, the natural sight beholds. This is the word that perhaps a sister would use when she says, "Umph! What does he *see* in her?" That's just it; he sees something *in* her that our eyes looking on the outside cannot see. Multitudes saw Christ during His earthly ministry. But they were divided in their opinions about Him.

Some said He is a prophet, claiming: He is Elijah! He is Isaiah! He is Jeremiah! Others called Him a deceiver! A good rabbi! John the Baptist risen from the dead! He's crazy! Possessed with a demon! In league with the Devil! He is but a carpenter's son. He is a healer. He speaks with authority. He is a blasphemer! A visionary, Sabbath-Day desecrator! He is a breaker of Moses' law.

Despite the confusion as to His identity at His first coming, there will be no doubt in the minds of men and women when He comes again as King to reign and rule. For when He comes with clouds every eye shall see Him (Revelation 1:7). Rest assured of this: All men, every human being from Adam's day until the last child is born into this world shall see Jesus Christ.

All who have died shall be made alive by Christ (John 5:28-29; 1 Corinthians 15:22); indeed every human creature shall see this King, the Creator who made all of us. This Sovereign King is the Resurrected Lord before whom every knee shall bow to be judged. God grant that we can truly say, "King of my life, I crown Thee now!"

Awake, my soul, and sing
Of Him who died for thee,
And hail Him as thy matchless King
Thro' all eternity. (Matthew Bridges)

May 2

Your eyes will see the King in His beauty. (Isaiah 33:17)

God promises a glorious future awaits us. Men scoff at the idea of God running this world. They think that by their elections, democratic or otherwise, by their plebiscites, their military coups, rebellions, assassinations and political maneuverings that they are the ones who decide the fates of the nations. However, the God of wisdom has said, "By me kings reign, and rulers decree justice" (Proverbs 8:15).

He removes kings, and sets up kings, makes and unmakes them (Daniel 2:21). Paul said in his sermon on Mars' Hill that God "has made from one blood every nation of men to dwell on all the face of the earth, and has determined their preappointed times and the boundaries of their dwellings" (Acts 17:26).

The idea of a baby boy being born of a Jewish virgin and growing up into manhood, then dying an ignominious death on a cross, shedding His blood for our sins—the idea that this One was buried, resurrected and is coming back again to rule and reign with a rod of iron is simply too much for the world to take. But God promised, "The scepter shall not depart from Judah, nor a lawgiver from between His feet, until Shiloh comes; and to Him shall be the obedience of the people" (Genesis 49:10).

When He comes His rule in Judah will be expanded to include the entire world, so that our eyes shall behold not just the hills of Judah, or the cedars of Lebanon, or the valley of Jehoshaphat, the sand of the Negeb, the Dead Sea, the river of Jordan or the walls of Zion—but the land that is very far off, a land that stretches afar in all directions.

God is not a man that He should tell a lie. The King is coming! Let the nations rage, the King is coming. Let the peoples imagine a vain thing! The King is coming. God has set His King upon His holy hill of Zion. He whom the Lord promised will come. Look for Him today!

May 3

Thus says the LORD: "Set your house in order, for you shall die and not live." (Isaiah 38:1; 2 Kings 20:1)

<u>*The Report of the Seer*</u>: Hezekiah, king of Judah, was basically a good king. Here we find him mortally ill, and lo, the prophet Isaiah comes and says, "King Hezekiah, I've got a message for you from Jehovah." "What is it, Isaiah?" "Thus says the LORD, 'Set your house in order; for you shall die and not live.'"

Now the command to set your house in order is found on two occasions only: once in Hezekiah's life, and once in the life of a man named Ahithophel (2 Samuel 17:23) who was a trusted adviser of David but supported David's rebellious son, Absalom. Ahithophel's advice was not followed, for Hushai a friend of David, convinced Absalom of another plan by appealing to Absalom's vanity.

Ahithophel had the foresight to realize that defeat would result. "Now when Ahithophel saw that his advice was not followed, he saddled a donkey, and arose and went home to his house, to his city. Then he put his household in order, and hanged himself; he was buried in his father's tomb" (2 Samuel 17:23).

To set your house in order means to command, or to give charge to your household. It is to make a will or testament; tell what you want done after you leave these mundane shores. It is to dispose properly of your earthly possessions, give orders as to what you want done with your house, its contents, money, automobile, and other material goods. So you see what Hezekiah was commanded to do.

It probably would not do well for some folks to know the date of their death. Their concern might hasten the appointed hour! But what would *you* do if told, "Set your house in order!"? Or is it in order already? May all that you do today be done with the awareness that it is well with your soul.

May 4

Thus says the LORD: "Set your house in order, for you shall die and not live." (Isaiah 38:1; 2 Kings 20:1)

<u>*The Remedy for the Saints.*</u> A preacher said to me, "You can't make those people do anything. They must come to the realization themselves that they are in a mess. Then when they want to do something about it, you'll get something done!" That's an interesting point of view, isn't it? There must be in the heart of the church the sincere desire to live and not die. But if people are not convinced that they are dying, or will die, no spiritual progress will be made.

What is the remedy? We need a huge dose of prayer medicine, crying out of the depths of our hearts, "Lord, spare us. Give us another day, another opportunity to witness, pray, give of our money, time and talent, support missions; to teach Your Word, observe communion, distribute benevolences, visit the sick, clean up our lives, become more stable, break bad habits, stop wagging tongues, remove the garbage pail from our ears, and stop *playing* church.

"Give us another day to demonstrate that we need not confuse love and discipline, or mix up authority and function. Let us be a church where the family of Christ is more important than our family of flesh; where the Bible is seen as more than just another book, and the church is more than a social club but becomes the fellowship of believers."

I assure you that when we take the prescription the Lord provides that we will live and not die; our light will shine; our salt will be salty; souls will be won to Christ; saints will be edified, and the Lord Jesus exalted. Hearts will be fixed, glory will come down, peace will flow like a river, and joy will flood our souls. We will see in a better way the truth of the fact that we have eternal life even now. Jehovah promised to deliver Hezekiah and the city of Jerusalem out of the hand of Assyria, and to defend the city. Surely He is willing to do no less for His own today.

Thus says the LORD: "Set your house in order, for you shall die and not live." (Isaiah 38:1; 2 Kings 20:1)

<u>*The Response of the Savior.*</u> Now we know from Job and other Scriptures that the day for our death has been set already. We cannot go beyond that time. Our steps have been numbered, the year appointed, the month already ordained, and the day already programmed. However, the possibility of falling short always remains, for there are those of us who live dangerously beneath our Christian heritage, who live carelessly and who live in disobedience.

Now do not think the Lord did not know ahead of time what Hezekiah would do. The God of the Bible is omniscient and no surprises are sprung on Him; no hidden, unforeseen events cause Him to change His mind or alter His plans. No. He knows all along what men will do. Before Isaiah had gotten very far, the prophet was directed by Jehovah to return to King Hezekiah and tell him, "Thus says the Lord, the God of David, your father..."

You see from this statement alone that you may be blessed by God because of the good relationship someone else had with the Lord. This point is often brought out in the Bible with respect to Abraham, Isaac, Jacob and David, and their relationship with the Lord God. So it is that you may be blessed right now because someone else lived close to the Lord. By God's grace it may well be that one reason you are alive and doing well is that people truly born again prayed for you and the Lord honored their prayers.

Even though some 300 years intervened between their reigns, we find the Lord blessing Hezekiah because of David. Who knows the effects of a godly father and mother in the lives of their children? What has the Lord wrought on your behalf because someone in your family lived all out for the Lord? What benefits have you reaped? What doors have been opened, how many years added?

May 6

But those who wait on the LORD shall renew their strength; they shall mount up with wings like eagles. (Isaiah 40:31)

Many different birds are mentioned in the Bible. Quails fell from heaven supplying meat for the Israelites wandering in the wilderness (Exodus 16:13). Job spoke of the beautiful plumage of the peacock, and the feathers of the ostrich and stork, and the sharp eye of the falcon (Job 39:13, 28:7). Commanded by God the ravens fed the prophet Elijah bread and meat both morning and evening (1 Kings 17:4).

Jeremiah said, "As a partridge that broods but does not hatch, so is he who gets riches, but not by right. It will leave him in the midst of his days, and at his end he will be a fool" (17:11). King Hezekiah described his illness "like a crane or a swallow, so I chattered; I mourned like a dove" (Isaiah 38:14). Jeremiah voiced Jehovah's complaint, "Even the stork in the heavens knows her appointed times . . . But My people do not know the judgment of the Lord" (8:7).

Overwhelmed by affliction and troubled by enemies, the psalmist said of his solitary desolation and dreary loneliness, "I am like a pelican of the wilderness; I am like an owl of the desert; I lie awake and am like a sparrow alone on the house-top" (Psalm 102:6f). Finally, we hear the voice of the Lord Jesus saying to His disciples, "Behold, I send you out as sheep in the midst of wolves, therefore be wise as serpents and harmless as doves" (Matthew 10:16).

Thus in our biblical aviary we have the quail, peacock, ostrich, falcon, raven, partridge, crane, swallow, dove, stork, pelican, owl and sparrow. Many more are mentioned in Leviticus 11, the chapter spelling out what birds could be eaten by the Israelites. But here in our devotion text, the promise is: They that wait upon the Lord shall mount up with wings like eagles. Imagine flying through this day on the strong pinions of an eagle!

May 7

But those who wait on the LORD shall renew their strength;
they shall mount up with wings like eagles. (Isaiah 40:31)

A primary characteristic of the eagle is speed; another is incredible eyesight. High in the sky the eagle is able to spot a mouse, rabbit or snake on the ground. With wings tightly folded together and the head pointed downward, it goes into a deep dive to pounce upon its prey; and the speed of those dives is estimated at 100 miles an hour.

Is it any wonder that Job (9:26) speaks of "an eagle swooping on its prey"? Or that those soldiers permitted by God to invade disobedient Israel would come as "swift as the eagle flies" (Deuteronomy 28:49) with horses swifter than eagles (Jeremiah 4:13); they shall fly like the eagle that hastens to eat (Habakkuk 1:8); our persecutors are swifter than the eagles of the heaven (Lamentations 4:19).

Why the eagle? Because this large, fearless, fierce-looking feathered creature is the strongest of birds. The female golden eagle may have a wingspan more than seven feet and weigh about 12 pounds. Soaring (Proverbs 30:19) on flat, outstretched wings it rises to catch thermal updrafts and with seemingly effortless ease glides and planes with great speed in its chosen direction. Within a short time its powerful flight carries it so high in the air that the human eye sees only a speck if it sees the eagle at all. No wonder Solomon warns us not to labor to be rich, for riches make themselves wings and fly away like an eagle (Proverbs 23:5).

When the Lord asserted His omnipotence, He asked Job (39:27): "Does the eagle mount up at your command, and make its nest on high?" To proud Edom God said, "Though you make your nest as high as the eagle, I will bring you down" (Jeremiah 49:16; Obadiah 4). Yet God's tender providence for Israel is heard: "As an eagle stirs up its nest, hovers over its young . . . So the Lord alone led" Jacob (Deuteronomy 32:11). So He will lead you today.

May 8

But those who wait on the LORD shall renew their strength; they shall mount up with wings like eagles. (Isaiah 40:31)

The Bible pictures the eagle as a symbol of strength and swiftness. Can you imagine now such a creature being caged or having its wings clipped, no longer able to display its vigor, its speed or its powerful flight? Well, eagles were not created to be caged, but to soar in the vast, limitless sky. And so are the souls of human beings meant for higher things.

Think back over the past days. Were you a caged Christian? Did the Devil clip your wings? Were you kept earthbound by shackling habits, twisted values, unholy ambitions, bad company, desire for revenge, a hot temper, a quick tongue? We saints have no business being thus imprisoned, for by the blood of Jesus Christ we were set free from the penalty of sin, and given the privilege of soaring free from the power of sin!

To all then who sincerely believe in the Lord Jesus Christ there is the command, wait on Him. What does it means to wait for the Lord? I thought I knew but discovered it is a lesson I still must learn. I am still in school. For sometimes in what I consider an emergency, I want an instant answer and I treat God as if He were running a fast-food restaurant. When the answer does not come right away, I panic and pout, and depressed begin to question God.

Since this never happens to you, I hope you will have pity on this poor preacher. After all, you have heard it said that what God commands He supplies. He provides us with waiting power, patience and perseverance. Waiting involves trusting in the Lord for His help; those who wait for Him hope in Him. This waiting is full of expectation of good, for our God is the God of hope. Wait on Him today, and you will mount up with wings like an eagle and soar above the storms of life. Rise up! Rise up! Fly high into the sky!

May 9

But those who wait on the LORD *shall renew their strength;*
they shall mount up with wings like eagles. (Isaiah 40:31)

Just wait on Him and in His good time He will move. Wait
on Him and you will mount up with wings like eagles! You
will be living evidence that the God of the Bible does not
want His children to face the future either caged or with
clipped wings. If your lifestyle has Christ as its object you
are possessed with the pinions of an eagle. Yea, if you wait
on the Lord Jesus, He gives strength to mount up and soar.

Do not then put trust in men. Not in the pope, preacher,
politician or president, for they will fail you. Even the youths
with their seemingly boundless supply of energy shall faint
and be weary. Yea and the young men will utterly fall. But if
you wait on the Lord, if you believe in Him, trust Him, hope
in Him, you will gain fresh strength.

If you wait on the Lord you will follow in the footsteps
of Christ. He waited until the fullness of the times; then
came forth from heaven born of a virgin. He waited until the
proper time to break forth in His public ministry as the
beloved Son of God in whom the Father was well pleased.
He waited on the Father as each day drew Him nearer to
Calvary, until that day ended, and the night came when no
man can work.

They laid His body in the tomb; three nights and three
days He waited, and on the third morning His spirit flew
from Hades on eagle's wings and joined that uncorrupted
body. For forty days He waited, going back and forth from
earth to heaven, until that final day He stepped on a cloud
there at the Mount of Olives, and ascended into heaven as on
the wings of an eagle. He sat down at the right hand of the
Father and He is still there waiting. Now we are waiting too,
looking for His return. And how strengthening it is to wait!
Even so, come Lord Jesus.

May 10

A bruised reed He will not break, and smoking flax He will not quench. (Isaiah 42:3; Matthew 12:20)

The *bruised reed* represents the poor, oppressed and needy; it signifies a condition of weakness that is close to dissolution and death. Applied to our human condition we find that it does not take much to break us. Force may cause us to collapse like a bruised reed that is easily snapped.

Christ is described as One who restores, mends, heals, strengthens, encourages, forgives, blesses, pities, and pardons. The soul that is broken in contrition, weeping because of transgression, truly repentant, He will not break.

The *smoking [smoldering] flax* pictures the fine fiber of a plant used as a wick in a lamp. To quench means to put out or extinguish; the smoking wick is one expiring, about to give up the ghost, more smoke than fire. It represents those who are at the end of their rope. Our feebleness, frailty and infirmity are pictured in the flickering flame and rising smoke. As a boy I hated having to clean the soot from those lamps, primarily because I was scared to death I would drop one and shatter it to pieces.

Reading the Gospels we find the non-provocative ministry of Christ is consistent with the prophecy Isaiah makes of the Messiah. There are religious leaders who think they advance God's kingdom by their in-your-face marches, loud public haranguing and demonstrations of political "clout" and demagoguery.

This is not so with Christ. He speaks, prays, teaches and preaches with a quiet spirit motivated by love. When our faith is weak, He encourages us; He bids us come to Him to find rest for our souls. It may be that you are ready to give in and give up, and feel as Jacob said to his sons on one occasion, "All these things are against me." Christ comes to lift you up, to cherish the feeble flame in your lamp, supply the oil of grace, and rekindle the wick into a blaze.

May 11

Kings shall shut their mouths at Him. (Isaiah 52:15)

Because of the Suffering Servant many nations shall be drawn to the Lord God and be cleansed. But note now that on account of Him the lips of the kings of the earth will be dumb; the kings will be speechless, in silent awe. Micah (7:16) says, "The nations shall see and be ashamed of all their might; they shall put their hand over their mouth."

Why this shutting of the mouth, this sealing of the lips? It is more than an act of amazement. Job said to Zophar, one of his 'friends,' "Look at me and be astonished; put your hand over your mouth" (21:5). We learn that the kings of the earth will be silent because they will have no valid basis for justifying their deeds. The nations of this world will be unable to speak, either to condemn and blame God, or to justify themselves, when they look upon the victorious Jesus Christ, the Suffering Servant seated as Sovereign Savior.

Paul said: "Now we know that whatever the law says, it says to those who are under the law, that every mouth may be stopped, and all the world may become guilty before God" (Romans 3:19). In very general terms the law is the revealed will of God given to mankind in order that we might have a standard whereby to live. It seeks to tie us to a certain living standard. Now God has revealed His will to us through many channels: in nature, conscience, history, the Ten Commandments, the Bible or Word of God, the Holy Spirit, and certainly in Jesus Christ Himself, for you note they, the kings shall shut their mouths at *Him.*

We learn that God has so fixed it that every mouth may be closed, stopped, shut up, fenced in, blocked and silenced. When God reveals Himself through his Suffering Servant there is nothing that man can say; as they look and see victory rising up out of Tribulation, they will be unable to speak. In the meantime, thank God the redeemed *can* speak (Psalm 107:2).

May 12

All we like sheep have gone astray. (Isaiah 53:6)

However much it may offend some people, the Bible describes some human beings as dogs (Psalm 22:16, 20; Isaiah 56:10; Philippians 3:2; Revelation 22:15), wolves (Matthew 7:15; Acts 20:29), a fox (Luke 13:32), snakes and goats (Matthew 23:33, 25:31-33). It should come as no surprise then to hear humans described also as sheep.

The sheep is a very stupid animal. It has a mind that causes it to wander about, easily going astray, head down, nibbling along and unmindful where it is going. A sheep is defenseless: It has no horns to butt; and no sharp teeth or fangs to tear. It cannot fly or climb a tree to escape; it cannot blow or puff up to prevent being swallowed; it has no poison to inject or putrid smelling liquid to eject.

It has no ability to jump high; no swift legs with which to run; no protective coloring or camouflage to hide. The sheep has no tough skin for armor; no awesome roar to intimidate; no rattle to frighten away enemies. It is simply helpless. By all standards of the animal kingdom and all human common sense, who would want to be a sheep? No one; but such we are. And therefore we need a Shepherd.

Well, I am glad to announce Jesus Christ is the Good Shepherd (John 10:11-18), the Great Shepherd (Hebrews 13:20), and the Chief Shepherd (1 Peter 5:4). Simon Peter also said, "For you were like sheep going astray, but have now returned to the Shepherd and Overseer of your souls" (1 Peter 2:25). And so that's my hope. Is it yours?

My hope is not on what men can accomplish in this world. Thank God for good politicians, but my hope is not in them. Humanitarians, philanthropists—we need them all. But one day the clouds will break, the trumpet shall sound; and I expect to be snatched up to meet the Shepherd who saved this sheep by His grace!

For thus says the High and Lofty One who inhabits eternity, whose name is Holy: "I dwell in the high and holy place, with him who has a contrite and humble spirit, to revive the spirit of the humble, and to revive the heart of the contrite ones." (Isaiah 57:15)

His Promise: A pompous fellow walked into an office and demanded to see the manager immediately. "I'm sorry, but he's not here," replied the secretary. "May I be of any help to you?" "No!" he snapped, "I never deal with subordinates. I'll wait unto the manager returns!" "Very well, take a seat," said the secretary. About an hour later the man fuming with impatience said, "How much longer do you think the manager will be?" "About two weeks. He went away on his vacation yesterday," was the reply. How sad to fail to benefit from God's promise to give the humble honor and peace.

His Person: What God discloses about Himself thrills our hearts. Our foreparents summed it up perfectly when they said, "He sits high and looks low." The psalmist talks about God's transcendence and immanence, and says, "The Lord is high above all nations, and His glory above the heavens. Who is like the Lord our God, who dwells on high, who humbles Himself to behold the things that are in the heavens, and in the earth?" (Psalm 113:4-6; cf. 138:6).

His Presence: God who is also far away draws near; remoteness becomes nearness; glory on high is manifested in grace below. See both at the same time, and realize that Jehovah dwells on high *and* with the lowly. What love! What mercy! He who is at home in eternity is found in the company of temporal man. The Creator is found hobnobbing with the creature. Ephemeral man, the creature of a day, knows little about the past, is not too good at interpreting the present, and knows nothing on his own about the future. "If we think we are something, we have only to turn our eyes to God, and immediately we are nothing" (Calvin).

May 14

For thus says the High and Lofty One who inhabits eternity, whose name is Holy: "I dwell in the high and holy place, with him who has a contrite and humble spirit, to revive the spirit of the humble, and to revive the heart of the contrite ones." (Isaiah 57:15)

His Purpose: Why would one enthroned in heaven bother with earth His footstool? Why would One so high look so low? Why would the Creator be so concerned with the creature? Why would He who lives in eternity also dwell with feeble slaves of time? In short, why did Jesus Christ come? His coming was predicted; He came to fulfill the Scriptures, and because the Father sent Him. Because He loved us he came to seek and to save the lost. He also came to destroy the Devil; and to die on the cross for you and for me. Furthermore, Christ came to revive the spirit of the contrite. This was His goal.

Study of the meaning and use of the word rendered *revive* helps us to see His purpose of keeping alive that which is already living, and restoring to life that which is dead. God used Elijah the prophet to revive the dead son of the widow of Zarephath; a dead man's body touched the bones of the prophet Elisha and the man revived. Revival describes causing grain to grow; Naaman recovering from leprosy, a ruined city restored, and rejuvenation of Jacob's discouraged spirit upon learning Joseph was still alive.

Hezekiah used this word when he cried, "Lord, restore me and make me to live." In Moses' day those who were bitten by serpents looked at the bronze serpent and lived. Thirsty Samson's spirit was revived when he drank of the water God provided from the donkey's jawbone. The appreciative humble saint realizes that although he or she serves a big God, no heart is too small for Him to dwell in. Humble yourself today beneath the mighty hand of God and see Him work in your life as never before.

May 15

Behold, the LORD's hand is not shortened that it cannot save; nor His ear heavy that it cannot hear. (Isaiah 59:1)

God has been dealing with sinners for a long time. He dealt with the disobedience of Adam and Eve, the murder of Abel by Cain, the drunkenness of Noah, disrespect of Ham for his father, the immorality of Canaan, lies told by Abraham and the covetousness of Balaam. He dealt with the homosexuality of the men in Sodom and Gomorrah, the jealousy of Joseph's brothers, the trickery of Jacob, the carnality of Esau, the hard heart of Pharaoh, the magic of Jannes and Jambres, the murmuring of the Israelites in the wilderness, and the prostitution of Rahab.

He handled the deception of Delilah, the self-destructive nature of Samson, the instability of king Saul, the arrogance of Goliath, the adultery of David and Bathsheba, the cursing of Shimei, the rape of Tamar by Amnon, the conspiracy of Absalom, and the foolishness of Solomon in all his wisdom.

He dealt with the bad advice given to Rehoboam, the blasphemy of Rabshakeh, the weakness of King Ahab, and the vengeance of Jezebel. And what about the presumptuousness of Uzziah, the hatred of Haman, the schemes of Sanballat, the hypocrisy of the Pharisees, the vindictiveness of Herodias, the demoniacs, the riotous living of the prodigal son, and the impetuousness of Simon Peter!

Do not fail to include the treachery of Judas, the deceit of Ananias and Sapphira, the worldliness of Demas, the evil of Alexander the coppersmith, and the unholy ambition of Diotrephes! And what about *you*? Yea, what about *me?* Where did God's long arm and good hand find us? Where were we when He heard our cry? What were we doing when Christ came into our lives? Oh, the wonderful grace of God!

May 16

Yet they did not obey or incline their ear, but followed the counsels and the dictates of their evil hearts, and went backward and not forward. (Jeremiah 7:24)

Backsliding is for those who have gone ahead far enough to have some place or space to slide back. It indicates that at one time some progress was made, whether in knowledge, experience, conscience or ceremony, but in some degree in relation to God. In other words, in order to slide back you must have some "sliding room."

Otherwise you will be like the little boy who fell out of his bed onto the hard floor. His mother heard the loud bump in his room and ran up to ask what happened. His reply was, "Aw, mom, I fell asleep too close to where I got in." So backsliding has to do with folks who have some knowledge of God, some dealing with Him. He lifted them up, rescued them, blessed them, delivered them or enlightened them.

Those who are up backslide and come down; the delivered are re-shackled; the enlightened are headed back to the darkness; those in the know return to ignorance. Unfortunately, in the moral realm there is no fence-walking, no fair-to-middling, no in-between, no "no-man's land" or buffer zone. For if you are not growing in Christ you are growing away from Him.

I am not talking about losing salvation; that's not possible. But backsliding in the moral aspect indicates we are either getting better or we are getting worse. There is no in-between place. To the believer who may be despondent because of his mistakes; to the saint whose conscience is pricked, the Lord pleads "Come to Me." To the weary and faint, He bids, "Come, and I will give you rest." No genuine Christian is so far back that he cannot be brought forward again to the joy and peace once experienced. Christ's blood still cleanses us from sin; and guarantees that the backslider can reverse his or her direction and go forward again.

O LORD, the hope of Israel, all who forsake You shall be ashamed. Those who depart from Me shall be written in the earth, because they have forsaken the LORD, the fountain of living waters. (Jeremiah 17:13)

Those who forsake or abandon the LORD shall be written in the dust or ground of the earth. To forsake God is to disappear like the writing on the sand at the seashore. To print anything in dust, dirt or sand is to suggest that which is not enduring or lasting. One Sunday someone got his or her finger dirty by printing WASH ME and WASH ME PLEASE on the door and hood of my car. I announced from the pulpit that if I find out who did it, I would be glad to oblige and give the culprit a bath! Once the car is washed, the dirt disappears and the message is no more.

To forsake God is to have your name written down upon that which is not permanent. To be written in dust is a forceful figure for that which is folly, futile, foolish, and fragile. It represents that which is transitory. This figure of speech reminded me of the Lord Jesus who stooped and wrote on the ground in front of the men who brought to Him the woman caught in the very act of adultery. Whatever He wrote He conveyed to the hypocrites the flimsiness of their charge, their bad motives, and their failure to bring the man in too. The passing nature of the Law was brought to their notice.

Where is your name written? Christ said to the joyful seventy disciples returning from their victorious mission, "Nevertheless, do not rejoice in this, that the spirits are subject to you, but rather rejoice because your names are written in heaven" (Luke 10:20). Rejoice today that your name is not written in dirt or the sand of the earth, but praise God, in the Lamb's book of life in heaven.

May 18

Ah, LORD GOD! Behold, You have made the heavens and the earth by Your great power and outstretched arm. There is nothing too hard for You. (Jeremiah 32:17)

Zedekiah king of Judah had Jeremiah imprisoned for predicting Babylon's army would besiege Jerusalem and capture Zedekiah. While in prison Jeremiah received a message from the Lord to buy family property situated in Anathoth, land then occupied by the Babylonian army. The prophet did immediately what God told him to do, then puzzled and asked questions afterward.

Some folks never get this far in their spiritual journey because they ask questions *before* they do anything; they have never learned to take God at His word. Because they disobey *first* they don't know what it means to *obey* **and** have problems. All they know is *disobeying* **and** having troubles, unaware that faith makes the difference.

Jeremiah's life was no bed of roses. Commanded not to get married, he never knew the joys of family life; what relatives he had conspired against him. Friends betrayed him; he was falsely accused, lied on, and beaten, mocked, derided, ridiculed, and thrown into prison, once into a dungeon of mud. Somehow even in the midst of troubles, and desiring to give up, he could not, for the Word of God was like a fire shut up in his bones and he had to keep on preaching.

Look at the situation. King Nebuchadnezzar's soldiers are pounding on the door; the siege of Jerusalem is in its final stage; fire has devoured, the sword cut down, pestilence devastated, famine has ravished; and the city is falling even as the Lord predicted. Yet Jehovah ordered, "Buy the field with money; call in witnesses—although the city is given into the hands of the Chaldeans!" Well, nothing is too hard for You, Lord, even though I don't understand. Who in his right mind would purchase property already in enemy hands? But Jeremiah's mind was right because he trusted God.

Ah, LORD GOD! Behold, You have made the heavens and the earth by Your great power and outstretched arm. There is nothing too hard for You. (Jeremiah 32:17)

Jeremiah had enough faith in the Lord to believe that eventually God would reclaim the land for Israel. Buying the lot was daring proof to the Jews that Jeremiah believed what he prophesied. For nearly 40 years he had preached the fall of Jerusalem because of her wickedness and idolatry. Now it was happening. Look at the opening words of this prayer of anguish. How, Lord, can my purchasing a piece of property in enemy hands be reconciled with the fact that You already predicted the Chaldeans would surely conquer wicked Israel?

Jeremiah began by praising God as the Creator, a doctrine sadly neglected these days. He acknowledged and lauded Jehovah who by His great power and outstretched arm made the heavens and the earth, and redeemed Israel out of the land of Egypt. Surely there is nothing too hard for the Lord. The word translated "hard, difficult" is a gem, a real jewel for study. Translations of this word in various verses in the KJV of the Bible give us the following:

Is anything *extraordinary* for God? Is anything too *wonderful* for Him? Is anything too *miraculous* for the Lord? Is anything too *presumptuous* for God to do? Is there anything too *wondrous* for Him? What is *surpassing* or *beyond His power* to do? Is anything too *difficult* for the Lord? Is there something *hidden* that He cannot see or anything too *high* for Him? What is so *exceptional* that He cannot do it?

Our hearts respond, "No. He is able to do exceedingly abundantly above all that we ask or think." (Ephesians 3:20). May we realize today in a new way nothing is too difficult for God, and that through Christ we can do all things.

May 20

They will know that a prophet has been among them.
(Ezekiel 2:5, 33:33)

Ezekiel was no magician minister, no prestidigitating preacher-prophet pulling out philosophies from different pockets to fit the particular point of view of the people in the pews as he preached from the pulpit. He did not preach one thing in one place and just the opposite in another place. Folks who want to be massaged and not given a message look for entertainment and not edification; they desire syncopation but not sanctification; they would rather wriggle than worship. Programs that produce pecuniary profits are preferable to preaching and prayer meetings.

God said, "Ezekiel, it does not matter what people do with your sermons, don't you stop preaching the truth. In the end it will be recognized that a prophet has been in town in their midst." Ezekiel emphasized restoration, and when his predictions actually came to pass, the people came to hear him. However, their coming was hypocritical; they loved to hear good stuff, predictions about the defeat of the enemy, restoration to national glory, and peace.

But the moral implications were ignored. They would not do what was required of them. And so Jehovah told Ezekiel, "They love your oratorical ability and sweet sounding voice; they are impressed by the grandiloquence with which you employ polysyllabic words, the rhetorical splendor of the description of a beatific eschatological scene thrills their very hearts! But don't be fooled, for they hear but don't do. They don't really take you seriously, Ezekiel. But you keep on preaching, for Israel will never be able to plead ignorance. When the time comes, they shall know that a prophet has been among them" (Deuteronomy 18:21f; Jeremiah 28:9). If you have been blessed to have a prophet-preacher for a pastor, pray for him today, and thank Jesus Christ, the Prophet without Peer!

May 21

The soul who sins shall die. (Ezekiel 18:4, 20)

The problem Ezekiel faced more than 2500 years ago comes to us in new disguise. It is the matter of personal judgment for personal sin. And God's answer gives us insight for today. The principle spelled out is applicable to all nations, races, age groups, societies, classes, families and individuals.

Simply put: We cannot blame generations past for the evils of today; we cannot escape the responsibility of our own misdeeds. That events of the past may help shape the way in which sin will manifest itself cannot be denied. But the actual commission of evil is the sole responsibility of the doer himself. I may want to blame Adam and Eve for my plight, but I do not thus avoid the pain, sorrow and misery which result from my own personal folly and sin. Passing the blame to others will not keep the unbeliever out of Hell.

Unfortunately there are people who have attempted to use this passage to support what is called "soul-sleep." There is no such animal as "soul-sleep"! The soul represents the entire person. We often ask, "How many souls were saved?" This means how many people came to accept the Lord Jesus Christ as Savior.

The part—body, soul or spirit—represents the whole. So it is the person who sins that shall die; each tub stands on its own bottom. There is no proof that "death" means extinction of personality. Jesus Christ took our sins upon Himself, so that for believers there is no eternal death. Christ died for us, once for all. We may not even experience physical death (1 Thessalonians 4:15-17; 1 Corinthians 15:51). The only judgment we face is for rewards (2 Corinthians 5:10). Today, keep in mind that to be absent from the body is to be present with the Lord (2 Corinthians 5:8). What a joy in knowing where we stand with a holy God. Rejoice today knowing that there is no condemnation and no separation; we have *eternal* life right now!

May 22

Their features appeared better and fatter in flesh than all the young men who ate the portion of the king's delicacies. (Daniel 1:15)

There are all kinds of faces in the world. Job said, "My face is flushed with weeping" (16:16). The wicked man hardens his face (Proverbs 21:29). Cain's countenance fell (Genesis 4:5f); the skin on Moses' face shone (Exodus 34:29); and Jezebel's face was painted (2 Kings 9:30).

In the Bible are faces of impudence, shame, fear, awe, pride, paleness, confusion, blackness (gloom) and despair; we read of countenances which are fierce, angelic, beautiful, comely, fair, sad, angry, troubled, cheerful, etc. There is the face of Christ in *humiliation*: smitten, spittle-covered, blood stained and in pain and anguish. But John saw the face of the same Lord Jesus, and it was *glorious and majestic*: with eyes as a flame of fire, out of His mouth went a sharp two-edged sword and His countenance was as the sun shines in its strength (Revelation 1:14, 16).

By their faces you shall know them! How do you look when under pressure? When things don't go the way you want, do you look cross-eyed? When your will is frustrated, are your jaws puffed out? When something unpleasant is said to or about you, do you look mean?

The prince of the eunuchs was afraid that by not eating the king's food, the faces of Daniel and his friends would be in poor condition and cause him to lose favor with the king. He declined the responsibility. Daniel then spoke to Melzar the steward, and requested a ten day trial of eating a vegetable diet and water. This was granted and Daniel and his friends passed the test.

Today, make a special effort to sit down at God's table and eat His food, His Word. It will do your soul good. And peace, satisfaction, contentment, love and joy will all be seen in your face. And others will see Jesus Christ in you.

May 23

He delivers and rescues, and He works signs and wonders in heaven and on earth, who has delivered Daniel from the power of the lions. (Daniel 6:27)

From the words of King Darius we learn what biblical deliverance is. If when you are cast into the fiery furnace of destructive criticism you emerge unharmed by sarcasm and skepticism, but full of optimism and believing God is capable of making all things work out for your good—that's deliverance. When you are thrown into the lions' den of racism, hypocrisy and exploitation, and come out unbitten by bitterness—that's deliverance.

When surrounded by the fat cats of corruption and you come out uncompromised, unscratched by greed and the lust for power, not having stabbed anybody in the back—that's deliverance. When shackled by bad personal habits and addiction, and the Holy Spirit sets you free, enabling you to live a clean life in a dirty age—that's deliverance. When a man can see through all the wicked attempts to emasculate him, make him feel inferior, and cause him to hate himself, and can realize within himself that he is a man, and that in Jesus Christ he is God's man—that's deliverance.

When God convinces you that that boyfriend or girlfriend who is not a Christian is tearing you down, and you let him or her go—that's deliverance. When quick tempers and hot heads are permanently cooled off—that's deliverance. When truth has set free a lying tongue; when you get joy out of giving to the Lord's work, joy out of helping others; when there's a peace deep down in your heart—that's deliverance.

When you're walking in the light as He is in the light; and have absolute assurance His blood has washed away all your sins—that's deliverance. Walk on clouds of joy today as you recall how the same God that delivered Daniel delivers you also.

May 24

I will be to Ephraim like a moth . . . I will be like a lion to Ephraim. (Hosea 5:12, 14)

This text speaks of God's judgment upon the nation, here called Ephraim, another name for the ten tribes of Israel. Because of Israel's inveterate idolatry, Jehovah took steps to straighten out His people; and of course, He does many different things when He chastises, judges or punishes.

Here God threatens to destroy as does the moth. Would you believe that at one time I wanted to be an entomologist and work for the Government? More important, did you know that the God of the Bible is the God of insects? Yes, they are part of the hosts that do His bidding (Joel 2:25). And there are at least eleven references to moths in the Bible. Moths operate in silence and often in darkness; they represent God's slow but certain justice. Thus He likens the destruction that awaits Ephraim to the work of a moth, slowly and silently destroying the nation internally and externally.

A second way to accomplish His judgment is by the lion. Thus from a slow moving, silent, small moth to a fast moving, roaring, rapacious, ravening lion Jehovah warns Israel of imminent destruction. How has the Lord dealt with you who belong to Him through faith in the shed blood of Christ? Did He use an ant or an alligator? Did He use a caterpillar or crocodile? Did He use a bug or a bear? Did He use the grasshopper or turn loose the gorilla?

He speaks to our consciences and uses chastisements to get us to repent, confess, straighten up and "fly right"! When we harden our hearts, stiffen our necks the pressure is increased, the screws tightened, and the moth becomes a lion. And though saved, some of us have added unnecessary misery to our lives. And all the while the Lord Jesus bids us come with genuine contrition, have fellowship restored, and be made whole again.

May 25

Ephraim is a cake unturned. (Hosea 7:8)

Over the years I have had some bad restaurant experiences at breakfast time. I have had to request my sausage be cooked a little more; I have been given watered-down orange juice, bacon fried to a frizzle, burnt toast, and coffee that was nothing more than colored water. But never have I been given a half-baked pancake! Such a pancake is of no value; it is good for nothing. You cannot eat it.

God used this graphic description of Ephraim (another name of the ten tribe kingdom of Israel) to portray the nation's twisted values, inconsistencies, self contradictions, weaknesses and flabbiness of character, the pursuit of vanity and chase of worthless goals.

Imagine a pancake baked only on one side. It is a picture of the nation claiming Jehovah as its God, but still serving idols. It portrays one side of outward performance done up real nice, but inward there is raw indifference to the things of God. Some one has described the half-ruined nation as "a half-fed people, a half-cultured society, a half-lived religion, with a half-hearted policy."

This reminds us of Revelation 3:15-16, "I know your works, that you are neither cold nor hot. I could wish you were cold or hot. So then, because you are lukewarm, and neither cold nor hot, I will vomit you out of My mouth."

According to the dictionary a mess is a muddle; it is a disturbing, confusing, troublesome, chaotic state of affairs; a distasteful and unappetizing concoction. Picture then a church described as *half-baked,* "raw, incomplete, or not thorough-going" (Hendrickson). Finally, imagine a Christian being described as *half-baked!* Think about this today. Ask yourself, "Am I consistent? Am I dependable? Or am I really hard to swallow, a gooey, spoiled, carnal Christian? Am I a half-baked pancake?"

May 26

For thus says the LORD to the house of Israel, "Seek Me and live." (Amos 5:4)

The Creator of the Stars: Who is it that pleads thus? It is He who binds the chains of the Pleiades, and loosens the cords of Orion, who guides the stars, having appointed their number and called them all by their names (Psalm 147:4; Job 38:31). The heavens are the work of His fingers; He who ordained the moon and the stars cries, "Seek Me and live!"

The Controller of the Seas: It is He who encloses the sea with doors and determines its boundaries; who says to the ocean, "This far you may come, but no farther; and here your proud waves must stop!" (Job 38:11). It is He who gathers the waters of the sea together as a heap (Psalm 33:7), stills its noise, silences its waves, rules its raging, calms its storms and makes its billows cease to roll. He is the One who commands, "Seek Me and live!"

The Conqueror of the Strong: It is He before whom mighty nations are but the dust of the earth. He puts their armies to flight, snaps their bows, causes their arrows to fall short, their spears to melt, the wheels of their chariots to come off, their horses stumble, the gates of their cities fall flat, the walls thereof crumble, and all their plans go awry. This is He who orders, "Seek Me and live!"

The Christ of the Saved: Now hear the good news that God through Christ is the One who seeks with passionate plea, with nail-pierced hands. Christ begs: "Come to Me and live—abundantly, eternally." Rejoice today that you have found Him because He searched and found you first.

Thy truth unchanged hath ever stood;
Thou savest those that on Thee call;
To them that seek Thee, Thou art good,
To them that find Thee, all in all. (Bernard of Clairvaux)

And He knows those who trust in Him. (Nahum 1:7)

Believers are admonished *not* to put their trust in Egypt's shadow, Samaria's mountains, or any powers outside of God, for unholy alliances bring woe. Their horses and chariots will fail. There is no hiding place down here; walled fortified cities will be breached and torn down. Trust in idol gods and great shame will be your lot.

Do not trust in good works, for by grace are you saved in order to do good works. Do not put your faith in beauty, for physical beauty is vain; or in treasures and wealth, for thieves break through and steal, moths eat and rust corrodes; or in man, for the arm of flesh will fail; or in self, for he that trusts his own heart is a fool (Proverbs 28:26).

On the other hand, if you take refuge in the Lord, great will be your blessings on earth and your rewards in heaven. Trust in the Lord, and like Mount Zion which cannot be removed, you will abide forever; you will hear God's loving-kindness in the morning. Trust in the Lord, and find in Him everlasting strength. Seek refuge in the Lord and He will work goodness for you; and you will never be put to confusion or made ashamed.

He will be your shield, buckler, battle-axe and high tower. He will fight your battles for you. Trust in Him and rejoice, be glad in Him; He will deliver you, preserve you and your heart will be fixed. Trust in the Lord and God will be your help, mercy will surround you, fears will flee from you. Take refuge in Him, and He will direct your paths and keep you in perfect peace.

Under His wings I am safely abiding;
Though the night deepens and tempests are wild,
Still I can trust Him—I know He will keep me;
He has redeemed me and I am His child.
(Wm. O. Cushing)

May 28

Now Joshua was clothed with filthy garments, and was standing before the Angel. (Zechariah 3:3)

Joshua (not the Joshua who followed Moses) stood silent in the presence of God. The filthy garments he wore signified sin and impurity, pointing to the terrible character of the priesthood and to the condition of the nation Israel. Joshua's besmirchment was not a chance or unusual matter. Rather, his attire was a picture of habitual defilement.

Israel had learned its lesson and no longer dirtied itself with the fornication of idolatry. But a more refined and subtle idolatry had come, a self-righteousness and legalism, creating a generation pure in its own eyes (Proverbs 30:12). By the time of Christ such conceit and legalism had reached their zenith as illustrated by the deeds of the Pharisees, Sadducees and scribes.

Removal of the polluted clothing signifies forgiveness, acceptance and re-instatement. Joshua himself had no power to cleanse himself or to cleanse Israel. Yet cleansing is a prerequisite for blessing. So God who wants to bless us must cause iniquity to pass from us. But *He* must do it, and not *we*. So here the high priest, Joshua, had to be clothed with a robe befitting his office as the religious head and representative of a chosen people.

Such a festive garment speaks of purity, joy, and glory; it signifies re-instatement of the nation into its original calling (Exodus 19:6). Today, by faith in the shed blood of Christ we have on a robe of righteousness. Positionally our vestment is whiter than snow. Conditionally our robe of service is soiled, for we live in a polluted age. The Christian has the Holy Spirit wherewithal to live clean in a dirty age, however. And so, if we have a new robe, wear it pleasing to God. May our clean life represent well our righteous robe, as our condition slowly approaches our position.

May 29

So he answered and said to me, "This is the word of the LORD to Zerubbabel: Not by might nor by power, but by My Spirit," says the LORD of hosts. (Zechariah 4:6).

Zerubbabel's zealous desire to finish rebuilding the temple was commendable. But in the face of such formidable foes it would be folly for him not to recognize his own utter helplessness. He needed to hear what God told Jeremiah: "Do not be dismayed before their faces, lest I dismay you before them . . . They will fight against you, but they shall not prevail against you, for I am with you," says the Lord, "to deliver you" (Jeremiah 1:17, 19).

Zerubbabel needed to be told that the battle is the Lord's and He will prevail. Faced with the tremendous task of rebuilding the ruined Temple, he could not succeed on his own. But he is assured of success, for divine help is available. Only by the strength of the Holy Spirit can God's temple or spiritual community be built. So God spoke to Zerubbabel in order to get him to yield, to surrender, and to *let go and let God* the Holy Spirit do the work.

Indeed, the Holy Spirit is God, not just a breath, or a wind, or an impersonal force or influence. *We do great dishonor by calling Him "it"*. He is the third Person of the Godhead: blessed, invisible, eternal, omniscient, omnipotent and omnipresent.

If we desire to build a spiritual community, a holy temple, a Christian church, a beautiful home, a sanctified life, we must remember it is not by might, nor by power, but by God's Spirit. He sanctifies, he seals for all eternity, secures salvation, and speaks the truth; He strengthens the soul, strives against sin, and searches the heart. He teaches the Word, uncovers lies, and witnesses to the saving blood of Jesus Christ. May we remember Him today as we work on the building!

For we have seen His star in the East. (Matthew 2:2)

Hear the magi (wise men) state, "We have seen His star in the east!" *His* star? There is a definite article in the original language, and it is literally, "*the* star of Him." These astronomers first sighted the star in the eastern heavens. What countries the men came from is not certain. "Eastern" is a rather broad geographical term. And so there is speculation: Arabia, Mesopotamia or Babylon (present day Iraq), Persia (present day Iran); these are the places scholars have suggested. Wherever its origin the fact is: They saw His star. It appeared, then disappeared, then reappeared and hovered over the place where the child was in Bethlehem.

Micah (5:2) had predicted 700 years earlier, "But you, Bethlehem Ephrathah, though you are little among the thousands of Judah, yet out of you shall come forth to Me the One to be Ruler in Israel, whose goings forth are from of old, from everlasting." Men have devoted their energy and time to astronomy and the natural sciences. Skilled in such observation and aware that there was widespread expectation of the birth of a great monarch, they connected this celestial phenomenon with His birth. Recall that Balaam predicted, "A Star shall come out of Jacob, a Scepter shall rise out of Israel" (Numbers 24:17).

Men have dreamed of reaching the stars; they have sung about them, written poems about their "twinkling", their mysteriousness, distance, creation, and their wandering about in space; and have peered at them through giant billion-dollar telescopes. We have named some of the stars, built designs and patterns around them, inculcated their language with such terms as "star struck," star athlete, star wars, Hollywood stars, "he saw stars," "thank my lucky stars." Thank God our Father today for His Star, and for every piece of evidence and every pronouncement of the guiding presence of Him who gave Himself for us at Calvary.

May 31

It is written. (Matthew 4:4)

In the temptation story Christ used the Word of God to parry the thrusts of Satan. "Command that these stones be made bread!" said the Devil. "It is written," said Christ, "Man shall not live by bread alone, but by every word that proceeds from the mouth of God." "Cast Yourself down!" countered Satan, this time quoting scripture himself. Christ replied, "It is written again, 'You shall not tempt the Lord your God." "Fall down and worship me," the adversary pleaded. To this the Lord Jesus said, "Away with you, Satan! For it is written, 'You shall worship the Lord your God, and Him only you shall serve.'"

When Christ chased the money changers from the Temple, He said, "It is written, 'My house shall be called a house of prayer', but you have made it a den of thieves" (Matthew 21:13). After instituting the Lord's Supper, Christ foretold Peter's denial and said, "All of you will be made to stumble because of Me this night; for it is written: 'I will strike the Shepherd, and the sheep of the flock will be scattered'" (Matthew 26:31).

Satan hates the words, "It is written," but they are sweet to all who believe in going by the Book. It is a soul stirring refrain that reminds us of Christ's victory over Satan. It is a powerful thrust that blocks every thrust of Satan. It is written and no man can erase it. No man can truthfully deny its accuracy or comprehend the depths of its wisdom; or prevent its prophecies from fulfillment.

It is written and God has preserved it; it is truth; it is a fire whose words burn into the heart; a hammer whose words smash to pieces human error; it is bread come down from heaven; food coming out of the mouth of God whereby men live. Think of the fact that one day you will gaze into the eyes of the Author, and hold the nail-pierced hand of the Writer—the One of whom it is written.

June 1

Blessed are the poor in spirit. (Matthew 5:3)

Poorness of spirit is the human spirit deeply submissive, crawling to God completely empty, bankrupt, helpless, yea, stooping in the dust of self-abasement, crying for pure grace and pure mercy. It is humble-mindedness. Poor in spirit is not necessarily connected with lack of material possessions, cultural attainment, intellectual achievement, lack of political clout or position of authority.

No, we are not dealing with social and economic conditions or environment here. Emphasis is upon a relationship with God, a relationship of the human spirit with the Holy Spirit. This blessedness is neither circumstance-oriented nor environment-conditioned. Rather, it is God-conditioned and Christ-centered.

The poor in spirit are those whose sole help is the Lord. It is a poverty that things cannot satisfy or help. Flesh is flesh and spirit it spirit. When a man's spirit is hungry, a brand new $60,000 Mercedes Benz won't satisfy him. A brand new mink coat does not satisfy a woman who is empty or proud in spirit. Poor in spirit is the crying out from the depth of distress, defeat, degradation, and the dismal doomed heart.

It is the "woe is me" of an Isaiah; the cry of David, "Lord, come down; bend the heavens, and come down! Touch the mountains that they may smoke! Flash forth lightnings! Scatter the stars! Ride the wind! Push through the clouds! Stretch forth Your hand from on high! And pluck me out of the enemy's hand" (My rendering, Psalm 144:5-7).

Poor in spirit is the cry of a king Hezekiah told to get his house in order so that he may die; who turns to the wall, pours out his heart, and pleads for extended life. Poor in spirit is the scream of Simon Peter sinking in the water who cries out, "Lord, save me!" Only the Holy Spirit produces this humility and thereby brings joy. May such joy be yours today!

June 2

Your will be done on earth as it is in heaven. (Matthew 6:10)

Corrective for the Church: We accept the fact God's will is done in heaven, God's throne. The angels there are holy, excelling in strength, doing His commandments, and hearkening to the voice of His word (Psalm 103:20). Believers there wait for the resurrection day to receive their bodies of glory (1 Corinthians 15.51-53). So there is no problem accepting the belief God's will is done in Heaven.

What about His footstool? I regret to inform you this morning that this divine imperative is not entirely obeyed on planet earth. Rest assured some day this earth shall see God's will done, for the words of our text guarantee it. It must be done! It is mandatory. The corrective brought to our attention is the fact that this Kingdom Age prayer is tied in with the Lord's return. It begins when He sets up head-quarters in Jerusalem and rules with a rod of iron.

Presently God's plan is to let the world sink inexorably deeper into immorality, headed for the leadership of the Beast, the Man of Sin. There is no indication that prior to the Millennium or Kingdom age that the will of God shall be done on this terrestrial ball as it is done in that celestial realm called Heaven.

What is called the "Lord's Prayer" (Matthew 6:9-13) is part of the Sermon on the Mount and describes principles of the kingdom Christ declared "at hand." His disciples were taught that whatever God's will is, submit to it. When the kingdom does come, God's name will be sanctified, and His will realized. However, only the King (Jesus) will bring in the kingdom! But seek no worldwide fulfillment of this text before the true Church is caught up to meet the Lord. Do seek, however, that His will be done in our lives today.

June 3

Your will be done on earth as it is in heaven. (Matthew 6:10)

Challenge to the Christian: We did not say yesterday that this verse has no meaning for the church saint. It does have relevance, significance and importance. It is a challenge to every believer because of the terrific spiritual battle going on, waged by all who are determined to have their own way. It is a challenge because it requires we make some conscious effort to know God's will and to do that which we know.

In an age when the individualistic, atomistic approach is hated and men love to turn the spotlight on whole nations and societies, and condemn collective racism, militarism, and delight in transferring guilt to some impersonal agency, seldom is much said against specific personal sins. I do not think a believer can honestly pray these days without having some desire that God's will be done in his or her own life first of all. The challenge is inescapable.

This text expresses a yielding to the sovereignty of God, a declaration of obedience, a pledge of allegiance, and a profession of submissiveness. The challenge comes because any genuine, valid relationship with God in Christ includes opposition to those who oppose God. If you join Him you oppose His enemies. They become your enemies.

Christians are challenged because there is a tendency to confuse God's permissive will with His directive will. His directive will includes such doctrines as election, pre-destination, and foreordination. Creatures are compelled to do certain things, and God is not thwarted. There is no choice about such decrees. What He directly wills is done, and that is it.

Then there is the permissive will of God, in which God is seen as allowing us to do as we please. Indeed, there are those who assert "I did it *my* way!" They believe their will *is* God's will. But the time is coming when only the will of God shall be done on earth as it is done in heaven!

June 4

Your will be done on earth as it is in heaven. (Matthew 6:10)

Characteristic of Christ: The believer who sincerely utters this text expresses a desire to be like the Lord Jesus, for one major characteristic of the Lord Jesus is doing the will of God the Father. Hear Him even before the incarnation; "A body You have prepared for Me . . . I have come to do Your will" (Hebrews 10:5-9). Hear Him say during His earthly ministry, "My food is to do the will of Him who sent Me— for I have come down from heaven, not to do My own will, but the will of Him who sent Me" (John 4:34, 5:30, 6:38).

In the Garden of Gethsemane He said, "O My Father, if it is possible, let this cup pass [**hasten**] from Me; nevertheless, not as I will, but as You will . . . Your will be done" (Matthew 26:39, 42). From this basic attitude, this essential lifestyle of habitual openness to the Father, we too realize our purpose in life, namely, to do the will of God. There is no higher goal. God's will is right, an expression of His holiness. God's will is good, acceptable, and perfect.

Doing the will of the Father led the Lord to Calvary. It led to the shedding of His blood. And He who knew no sin became sin for us, for this was the will of God. In the midst of crosses, hard times, inflation, recession, unemployment, ingratitude, trials, tribulations, family strife, accidents, broken marriages, cancer, and the deaths of loved ones, do I still say, "Your will be done"?

O grant it, Lord, for "You are worthy, O Lord, to receive glory and honor and power; for You created all things, and by Your will they exist and were created" (Revelation 4:11).

Have Thine own way, Lord! Have Thine own way!
Thou art the Potter, I am the clay.
Mould me and make me After Thy will,
While I am waiting, Yielded and still.
(Adelaide A. Pollard)

156

And behold, a leper came and worshiped Him, saying "Lord, if You are willing, You can make me clean." (Matthew 8:2)

This leper had no doubt whatever concerning the fact that God is able; he had no question about the Lord's ability. His words show a humble submission to the Lord Jesus, a complete giving over into His hands, a faith of the highest type. He indicated also his willingness to remain in his living physical death of leprosy if Jesus Christ so willed it.

Our sovereign Lord does as He pleases, as He chooses. Although we speak of God's directive will and His permissive will, we recognize that one way or the other, His will falls into actuality—His will is done. Thus for the believer, all that counts in life is God's will, the standard by which all is measured. The highest good or end in life is found only in conformity with the mind and will of Christ.

Nothing else is more important. Therefore we thank God for the Bible, and for prayer, two channels whereby we may know His will. We thank Him for the circumstances He makes work together for our good.

But now, what happens when you ask and God says no? When you pray for health and take sick; or pray for economic aid and the bills pile higher; or pray for peace in the church and the Devil breaks loose—what then?

You pray for genuine friends and enemies multiply. You pray for more love in *your* heart and *their* hatred increases. You seek joy and sorrows overflow. You pray for patience and irritating experiences test you. You ask for humility and the proud step on you!

What then? Are you still willing—am I willing—to say to Him who bought us, "Lord, do with me whatever You please"?

June 6

And I will give you rest. (Matthew 11:28)

This is an invitation of *condescension*, God speaking to man. It is an invitation of *compassion*, God showing His concern. It is an invitation of *communion,* God requesting fellowship—come unto Me! How thrilling to know that an Almighty God makes such a gracious request to the children of men. Who is able to provide rest for the weary, medicine for the sin-sick, a haven for the afflicted, comfort for the bereaved, relief for the distressed, and a solution for every problem? It is none other than the Lord Jesus who said, "I will give you rest."

His language is emphatic: I, I myself will give you the rest you desire. This is strong language; they are words no mere mortal man could speak. Anyone else who claims to give such rest is a phony, a charlatan, a thief and a robber. This is Christ who said in Isaiah 45:22, "Look to Me, and be saved, all you ends of the earth! For I am God, and there is no other."

What men offer makes matters worse. And the grief is compounded. But when Jesus Christ calls, and the heart recognizes its need for newness, the proper response is made. As David said, so we recognize: "Nor [is there] any health (rest) in my bones because of my sin. For my iniquities have gone over my head; like a heavy burden they are too heavy for me" (Psa 38:3f). When Christ calls do not turn Him away, for He has what you need. He has relief, recovery, recreation, resurrection, righteousness and rest.

When I can read my title clear To mansions in the skies,
I'll bid farewell to every fear, And wipe my weeping eyes.
There shall I bathe my weary soul In seas of heav'nly rest,
And not a wave of trouble roll Across my peaceful breast.
(Isaac Watts)

June 7

A bruised reed He will not break, and smoking flax He will not quench, till He sends forth justice to victory. (Matthew 12:20; Isaiah 42:3)

The Charge of Christ: Christ the Lord of the Sabbath healed a man with a paralyzed hand on the Sabbath. This act outraged the Pharisees, moving them to plan to destroy the Lord. Christ discovered their plot and withdrew Himself. However, great crowds followed Him. Moved by compassion He healed them all; and then sharply charged them not to broadcast Him. He had no desire that His miracles be used to stir up more opposition. He knew that hatred moved people to misuse even the good He did. Instead of rejoicing that folks got healed, His enemies became more furious.

Meekness was His way, not rebellion, wrangling, striving, shouting or agitating. Such acts were not needed in order to save perishing souls. Our nature is just the opposite in this respect. We break off bruised reeds and we snuff out smoldering wicks. We discourage new converts; despise new church members; crush the fallen, chastise the contrite, trample the bruised conscience, browbeat the back-slider, refuse the repentant, chide and ridicule the misfortunate righteous, and step on others to build up ourselves.

Callous men will step on a wounded conscience, play on feelings of guilt, and never let you forget the time you slipped up and sinned. They "I-knew-you-when" to death, to keep you subject to them, a sort of spiritual blackmail. Satan wants you to keep on singing the blues rather than exercise the joy of your salvation. Some folks find out something bad on you and squeeze every juicy morsel out of it they can. But this was not the nature of our Lord. He avoided all such for He knew that in the Father's own good time, through the forgiveness of sin, justice would be sent forth unto victory.

A bruised reed He will not break, and smoking flax He will not quench, till He sends forth justice to victory. (Matthew 12:20; Isaiah 42:3)

The Character of Christ: The reed is a stalk or cane, of various specific tropical Asiatic palms. It may stand straight, looking strong, however looks are deceiving. Some people give the appearance or impression of being unflappable, self-sufficient, independent, collected, cool, and calm. Beneath appearances they are like the reed: easily bruised, bent and battered. Like the stalk that is trod upon by human feet or animal paws, or bent by the blast of a strong wind, or by a storm passing through, our lives sometimes are in bad shape that not much is needed to snap or to break us.

Literally, to "bruise" means to rub together, grind, smash, break, destroy, twist or crush. Figuratively, the bruised reed is the person who is at the end of his rope, weak, feeble, in despair, but by the grace of God aware of his sad plight, cries out, "Lord, help me!" Christ compassionately looks at the bruised reed and does not snap him in two or break him off, but heals, helps, and makes him whole.

The word for flax is rendered "linen" in Revelation 15:6; the wick (flax) was made of linen. Unless it was well cut and trimmed constantly, the light would not be bright and sometimes would cause smoke and die out. Picture a lamp with the oil about to run out. It does not take much to snuff out the light at that point (Isaiah 43:17). So the smoking wick indicates that the fire is almost gone, smoldering, glimmering and flickering. Christ will not extinguish, quench or put out even the smoking wick. What a beautiful picture of the graciousness of His ministry. For here the smoking flax represents the smallest hope. With all of our faltering and stumbling, our fears and doubts, mistakes, and backslidings, the Lord does not come along and snuff out the flickering flames.

June 9

A bruised reed He will not break, and smoking flax He will not quench, till He sends forth justice to victory. (Matthew 12:20; Isaiah 42:3)

The Compassion of Christ: We learn that Jesus Christ is compassionate. When we Christians truly confess our sin, repentant and contrite of heart, He does not crush us. When we cry out to Him from the very depth of our soul, He hears. He is gentle to the weak and kind to helpless.

There must be within us, however, that genuine spark of repentance. This is more than feeling sorry we got caught. This is a crying as did David, "Against You, You only, have I sinned" (Psalm 51:4). He knows our frail, feeble frames, that we are but dust, bruised reeds, smoldering wicks, earthen vessels and tents of flesh. He knows that in times of testing, we often are deceived and discouraged. Yet He forgives, encourages and restores. Why? It is because He bought us out of the slave market of sin; He owns us; we are His. Having done this great thing for us when we were dead, what is there He won't do for us now that we are alive?

We can depend upon Him. His zeal will not be extinguished nor His strength broken until He accomplishes His purpose. He came to build, not destroy. Not to crush life but to give life eternal and abundant. Not to despise the weak, but to empower them. He is our ever persevering Savior who never flags and never fails. What mercy! What love! What compassion! He who was wounded for our transgressions does not snuff out the flickering flame of the wounded soul; He who was bruised for our iniquities does not break off the bruised reed. He cares for us!

O yes, He cares; I know He cares,
His heart is touched with my grief;
When the days are weary, the long nights dreary,
I know my Savior cares. (Frank E. Graeff)

June 10

He who is not with Me is against Me; and he who does not gather with Me scatters abroad. (Matthew 12:30)

Whereas the common people proclaimed Him Son of David, the Pharisees considered Him a son of the Devil: "This ---- does not cast out demons, but by Beelzebub, the prince of demons." Note the contempt in not calling Him by name! This was not the first time they had made such an accusation; and of course, the Lord knew their thoughts (Matthew 9:34; 12:25). You cannot hide anything from Him.

Men scheme and hold their secret meetings and private conversations, all the while ignorant of the fact that the Lord Jesus knows every thought before it is spoken. And so it is as if He said, "You all don't make sense! If I'm casting out demons with the help of the Head Demon, then the Devil is dumb; if Satan expels Satan he is schizophrenic.

"Because a divided kingdom cannot stand; a divided house will fall. On the other hand, if what I've done is by the power of God, it means the kingdom is in your midst. You don't go into a man's house while he is there to rob him without first tying him up. My point is: If you're not with Me, you're against Me; and if you're not gathering with Me, then you're scattering. It's got to be one way or the other."

Whose side are *you* on? There is no middle or neutral ground. Indeed, there are no inactive Christians; all are busy, either for or against. I spoke in Willingboro, N. J. and the minister told the audience how he was working for one of the members of my church and asked her, "How's your new pastor, Reverend Banks, doing?" "Oh, he's all right, I guess. But he's always preaching from the Bible," was her response. This was the opportunity, said the preacher, for him to witness to this good member.

June 11

He who is not with Me is against Me; and he who gather with Me scatters abroad. (Matthew 12:30)

Scatterers fight for money; gatherers fish for men. Scatterers are interested in programs; and gatherers are interested in people. Scatterers love a big splash, a big show; gatherers love the Scriptures. Scatterers are more interested in beauty-fying the church building; gatherers, in building up believers. Scatterers smite the shepherd; gatherers pray for the pastor.

Scatterers desire to be heard by the crowd; gatherers want to hear Christ. Scatterers spread gossip; gatherers spread the Gospel. Scatterers like mindless robots agree on a common course of evil; gatherers are led by the Spirit of God to think on that which is good. Scatterers are drunk with human power; gatherers are sober with godly peace. And scatterers are disintegrated by Satan; and gatherers are integrated by the Savior.

I prefer to be a gatherer, for then I am among those who will come together at the sound of His voice, at the blast of the trumpet of God to be with Him who said, "Gather My saints together to Me" (Psalm 50:5), to be with Him who shall feed His flock like a shepherd, gather the lambs with His arm, and carry them in His bosom (Isaiah 40:11).

If you are a gatherer rejoice with Him who said, "Come unto Me." Let that truth crowd out the adversities of life. When the blues would prevail, when I would feel down in the dumps, the thought comes, "Hey! I'm on the Lord's side and He's on the inside!" Joy of my salvation, return my joy. Prince of Peace, give me Your peace that passes all under-standing. Lover of my soul, help me to love. Almighty Savior, give me power. Precious Lord, take my hand. Heavenly Light, lead me on. Elevator of the fallen lift me up! Let all who gather with the Gatherer, rejoice. For to be with the Lord who cleansed us with His own blood is life eternal and life abundant.

June 12

Then some of the scribes and Pharisees answered, saying, "Teacher, we want to see a sign from You." (Matthew 12:38)

It appears more and more that folks professing Christ are becoming Sign-Seekers! Why is this? Why is it becoming increasingly difficult for church members to remain steady, steadfast with fixed hearts and made-up minds? I think in part the answer is that the world is going crazy. Taxes are going up; more people commit suicide; crime increases; noise is noisier; music is jumpier; and tempers are shorter. The sun is hotter, winters are colder, racism is rougher, unemployment nags and strikes threaten.

We are influenced by it all. In such distressful times of change, complexity and restlessness, professed Christians become dissatisfied with the tried and the true. Their minds wander off into the spectacular, the sensational type of showy religion that stirs up the emotions. What is worse, they think this is spirituality! I have noticed their lack of consistency, dependability and perseverance, deficiencies that demonstrate not spirituality but carnality.

Like the Athenians of old they are ever anxious to hear something new (Acts 17:21). Their attitude signifies they are not satisfied with what God has done already or is still doing. For them the old way is too humdrum, unspectacular, non-sensational, too slow, too small, and too quiet or cold. And so they seek signs. They scream, "Master, do something new! Show us a sign!" They think that a passive approach does not take advantage of what God has to offer, and causes them to live beneath their privilege as children of God. Their request for signs is a lack of faith, unspiritual, an attempt to bargain with God, and possibly smacks of ingratitude. If God chooses to give me signs along the way, that's His business. In the meantime, I thank Him for what I do see, for what He has given. I am satisfied with the Lord Jesus. Are you?

June 13

Now He did not do many mighty works there because of their unbelief. (Matthew 13:58)

The statement is blunt: He did not do many mighty works there. Note the text does not say He *could* not or that He was incapable of doing many miracles, but that He *did* not perform many works of power there. It does not say He did not do *any*. There is a difference between many and any. Mark 6:5 helps here: "Now He could do no mighty work there, except that He laid His hands on a few sick people and healed them." So you see *something* was done.

We do not suggest that the Lord's power depended on man's faith alone. No. After all, the man born blind in John 9 had his eyes opened first and later wanted to know "Who is the Son of God?" that he might believe on Him. The son of the widow at Nain was raised from the dead by the Lord and delivered to his mother. No faith whatever was required. The same is true of the raising of Lazarus (John 11).

We learn that because of their unbelief very few people at Nazareth even bothered to come to the Lord. It is not that He was powerless but that they were faithless. He who commanded winds to cease their howling and boisterous waves to stop their frenetic frothy dance had only to speak to demons and demand they leave their tortured victims.

No disease could withstand the touch of His healing hand. No, His ability is not in question. In most cases of human infirmity the distressed came to Him; and in their very coming demonstrated faith. But the folks at Nazareth would not let God help them.

Let us boldly declare that Jesus Christ is all right! May our hearts respond, "Come, Lord, do as you desire. Here's my hand, my head, and my heart. I'm yours!" And let not unbelief in any form hinder us from receiving all that the Lord wants to give us here on earth right now! Even this day!

June 14

Then Jesus said to His disciples, "If anyone desires to come after Me, let him deny himself, and take up his cross, and follow Me. (Matthew 16:24)

<u>*Deny Yourself*</u> (Mark 8:34): Our Lord commands that we say no to ourselves, make a disavowal of our previous relationships of obedience and loyalty to self, sin and Satan. This is a renunciation of self, turning self off, refusing self. If we desire to follow Christ, there must come first our acknowledgment that self is a sinner on its way to Hell. Turn from it in utter dismay, cast out self, and accept Jesus Christ in a new relationship with Him. How? Through faith in the blood shed at Calvary that washes and cleanses from all sin.

    <u>Judge Yourself</u> (1 Corinthians 11:31): Christians must also closely, carefully, search or examine their own lives. Because of bad attitudes, a lack of solemnity, irreverence at the Lord's Supper, some saints at Corinth were sick and some died. Such need not befall us, said Paul, if we would judge ourselves and confess; and acknowledge what we find. This self-judgment helps us to avoid God's disciplining. But failure to discipline ourselves may result in chastisement (but not condemnation).

    <u>Show Yourself</u> (2 Timothy 2:15)—approved by God. A little boy feeling rather rambunctious just did all kinds of things. He outdid himself with a somersault, rolled on the floor, made faces, stood on his hands, then stood on his head, did a cartwheel—and finally, his mother grabbed him and said, "You don't know what to do with yourself, do you!"

    To be tested and approved, recognized as genuine after examination, yea, to hear the Lord say, "Well done!" is a goal towards which we should strive or be diligent. If any man desires to come after me, let him deny himself, judge himself, and show himself approved. Let this be our desire today.

June 15

Therefore you also be ready, for the Son of Man is coming at an hour you do not expect. (Matthew 24:44)

What makes people members of the Think-Not Club? Why would men think not? The word rendered "think" or "expect" expresses the subjective mental estimate or opinion; it may be right but also may be wrong. Take, for example, Galatians 6.3: "For if anyone *thinks* himself to be something, when he is nothing, he deceives himself." His own mental estimate of his spiritual condition is altogether erroneous. Thus "think" is a subjective judgment which may or may not conform to objective fact.

When the Lord Jesus came walking on the water the disciples *supposed* they had seen a spirit and screamed out in terror (Mark 6:49). In James 1:26, we read: "If anyone among you thinks he is religious, and does not bridle his tongue but deceives his own heart, this one's religion is useless." You see then that we are talking about members of the Expect-Not-Think-Not-Suppose-Not-Seem-Not Club.

There are those who think not because they prefer to think not. If men don't want the Lord Jesus to come, then it is easy for them to think He won't come. And they don't want Him to come if He is going to crack down on looseness, limit their license, deprive them of their liquor, stop their larceny, uncover their lies, return their ill-gotten loot, alter their lifestyles, and bring to naught their labors.

May our prayer be that of David, "Cleanse me from secret faults. Keep back Your servant also from presumptuous sins; let them not have dominion over me. Then I shall be blameless, and I shall be innocent of great transgression" (Psalm 19:12-13). May it be that the uncertainties of life keep us on our toes, yet with bended knees, remain watchful and prayerful. And realize that in not knowing what a day may bring forth, there is indeed the Lord's opportunity to display His grace.

June 16

For you have the poor with you always. (Matthew 26:11)

There are many causes of poverty. Proverbs 21:17 says that he that loves pleasure shall be a poor man; he that loves wine and oil shall not be rich. Thus frivolity and shackling habits of drink, nicotine, gambling and dope addiction help keep some men poor. "For the drunkard and the glutton will come to poverty, and drowsiness will clothe a man with rags" (Proverbs 23:21).

Then too some folks are poor because they are lazy. To the sluggard come the words, "So shall your poverty come on you like a robber (prowler) and your need like an armed man" (Proverbs 6:9-11). Bad company also tends to poverty: "He who follows frivolity will have poverty enough!" (Proverbs 28:19). Some people are poor, or kept poor, or plunged into poverty through the effort of others.

Widows' houses are devoured. Greedy men, envious and covetous, do not hesitate to defraud, deceive, steal, rob, flimflam, embezzle, swindle or through acts motivated by racial prejudice keep people beneath them. Then too, lack of education, recession, sickness, accidents, natural calamity and war—all these things combine to echo the truth, "Ye have the poor always with you." What an incentive to benevolence this is for us today. Christ gave, so ought we to give. He helped us, so we ought to help others.

Throughout the Scriptures believers are commanded to consider the poor (Psalm 41:1), to deal justly with them (Exodus 23:6) and not oppress them (Proverbs 14:31). We are told do not mock them (Proverbs 17:5) or stop up our ears at their cry (Proverbs 21:13). We are to have pity and mercy upon them (Proverbs 19:17; 14:21); to defend and deliver them (Psalm 82:3, 4). In short, "remember the poor" (Galatians 2:10), for the God we serve not only gives us enough for ourselves, but enough to help others—for we are rich in Jesus Christ!

June 17

Then Jesus came with them to a place called Gethsemane, and said to the disciples, "Sit here while I go and pray over there." Matthew 26:36)

Gethsemane (oil press) was an olive orchard, on private property, on the western slope of the Mount of Olives. Evidently the Lord often stopped there, but this time would be His last. Having asked eight of the disciples to remain at a certain place there in the garden, He took Peter, James and John (sons of Zebedee) with Him a little farther. Beginning to feel oppressed, He then told the three men to wait, to watch, and to be alert. Then He withdrew from them in order to pray by Himself.

Note that this prayer in the garden was *secret*. This was not the first time that He had prayed in secret. Soon after healing Simon Peter's mother-in-law the Lord rising up very early the next day, went out and departed into a solitary place and there prayed (Mark 1:35). After feeding the 5,000 men He departed into a mountain to pray (Mark 6:47) and was alone on the land while the disciples were at sea.

After the cleansing of the leper (Luke 5:16) He withdrew into the wilderness and prayed. Following the healing of the man whose right hand was paralyzed, He went out into a mountain to pray, and continued all night in prayer to God the Father (Luke 6:12). It is interesting to note how these four miracles were followed by secret prayer.

At times after God has wrought miracles in our lives, has granted deliverance, given victory, turned us away from a trap, recovered us from a pit, opened doors, healed bodies or defeated Satan—that instead of throwing a party and celebrating with the saints, we should go off to our secret room and spend much time with the Lord in prayer. "Go into your room, and when you have shut your door, pray to your Father who is in the secret place; and your Father who sees in secret will reward you openly" (Matthew 6:6).

June 18

Then Jesus came with them to a place called Gethsemane, and said to the disciples, "Sit here while I go and pray over there." (Matthew 26:36)

In talking to you yesterday about prayer in secret, I did not mean to disparage or discourage praying in public. The corporate witness has many advantages. We are able to pool our money, give to missions, help in emergencies; there are opportunities to exercise gifts, combine talents; there is mutual encouragement, celebration of the Lord's Supper, the public witness of water baptism; and the preaching and teaching of the Word. There is always something extra to be gained when we unite in prayer.

But some strange things go on in prayer meetings. Sometimes we hear announcement prayers, like the one a preacher gave: "O Lord, we trust that we will have a goodly attendance at our church supper on Wednesday night at 6:30 p.m., the price of which is $5.00!" In one church there was a member who constantly pleaded every Wednesday evening in prayer meeting for the Lord to clean out the cobwebs. One member, upon hearing, "Lord, clean out the cobwebs in this church!" responded, "Lord, kill that spider!"

Public prayers sometimes contain choice bits of gossip; or they are used to tell someone off, to cast aspersions, insinuate, even to shock. Nonetheless, there is great value in praying publicly. However, even public prayers mean little if there is no private practice. It does not make sense to pray in God's house if we never spend time in prayer in our own homes. Praying in private is a splendid training ground for praying in public.

We live in times when it pays to get away from the hustle-bustle, the much-ado-about nothing, the hurry-scurry, the make haste to waste, and the run and wait syndrome. There are those sacred times when the heart yearns to be all alone with the Lord.

June 19

Then He said to them, "My soul is exceedingly sorrowful, even to death. Stay here and watch with Me." (Matthew 26:38)

Our Lord's prayer-life was deeply sincere and serious: "And being in agony, He prayed more earnestly" (Luke 22:44)-- fervently, stretched-out, assiduously, zealously, intently, with earnestness of mind. I am reminded of Preacher Brown of Baltimore who gave the invitation to sinners to accept Christ, and unchurched Christians to join the local assembly, repeatedly urging, "Pray hard, saints! Pray hard!"

Our prayers are not to be doubting, wishy-washy or half-hearted, but sincere and zealous. We marvel when we think of the circumstances under which Christ labored in prayer. In Matthew 26:38 we read His soul was exceedingly sorrowful, even unto death. In Mark 14:33f we are told that He began to be greatly amazed and very depressed with an exceedingly sorrowful soul.

His sweat was red in color like blood, as if His sorrow were crushing the life out of Him. Surely, He is despised and rejected of men, a man of sorrows, and acquainted with grief, despised and held in no esteem at all. He came unto His own and they received Him not. He was hated by the world. He offered up "prayers and supplications with vehement cries and tears" (Hebrews 5:7).

I do not suggest that every prayer all the time be emotionally draining, but surely there are times when we must cry out from the depths of our souls. Our Lord's prayer there in the Garden of Gethsemane was answered. Strengthened by an angel, He went forth boldly to meet Judas and the gang that came to arrest Him. He drank of that cup willingly, wholeheartedly and freely. Proof that God the Father heard that secret, submissive, sincere prayer lies in the fact that on the third day the Father raised His Son from the grave, and we serve a living Savior!

June 20

O My Father, if it is possible, let this cup pass from Me; nevertheless, not as I will, but as You will. (Matthew 26:39)

Physical suffering was not the primary ingredient in this cup, for it also contained rejection, hatred, the ridicule of religionists, and betrayal. Even at that very moment, Judas was on his way, bringing with him a great multitude with swords, clubs and torches. For many ancient peoples the word cup was a figure of speech meaning experience, lot, fate, fortune, whether good or bad, joyous or adverse, favorable or not.

God is pictured as giving a man a cup to drink, and in that cup are the circumstances of life. What then was in the cup given to our Lord? Was it the confrontation of a cruel fate at the hands of men? No. Rather, the judgment of God upon sin. Hell was in the cup. Separation from God was in the cup. The horror of being forsaken was inevitable for God's Son who would experience the terrible dread of having our sins placed upon Him.

He who utterly abhorred sin was soon to be made sin for us. He could see in the cup at Gethsemane what would be poured out at Golgotha. There was never any doubt about doing the Father's will. It is difficult for us to fathom the Lord's soul naturally shrinking from what was in the cup. As Isaiah predicted, His soul would be made an offering for sin.

Christ saw bruising in the cup; the hiding of the Father's face was in the cup. We can describe some facts, but such articulation by no means indicates we understand what it is for Life to die, for the Sun to be eclipsed, the Rose of Sharon to be plucked, the Light of the world extinguished, or war declared upon the Prince of Peace! Only within the framework of always doing the Father's will comes the request that, if possible, within the carrying out of that will, the contents of this cup be drunk **hastily**. What a way of life for us to follow—not our will, Lord, but Yours.

June 21

Not as I will, but as You will . . . Your will be done.
(Matthew 26:39, 42)

Now the act of surrendering is not mindless robotry. The request for the cup—and all the horror in that cup—**to pass rapidly** from Him must not be seen as a bit of cowardice or cold feet. By no means is the plea rebellion. In fact, Christ realistically assumes the possibility of the rapid fulfillment of Calvary if it so pleased the Father. But whatever is done, the will of God the Father is to be carried out. Thus from beginning to end, Christ's prayer was submissive to the Father's will. Christ *came* to do the will of the Father; this prayer is but another expression of that determination. This was no grudging concession; no resignation to fate, no philosophy of "that's the way the ball bounces," or "the way the cookie crumbles."

No. There was no attempt to avoid death! His heart demonstrates the ready acceptance of the Father's will. Christ knew fully well what was in the cup, and the Father strengthened Him. Our Lord drank that cup, wholly submissive to the Father in His prayer, "Not as I will, but as You will, Your will be done." Here is the soul of perfection shrinking from a cup containing the imperfection of humanity. Here is the Righteous One soon to taste what it is like to be made unrighteousness. Lostness (perdition) is about to be put upon the Savior of mankind; His holy nature shrank from evil in that cup. He who was a blessing to all men saw a curse for the world's sin in that cup.

Sometimes I hear people *demanding* something of God, and they tack on the words, "In the name of Jesus" as if that will *make* God give them what they demand. The repetition of their desire often sounds pagan or that God is either deaf or dumb or both. Oh, that the motto for our prayer life would be: Not my will, Lord, but Your will be done!

June 22

And Jesus came and spoke to them, saying, "All authority has been given to Me in heaven and on earth." (Matthew 28:18)

Some fellow-seminarians called me a bibliolater—one who idolizes the Bible, thus accusing me of bibliolatry—that exceeding adherence to a literal interpretation of the Bible, thus leaning upon a paper crutch, relying on a paper pope. I stated I needed an authority; they said this was a sign of weakness. I asked them their authority for saying that. They replied, "We don't need any."

I answered, "Well, why should I listen to you?" I was then accused of "always absolutizing things!" I said, "Are you sure about that?" They answered yes. I then asked, "Are you absolutely sure about that?" While authoritatively renouncing authoritarianism and dogmatically rejecting all dogmatism, some men consider their rebellion and rejection of authority signs of strength.

In essence they make themselves their authority. Having enthroned self, their egos rule like tyrants. However, being born in need of an absolute standard is not a sign of weakness. Sin deceives us and the unreal, relative, valueless, temporal, immoral and wicked are made authoritative. We come into this world full of uncertainties; failing to submit to Christ, our dissatisfaction increases, our uncertainties multiply. No hand-me-down, rummage sale, patched-up religion can do our souls any good. He who wants the best from us gave His best to us and for us—His Son. In the midst of restlessness, He sent the Comforter. Where there was darkness, the Light of the World penetrated. In the midst of sadness came the Joy of Salvation. To the weak and anemic came the Almighty; those befouled with sin were washed clean in the blood of the Lamb of God. Thus He who authoritatively announced He had all authority in His hands is our Lord and Savior this day!

Yes, a sword will pierce through your own soul also. (Luke 2:35)

Simeon predicted Mary would suffer deep sorrow because of her Son. Imagine telling a mother that her heart will break with grief like the thrust of a sharp sword. Amazed at first by what Simeon said, Mary kept the words in her mind. But in those early days there was nothing to indicate a great sword was coming, for her Boy grew, and became strong in spirit, filled with wisdom, and the grace of God was upon Him.

Mary heard reports of His increasing controversy with the religious leaders. Every encounter He had with them led to their defeat and humiliation. Hatred smoldered, envy festered, plots were hatched, murder was conceived, demons were hyperactive, and the Devil instigated as never before. Soon betrayed, Christ was taken by cruel hands, tried, beaten, mocked, cursed, spat upon and crucified.

Men try to blunt or mask the attack by taking it out on the preacher; maddened by the message they mess up the messenger. It is easy to see through attempts to camouflage our souls' desires. Mary herself was not exempt from spiritual heart trouble. As a sinner she said, "My soul magnifies the Lord, and my spirit has rejoiced in God my Savior" (Luke 1:46-47). She needed a Savior.

In the Bible Mary is never worshiped. Honored among women, still she suffered because of sin. See clearly the error of calling her the mother of God. Yes, Jesus Christ is God, but He always has been God. As a Man He had no father; as God He had no mother. Only as a Man has He a mother; as God the Son, He has a Father. It was of the physical part that Mary became mother. Since no blood of the mother is passed on to the child, Jesus Christ inherited no sin nature from Mary who was indeed a sinner. Today Mary rejoices in Heaven. And we are reminded that though the heart is broken down here, there are no broken hearts in Heaven!

And they were all amazed at the majesty of God . . . while everyone marveled at all the things which Jesus did. (Luke 9:43)

We traced the use of the words "amazed, astonished, wondered, marveled," as they are used in the KJV with respect to Christ and His deeds. For example, when Simon Peter was commanded, "Launch out into the deep, and let down your nets," the catch was so great that the net broke. When Simon Peter saw what happened, he fell down at the knees of the Lord, saying, "Depart from me; for I am a sinful man, O Lord," for he and all who were with him were *astonished* (Luke 5:9).

Soon after this incident, a man sick of the palsy, lying on a bed was brought to the Lord. Christ said, "Arise, take up your bed, and go to your house" (Matthew 9:6). And he arose, and departed to his house. But when the multitudes saw it they *marveled.* When a man possessed with a demon, blind and dumb, was brought to the Lord, He healed him, and all the people were *amazed* (Matthew 12:23). Luke (11:14) simply states, "And the multitudes *marveled.*"

On still another occasion, the Lord entered into a boat with His disciples, and being exhausted, He fell asleep. But then a storm suddenly broke loose, and the terrified disciples awoke Christ, saying, "Lord, save us! We are perishing!" The Lord muzzled the wind with the words, "Peace, be still!" and the howling ceased; He tied the hands of the angry waves and forbade them to clap any more in frothy, rhythmic frenzied beat. Is it any wonder that the men marveled? (Matthew 8:27).

I was lost in sin, but Jesus rescued me, He's a wonderful Savior to me; I was bound by fear, but Jesus set me free, He's a wonderful Savior to me.
(Virgil P. Brock)

June 25

Mary has chosen that good part, which will not be taken away from her. (Luke 10:42)

Perhaps in the market place in the village of Bethany, the Lord met Martha, and she immediately invited Him to her home, where she and her sister Mary lived. No mention is made of their brother, Lazarus. It is almost as if the visit was to strengthen them for the death of their brother which would occur within the coming weeks.

Mary too was delighted to see the Lord, and welcomed Him; after being seated at the feet of the Lord, Mary began to listen to His word. While Martha was busy preparing that food deemed so necessary to sustain the body, Mary was interested in that necessary food by which man shall live, the Word of God.

We should not be too harsh with Martha, and realize that she was sincere in what she was doing; she did it in love. Becoming distracted, worried about much serving, for she was putting on a big spread for the Lord, she just had to say something about Mary. Perhaps Martha also desired to be a pupil of the Lord, and sit at His feet, and take in His teachings. But the issue here is priority.

"Lord, do You not care that my sister has left me to serve alone? Therefore tell her to help me." He replied, "Martha, Martha, you're hustling-bustling about, worried and bothered and distracted about many things. There is need of but one thing." Mary chose the Word. That's the one needful thing. The Word enables us to establish God-pleasing priorities; the Word gives us discernment to make the correct choices; it calms the troubled breast.

When you choose the Word and believe it, all else falls in place, values are straightened, priorities and goals are set, life becomes worth living, and joy-bells ring in the heart. And the soul shouts Hallelujah to God who reigns throughout all eternity!

June 26

Then He spoke a parable to them, saying, "The ground of a certain rich man yielded plentifully. (Luke 12:16)

There are at least four outstanding characteristics of this rich man. First of all, he was a good **Farmer;** he was successful. We are not told how many acres of farmland he owned, or whether he purchased the ground or inherited it. Furthermore, there is no indication he was oppressive or illegally employed migrant workers or used and abused sharecroppers.

We read that the cultivated ground was fertile and brought forth plentifully. This, of course, was God's doings. Perhaps this man used good farming methods; he knew about rotating crops, the proper use of fertilizers, control of insects, good equipment, etc. It is obvious also that he was not lazy, but had initiative and progressive ideas. Give him credit for being a successful farmer, blessed by God with productive soil; with know-how, abundant sunshine and rain, and energy to work hard.

The fact then that he was rich is not held against him. It is no crime, no sin to be rich. Money talks. Folks make a big fuss over rich men today. Indeed, it seems only the rich can afford to run for or hold certain political offices nowadays. I think this is bad, but it does not mean necessarily that being wealthy is wrong.

Abraham was rich; so was Job. It was however *God's* blessings upon this farmer and his land. His mistake was to forget God and concentrate on his goods. Though a good farmer, he failed to thank God for the abundance of his crops and for all his wealth.

From the very beginning of this parable we learn that it is God's hand that blessed the work of this farmer; it was the Lord who caused the ground to yield abundantly.

June 27

Then He spoke a parable to them, saying, "The ground of a certain rich man yielded plentifully. (Luke 12:16)

Note secondly that this rich farmer's assumptions were **False**. Many things can happen in our lives which affect our values, the weights we attach to material goods, and the interpretations we give to events. This is true regardless of the cause of poverty or the manner in which we obtain our wealth. Sometimes hook and crook dealings have a way of twisting up our minds. Here we have a man honestly come by his riches, yet fallen into the trap of false assumptions. Obviously he assumed what counted most in life is what you *have,* not what you *are.*

Even if this assumption were true, there is still the fact that life's values depend upon what we *do* with what we have. He not only wrongly assumed that *things* can satisfy the human soul, but presumed that *he* was the very center of life; he was like the rooster who thought the sun rose every morning just to hear him crow!

Note his selfishness. Twelve times he used the personal pronouns 'I' and 'my'. "What shall **I** do – **I** have no room to store **my** crops – **I** will do this -- **I** will pull down **my** barns – **I** will store all **my** crops and **my** goods – **I** will say to **my** soul – take **your** ease!" (Luke 12.17-19). What self-centeredness! What egocentricity! His selfishness blinded and deceived him, and caused him to think more highly of himself than he ought to have thought. He assumed that the abundance was calculated to be used for him alone.

Second, his selfishness moved him to imagine there was no one else in the world that mattered. Surely there were empty barns of farmers less fortunate than he; empty cupboards of widows and orphans; empty plates of the poor and the beggars; and mouths of hungry babies. But he saw only himself, and sad to say, this man's ancestors still live.

June 28

Then He spoke a parable to them, saying, "The ground of a certain rich man yielded plentifully. (Luke 12:16)

A third characteristic of this rich man is he neglected the **Future.** Now all of this begins to dovetail. Possibly his success went to his head, for he was a good farmer. And then too his false assumptions moved him to neglect the future. Let me put it this way: He made plans but they were short-ranged. He was reasoning (dialoguing) with himself but could see no further than self. His "I wills" were more immediate than eternal. And this is always a bad mistake for any man to make. It never entered his mind that the abundance of crops might not last. He never thought that he himself might die and not live.

One of the things about being a Christian is the emphasis upon the future. When you believe in the shed blood of Jesus Christ your future is guaranteed. We are so made that only when the hereafter is accented, can the here-and-now truly be enjoyed. The Christ we serve blesses right now, even in the midst of a sin-sick society headed by Satan, where death daily visits our homes and families, our circles of friends, and our churches.

The story is told that the late Bishop Edwin Hughes once delivered a stirring, rousing sermon on "God's Owner-ship". The sermon wrung the nose out of joint of one of the members of the church who happened to be quite wealthy. Later the rich man took Bishop Hughes out for lunch, and then walked him through his elaborate gardens, woodlands, and farm.

"Now are you going to tell me," he demanded when the tour was completed, "that all this land does not belong to me?" Bishop Hughes smiled and suggested, "Ask me that same question a hundred years from now."

June 29

Then He spoke a parable to them, saying, "The ground of a certain rich man yielded plentifully. (Luke 12:16)

The fourth characteristic of this man is given by God: He is called a **Fool.** Abruptly, suddenly challenged to give an account of his life, he was found sadly wanting. For him what you have was more important than what you are. This was foolish. From him came no thanks to God for material blessings. This was foolish.

He thought only of himself, "me, myself, and I," and not of others. This was foolish. He assumed that material things could perfectly satisfy an immaterial soul. This also was foolish. As Vance Havner says, "God does not give the soul a vacation; He gives it a vocation."

This man thought he would or could maintain his wealth, come what may. This was foolish. It never dawned upon him that he might take sick or even die. What a mistake! His chariot bumper sticker philosophy was, "Eat, Drink and Be Merry! Take It Easy!" This too was foolish.

And so that very night was a time of judgment! Sometimes the Lord *suddenly* reproves. He never wastes time, but here soon after the man had comforted himself with his own plans, God discomfited him with the divine plan. "You fool!"—you who are devoid of sense, and without mind or reason; you are stupid, without reflection or intelligence— this is very strong language.

We learn much from this story. To be called a fool may or may not mean anything. It depends upon *who* calls you a fool. If another fool calls you a fool, you may not pay him any attention. But if God calls you a fool you had better pay attention. Unless, of course, you are a fool for Christ (1 Corinthians 4:10); for then you would be a good farmer, bringing forth good fruit, with true assumptions, and facing a glorious future.

June 30

The one which is lost . . . which was lost . . . which I lost . . . he was lost . . . and was lost. (Luke 15:4, 6, 9, 24, 32)

Lostness is a fig tree with leaves but no fruit. Lostness is salt that is not salty. Lostness is to carry a lamp around without oil in it; it is a whitewashed sepulcher, spotless on the outside, but full of corruption within. Lostness is to make plans to tear down barns and build bigger ones, then be called a fool by God and required to give back to him the breath He lent; and then leave all your earthly goods here for others to squabble over.

Lostness is putting a piece of new cloth on an old garment, or new wine into an old wineskin or bottle. It is to have eyes and not see; to have ears and not hear; to have a tongue, but unable to speak. Lostness is destruction, darkness and delusion; it is weeping, wailing, gnashing of teeth—it is Hell!

Lostness is the stupidity of sheep that are without a shepherd, unable to find their way back to the fold. It is the uselessness of a coin that lies undiscovered in a hole in the floor. It is the miserable lifestyle of a prodigal son living among pigs. It is chasing after vanity and succeeding in catching it; it is separation from God!

What is the cure, the panacea for such perdition? It is the blood of Jesus Christ shed for us. The God of the Bible is not willing that any should perish or be lost. We have no business remaining lost, for God loves us. When we believe in Christ we are made right with God, declared children of the Most High, a royal priesthood, His very own possession and citizens of Heaven.

Thank God, Christ came to seek and to save that which was lost. Rejoice today that like the sheep, the silver, and the son, you too have been found.

July 1

So likewise you, when you have done all those things which you are commanded, say, "We are unprofitable servants. We have done what was our duty to do." (Luke 17:10)

Only those who receive the gift of God are eligible to receive the rewards of God. The gift is eternal life through Jesus Christ. If you have *not* been born again, changed in your heart through faith in His blood, all that you do means nothing. You have no foundation upon which to build. Since we are saved by grace, what we do by way of service puts no pressure on God to reward us.

If by our works we could make God commend us, the concept of grace would be destroyed. But a sovereign God recognizes indebtedness on His part to reward believers for their earnest service to Him. The rewards of men do not compare with the commendation of Christ. Folks who desire the praises of men, who hunger for man's recognition, will discover that satisfaction escapes them.

The rewards of men are temporal; those of Christ, eternal. Without Christ famous men and women become infamous; and the well-known, notorious. Without Christ plaques become plagues; golden watches are pawned; trophies become tarnished; commendations are discarded; citations crumble, awards are stolen, medals misplaced (and sometimes recalled), buttons burned, and all other evidences of man-made rewards are lost, forgotten, faded or buried in oblivion.

The best that men can give is nothing compared with God's praises. We are disqualified to receive divine rewards when we depend upon human rewards. What is there a mere man can give that is commensurate with the rewards of God in Christ? Why, just to hear Him say, "Well done, good and faithful servant!" surpasses all the glory that men might bestow.

July 2

Come and see. (John 1:39)

The two disciples answered a question with a question. To the query "What are you looking for?" they asked, "Rabbi, where do You live, where are You staying?" There is more to the question than meets the ear, for the two disciples wanted to have a private, undisturbed conversation with Him. "Sir, we have some questions to ask You; there are some things on our hearts, some matters on our minds that would take some time to go over. We don't want to waste Your time with foolish talk, but our hearts have been strangely stirred. What we want cannot be settled in a few minutes talk here on the roadside. Where do You live?"

And so the Lord extended an invitation, "Come and see!" Note His accessibility. It is as if He had been waiting all the time. Christ generously placed Himself at their disposal. It is not that easy to see the great men and women of this world. Potentates, popes, presidents, kings and queens, prime ministers, dictators—no, you must have an appointment, fit into their schedule, go through a security check, and be interviewed.

But there was more to this gentle command of our Lord. It was an invitation to stay with Him not only this day but to spend the night with Him. In that way they could have a long talk. Come and see. Hear the Samaritan woman at the well, "Come, see a Man, who told me all things that I ever did" (John 4:29). Come and see.

Argument has its place, but not here. Dialogue is good, but not here. Discussion and debate are excellent. Second-hand reports have their place. But you come and see! Nothing beats a personal following and abiding in His presence. Here is the very epitome of the Christian life—living in His presence, tasting and seeing that the Lord is good (Psalm 34:8). "Come and see the works of God" (Psalm 66:5).

July 3

Do not marvel that I said to you, "You must be born again."
(John 3:7)

Did you ever stop to think about what the Bible says concerning the condition we are in when we come into this world? It is not pleasant reading. Indeed, upon hearing the description of man's congenital nature, we become indignant and our very belligerence shows the truth of God's Word.

We are born *stark naked.* This is brought to our attention when upon hearing of the loss of his sons and daughters, servants and wealth, Job said, "Naked I came from my mother's womb, and naked shall I return there." Job (1:21)

The Bible also teaches we are born with a *sinful nature.* David made this known after Nathan spoke to him about his affair with Bathsheba. He said, "Behold, I was brought forth in iniquity, and in sin my mother conceived me" (Psalm 51:5). We come into the world with a sin nature in us. Sometimes called total depravity, it means the natural man in his own strength can do absolutely nothing to please God.

Third, we are born *spiritually needy.* From the moment we come into this world we are in trouble. We are children of wrath, hated by Satan, and at the mercy of all kinds of wickedness. This is why we need God, Christ, the Holy Spirit, the Bible, and angels to watch over us.

Such needs point to the fact of a birth that is *scripturally new.* The sin-sick man must be revived; the child of wrath must become a child of God; the earthly must become heavenly; the dead must be restored to life; the lost must be found; and the blind made to see.

There is only one way this can be accomplished. It is through faith in the finished work of Christ. Surely you can see now why Christ told Nicodemus, "You must be born again!"

July 4

The wind blows where it wishes, and you hear the sound of it, but cannot tell where it comes from and where it goes. So is every one who is born of the Spirit. (John 3:8)

This text came to mind when I read the 24-hour weather report for Philadelphia. Ordinarily I do not read such reports, but when I saw the great variety of wind directions I was astonished. Within 24 hours in our city the following changes in the wind's direction were made: nne, n, ne, se, s, se, s, n, se, ene, ne, ene and se. Along with those wind changes the temperature rose from 24 degrees to 36, and the humidity from 46% to 89%.

Wind is real, actual, and indisputably factual. It is invisible, but it is there. You cannot see it, but you see what it does. You observe how the wind whips the ocean waves, rustles the leaves, breaks branches and bends boughs; blows the tumbleweed, fills out sails, throws trash about in the streets, and causes fields of grain to ripple.

You see how it knocks off hats, inverts umbrellas, whips flames, raises kites, topples television antennas, creates drafts, whistles by the windows, swirls snowflakes, creates blizzards, twirls weathervanes, spins windmills, etc. And so it does not matter whether you can explain the wind. You may not understand it, or know its origin, the course it takes, the road it travels, how it builds up speed, why it changes, where it ends or why it stops—but you know the wind is there.

As the wind, so is he or she that is born of the Spirit of God! If the Holy Spirit is in us, He will give evidence of His presence. Once we believe Christ died for our sins, inner changes take place: attitudes, values, concepts, opinions, ideas, outlooks and thoughts are affected. And the redeemed life shows itself as something real, effective, and satisfying, as we bear witness to His presence.

July 5

God is Spirit and those who worship Him must worship in spirit and truth. (John 4:24)

Our response to God who is Spirit must be spiritual. There must be affinity between the Holy Spirit and the human spirit; otherwise there can be no real worship. God's very nature requires spiritual offerings. The Holy Spirit in us helps our human spirits to worship God the way God wants to be worshiped.

But truth is needed also, for while some people are sincere, earnest and zealous, their worship is false, idolatrous and an abomination. Absolute objective truth and reality is needed. Otherwise the worship becomes self-deception, even demonic. Without spirit you have mere formality, cold ritual. But without truth you have a lie. And so it is not optional, but mandatory, absolutely necessary that we worship in spirit and truth.

God can be worshiped in no other way. He must be worshipped in accordance with His nature, befitting His very being. Only true worship pleases Him, for true worship seeks to have the outside fall in line with the inside. Thoughts are concentrated. Eyes sparkle. How real He makes Himself to us in true worship. How sweet the taste.

How good the company. How victorious the battle. How still the water! How green the pasture. How strong the everlasting arms. How calm the ocean. How lovely the dwelling place. How wondrous His blessings. How great the benefits. How eternal His salvation.

How precious the blood. How cleansing the fire. How consoling His Presence. How sure His promise. How secure under His wings. How long endures His mercy. How true His Word. How amazing His grace! Today determine to worship God in spirit and truth.

July 6

Jesus said to them, "My food is to do the will of Him who sent Me, and to finish His work." (John 4:34)

When obedience to His will is our major concern in life, only then are we truly living. Only then will we discover a sense of achievement, a satisfaction of the soul, a joy of living, a feeling of usefulness, a goal worthwhile having, and a commitment that edifies. Knowing God's will and doing it equips us to face reality, not fearing the future, and will give a heart satisfaction that is unattainable otherwise.

When doing the will of God is our daily food, dreams become reality. Only then can we tunnel through the mountain of despair, or cross over troubled waters on a bridge of hope. When we know and do God's will it enables us to face the storms of life, the adversities, the lonely days and dark nights.

At times you sit all alone in your room and wonder about the things that have happened to you in life, things over which you had no control—but because you believe in doing God's will, somehow you are enabled joyously to go on to see what the end will be. In God's will your giving will cause you to get. In God's will, ministering to the needs of others satisfies your own needs. When you seek to establish peace in the lives of others you forget the war raging around your own life.

In God's will when you provide living water for the spiritually thirsty soul, you forget the physical condition of your own body. And God so blesses you that in spite of your bad situation, you shine as the sun above the storm clouds. Oh, I tell you there is good food on the table when you do God's will. Yea, doing His will is delicious!

One thing I know. (John 9:25)

Can you say with Holy Spirit assurance, "Now I see!"? Just what do you *know*, of what are you certain in this life? What do you know about the God of the Bible? *Noah:* I know He's an ark of safety in time of flood. *Abraham*: I know the Lord will provide. *Job*: I know that my Redeemer lives. *Joseph*: I know He pulled me out of a pit, plucked me out of prison and placed me in Pharaoh's palace.

Moses: I stood still to see His salvation; I know He can make a way out of no way. *Joshua*: I know He can make the sun stand still and cause the walls of opposition to crumble and fall. *David:* I know the Lord is my Shepherd. *Isaiah*: I know that in the year king Uzziah died, I saw the Lord. *Daniel*: I know He answers prayers. *Thomas*: I know He rose from the grave.

Paul: I know that what He started in me on the road to Damascus He is going to finish. *Slaves* working the cotton fields: "I know de angels in hebbin' done changed my name; and I know de Lord's done laid His hands on me."

You see, our God wants us to know right now our relationship with Him. This is why He gave us the Bible (I John 5:13). We can be certain of what is written. This is why He gave us the Holy Spirit to live in our bodies. We have the assurance that what He started in us He is going to complete.

Consequently though we are not now what we used to be, neither are we now what we shall be. The point is we should know what we are in Christ. If He opened your eyes at all, you know it and can say:

Amazing grace, how sweet the sound
That saved a wretch like me.
I once was lost, but now I'm found,
Was blind, but now I see.
(John Newton)

July 8

And he worshiped Him. (John 9:38)

The word rendered *worship* here means to kiss the hand to (towards) someone, in token of reverence. However, only God is to be worshiped. I confronted two "Witnesses" with this fact, only to be told that Jehovah gave Jesus permission to accept worship for Jehovah. But there is no Bible basis for such a belief. No mere man is ever to be worshiped, under any circumstances, at any time—be he pope, priest, preacher, peon, politician, prince or potentate.

Paul and Barnabas would not allow the people at Lystra to worship them; they cried out, "Men, why are you doing these things? We also are men" (Acts 14:15). No angel is to be worshiped. When John, overwhelmed by what was revealed to him, fell down to worship before the feet of the angel who showed him those things (Revelation 19:10; 22:9), the angel said, "Don't do it! I'm just a servant. Worship God!"

No one who worshiped Jesus Christ was ever told, "Don't do it!" The wise men from the east saw the star of the Lord Jesus, and when they found the baby Jesus with Mary they fell down and worshiped Him, not His mother (Matthew 2:2,11). When Christ came down from preaching the Sermon on the Mount, a man with leprosy came and worshiped Him, and the Lord healed him (Matthew 8:2). Jairus, one of the rulers of the synagogue fell at the Lord's feet and worshiped Him (Mark 5:22; Matthew 9:18), begging Him to heal his daughter. Likewise the Syrophoenician woman (Matthew 15:25), the demoniac at Gadara (Mark 5:6), the women who held the resurrected Lord by the feet (Matthew 28:9), and the disciples (Luke 24:52)—all worshiped Him. And so the man born blind had his spiritual eyes fully opened. He made progress in his recognition that this "man who is called Jesus" was not only "a prophet", and one who has disciples, or a "man of God", but the Lord to be worshiped.

July 9

And no one is able to snatch them out of My Father's hand.
(John 10:29)

God's hand formed the earth and the seas, the sun, moon and the stars. Underneath are His everlasting arms. What man is able to direct the wind out of God's hand? From His hands are hurled lightning flashes and thunderbolts. Who is able to shut up the hand which contains the breath of every living creature? So it is that no man is able to remove you from God's hand.

For one thing, God's hand is so big that if He had any dirt under His fingernails, I would suspect that we humans are living on just one little speck called earth. "Snatch" here means to rob, rape, pluck by force, or spoil. Who is able to pry loose the fingers of God? His hand is too strong. When He shuts doors no man can open them; when He opens doors, no man can close them!

What then can they do with God's hands? His hand is full of love; yea, He loved us so much that He gave His Son. His hand is full of mercy. He knows life's journey is uneven, full of traps, with mountain peaks and valleys, sickness, mental trouble, heartbreak, accidents, disease and death. But none of those can separate us from the love and mercy of God in Christ.

We serve a God who will never let us go. The gift of life is eternal, not two years, not ten years, or 40 years of life. It is not life until you backslide. It is eternal life, and the moment you accept Christ that life begins in you. So that *you* cannot even pluck *yourself* out of God's hand.

Rest assured this day that nothing is able to pluck or snatch you out of the Lord's hand. Be persuaded in your heart that absolutely nothing shall separate you from the love of God, which is in Christ Jesus, our Lord (Romans 8:38f).

And I, if I am lifted up from the earth, will draw all peoples to Myself. (John 12:32)

One of the first things that impressed my heart with this text was that the Lord Jesus did exactly what He said He would do. I can take Him at His word. Those are His words and He kept them. They are emphatic words, pregnant with meaning, highly personal, prophetic, predictive and prospective. And they indicate that the Lord Jesus was not ignorant of what was happening. He knew.

He was aware of Judas' treachery, of impending death; soon the days of His flesh would end. But if folks had seen Him in Person and did not believe, would they accept His word after He had gone? I recognize the Gospel not only draws but it drives. This is because some people love the sin they are in, their lifestyles have them trapped; recalcitrant, set, hard of heart, unaware they have become dupes of the Devil. They are blind and do not realize they cannot see.

Not every one who hears the Gospel story today believes it. Some insist there are many ways to heaven. Christ said, "I am *the* way." Some say Christianity is the white man's religion, but the Bible states God is no respecter of faces or races; He so loved the *world*. We hear, "Well, you know man wrote the Bible." But the Bible says it is the Word of God, "thus says the Lord," and that holy men of old spoke and wrote as they were moved by the Holy Spirit.

Still others say Jesus Christ stayed in the grave. But the Bible says He rose. The Disciples say He rose. Paul says He rose. The Church says He rose. My slave grandparents said He rose. The fact of His influence in the world today says He rose. And because I too one day met Him, I can attest, I can add my voice and say, "He rose!" Hallelujah! Be encouraged today to take God at His Word.

July 11

And I, if I am lifted up from the earth, will draw all peoples to Myself. (John 12:32)

The word "if" does not signify doubt or contingency. It has the force of "when", so that certain expectancy is indicated. Or as in John 3:14, "Even so *must* the Son of Man be lifted up." But now, what is this lifting up business? There is a double sense to the meaning of the word as it is used in John's Gospel.

First it speaks of exaltation to heaven. No mere mortal man was born on earth and then ascended up into heaven, ran all over God's heaven, collected information about God, and then returned to earth to disseminate that information. No. Rather, He who was in heaven, and came down from there, must now ascend and return there.

In honor, dignity and majesty, the Lord Jesus was lifted up, exalted to the right hand of God the Father and seated there. We call this His session; and there He is right now, making intercession for you and for me. And so, lifted up means He rose, ascended glorified and exalted, extolled, very high (Isaiah 52:13).

However, this is but one meaning, and within the context it is not even primary. For in verse 33 we learn the lifting up refers to the cross. In other words, this exaltation in heaven comes by way of elevation on the cross. Thus lifted up means death, and also describes the mode of death. This double meaning is fascinating and most informative. Indeed, the message given, the lesson learned, is one that encourages our hearts although tragedy may precede triumph.

Oh the world is hungry for the Living Bread,
Lift the Savior up for them to see;
Trust Him, and do not doubt the words that He said,
"I'll draw all men unto Me!"
(Johnson Oatman, Jr.)

July 12

And I, if I am lifted up from the earth, will draw all peoples to Myself. (John 12:32)

Whether you take the lifting up as death or see it as both death and exaltation to glory in heaven, it is through the lifting up that Christ promises, "I will, I shall draw all to Myself." What does He mean by *drawing*—not only the religious-but-lost like the Jews, but also the political-but-lost like the Romans—both Jew and Gentile, unto Himself?

Draw is a word used of fishermen bringing in a net full of fish (John 21:6); of the apostle Paul who was seized by the mob there in Jerusalem and *dragged* out of the Temple (Acts 21:30); of Simon Peter, having a sword, *drew* it, pulled it out, unsheathed it, and cut off the right ear of Malchus (John 18:10); of the owners of the fortune-telling slave girl who grabbed Paul and Silas and *dragged* them before the judges (Acts 16:19).

And so like fish in a net, a sword in a scabbard, a helpless victim of an angry mob, God has had to exert a force to bring us unto Himself. On our own we would not, could not come. I remember asking a man, "How're you doing?" and he responded, "I do as I please." Men like to feel that they are independent. But life doesn't work like that. No man comes to Christ except the Father draw him (John 6:44). How is it possible for a crucified Savior to draw men unto Himself? Is man a machine, turned on with a switch, the push of a button? Dragged to God kicking and screaming? No. I hear God saying, "Yes, I have loved you with an everlasting love; therefore with loving kindness I have drawn you" (Jeremiah 31:3).

'Tis done; the great transaction's done; I am my Lord's, and He is mine; He drew me, and I followed on, Charmed to confess the voice divine. O happy day! When Jesus washed my sins away! (Philip Doddridge)

July 13

And I, if I am lifted up from the earth, will draw all peoples to Myself. (John 12:32)

By the crucifixion Christ conquered. From death came life. From tragedy arose triumph. By lifting Christ up Satan was cast down. Out of entombment came enthronement. What was thought to be the Savior's doom turned out to be Satan's defeat. Gloom on the terrestrial changed to glory in the celestial. Lifted up to ruin He was lifted up to reign. Through shame the Savior succeeded.

Through darkness the Light of the Word shone bright. Through testing He was transfigured. The ugliness of Golgotha became the ultimate in glory. The end of an earthly mission became a heavenly ministry. From the cross He received a crown; and the crucifixion became a coronation. Those cruel nails were really pinions of love. The mocking taunts of men were exchanged for the hallelujahs of angels.

The helpless Man of Sorrows now reigns omnipotent! The symbol of hatred turned into a sign of love. That which was scandalous to men, driving them away became a magnet to draw them. A puzzle became the answer. And the bitterness of the sepulcher turned into the sweetness of salvation. What a sublime paradox!

The God of the Bible catches the crafty in their traps; wicked spiders are caught in their own webs; slicksters are made to slip up. Men appoint and God disappoints. They plot but their plans go awry. Some time ago some anti-Semites in a city in France planned to put a bomb in a synagogue. Something went wrong and it exploded prematurely and blew them straight into eternity! God is not asleep. All you have to do is wait on Him. I'm encouraged to do just that, aren't you? Troubles come and go. Sickness, aches and pains, disappointments, and heartbreaks—all the ills that flesh is heir to—surely we experience them. But Christ who drew me to Himself a long time ago won't let go!

July 14

Most assuredly, I say to you, a servant is not greater than his master, nor is he who is sent greater than he who sent him. If you know these things, blessed are you if you do them. (John 13:16-17)

All Christians are servants. Those who are followers are servants; those who are leaders are servants. Failure to accept this truth will decrease or lessen our effectiveness and usefulness to the Lord. It does not matter what field we are in; whatever our position, our profession, our work or our business, if we claim faith in the shed blood of Jesus Christ, we are His servants. We serve Christ, we serve other Christians, we serve those who are not Christians, yea, and we minister to all mankind.

Armed with such knowledge, motivated by such love, supported by such faith, we should not become discouraged or hardened or cynical professionals. Never mind the racism, ingratitude, immorality, lack of appreciation or recognition; the jealousy, lawsuits, power-struggles, unscrupulous behavior, the carnality or wickedness of those whom we serve. We remember that we too are but sinners saved by grace, and that acceptable service to God is to walk in the footsteps of our Savior.

God became a man; He who was rich became poor; the Master became a Servant; the Almighty a Slave. Yea, the Servant of Jehovah suffered! He served well, giving sight to the blind, hearing to the deaf, cleansing lepers, exorcising demons, and raising the dead. And yet He was wounded, pierced for our transgressions; bruised, crushed for our iniquities; oppressed, afflicted, put to death on the cruel cross of Calvary. Christians who are leaders in our society should not think it strange then that suffering is a part of the experience of the leader who serves. We sing: "Where He leads me I will follow, I'll go with Him, with Him all the way." Do you mean it? Good!

July 15

Most assuredly, I say to you, a servant is not greater than his master; nor is he who is sent greater than he who sent him. If you know these things, blessed are you if you do them. (John 13:16-17)

Four words are translated 'servant' in the New Testament. Each shows its own basic emphasis although often difficult to differentiate. Servant: *one holding a confidential dignified position* (*therapon*) used only once (Hebrews 3:5): "And Moses indeed was faithful" in God's house, serving nobly, tenderly, and willingly. Jesus Christ, superior to Moses, was a Son over His own house.

Servant, *as one who officially desires to do all that his superior orders* (*huperetes*): Recounting his conversion experience to King Agrippa Paul tells what Christ said to him on the road to Damascus: "But rise and stand on your feet; for I have appeared to you for this purpose, to make you a minister (servant) and a witness" (Acts 26:16; cf. 1 Corinthians 4:1). The root meaning is "under-rower" or "steerer", and came to refer to service loyally rendered by a subordinate, as an orderly attends a commander in war, or the herald who carries an important, solemn message.

Servant, *as one who personally serves in a labor of love* (*diakonos*) has given us the word 'deacon'. Emphasis is upon activity more than upon relationship. Any discharge of service in genuine love, any sacrificial advancement of the interests of another is the essence of this kind of ministry.

Servant, *as a slave, stresses subjection and permanent relation of servitude to another* (*doulos*); It suggests a total, utter belonging to someone else. He is a slave totally dependent upon his master, and has no choice in the matter. No wonder Paul delighted in calling himself a slave of Jesus Christ. And so should we delight, for our Master bought us, redeemed us, and owns us!

July 16

If you know these things, blessed are you if you do them.
(John 13:17)

It is important to act on what you know. This is what the apostle John meant by "walking in the light" (1 John 1:7). The light is the known will of God—knowing what is right and what is wrong. Walking in the light then signifies *doing* what is right and avoiding what is wrong. We are not to pat ourselves on the back for our knowledge of the Scriptures, or congratulate ourselves for our long-time church membership, our knowledge of church work, ability to get programs over, to raise money, etc.

The danger here is that we tend to become perfunctory, going through the motions, form and fashion. We know some things so well that we assume what is in our heads is automatically a force in our hearts, a power practiced in our hands, when in reality some truths are in the dormitory of our souls fast asleep. We fall into a rut because we have heard a thing so many times.

In other words, we can sing a hymn so often until the words mean nothing to us. This is self-deception. We can hear the gospel of the shed blood of Jesus Christ and become gospel-hardened. So that the message bounces off of our thick heads and rhinoceros skins. True happiness involves knowledge, but it also involves action. Act on the fact. Put into practice the truths you know and be blessed. Mere knowledge, however good or exalted, brings blessings only when put into action. Joy comes from the satisfaction of knowing God is pleased with our actions that are the outcome of what we know. Joy is seeing deeds to be done as divine opportunities. Joy is going through an open door He provides. Joy is hearing Him say, "Well done." Joy is perseverance that keeps on doing always and on every occasion the acknowledged will of God. Today, let the known will of God be demonstrated by our deeds.

July 17

Most assuredly, I say to you, he who believes in Me, the works that I do he will do also; and greater works than these he will do, because I go to My Father. (John 14:12)

<u>*To Do Greater Things for God Requires a Personal Commitment:*</u> Head belief is not the same as heart belief. Mere formal believers are people whose names are on the church rolls but who really don't know who Jesus Christ is. They don't believe Him and don't believe *in* Him. In other words, they don't believe what He says; picking their spots, the Bible is disregarded. For them He is not the Way, the Truth and the Life.

It is not just a matter of verbally rejecting the claims of Christ and saying, "I don't believe Jesus did this" or "I don't believe Jesus said that." The way a man lives is important. Life and lip should not be contradictory. Herein was one purpose of the miracles Christ performed: they backed up His doctrine. The healings authenticated His preaching. Thus the Lord could claim that the words He spoke were not of Himself, of His own initiative, but of the Father, so that it is really the Father who does the works.

Unless we understand who does the works our hands are tied when it comes to doing anything for the Lord. In order to do what Christ did we have to believe that He is in the Father and the Father in Him; and believe Him for the very works' sake, that is, on account of the works themselves.

If we do not trust God, we have no basis for trusting anything or anybody, thus making ourselves untrustworthy! The most suspicious-minded folks are those who least trust the Lord. Without faith nothing in life can be accomplished that pleases God. There must be a personal commitment in order to do greater things for the Lord. Without such commitment we will never reach the major league of God's team; we will only major in the minor league of moral midgets.

July 18

Most assuredly, I say to you, he who believes in Me, the works that I do he will do also, and greater works than these he will do, because I go to My Father. (John 14:12)

To Do Greater Things for God Requires a Proper Concept: Christ said the disciples would indeed do the works "I am doing." However, these are not the "greater works." From the Gospels we learn that Christ turned water into wine, directed the draft of fishes, cast out demons, and healed Peter's mother-in-law. He cleansed a leper, gave articulation of limbs to a paralytic, caused the bedfast man at the Pool of Bethesda to walk, restored a withered hand, cured the centurion's servant, raised the dead son of a widow, and made the dumb to speak.

He caused tempestuous howling winds to cease and calmed boisterous waves; healed the woman with the issue of blood, made the lame to walk, opened the eyes of a man born blind, fed 5,000 with five loaves and two fishes, and walked on water. He unstopped the ears of the deaf, fed 4,000 with seven loaves and a few little fishes, raised Lazarus from the dead, and loosed the woman bent over eighteen years from her infirmity. According to the record, the Disciples were given the power to heal also. Obviously, the greater things of which Christ spoke cannot be the same things which both He and the disciples did.

The attempt to support "faith healing" as something *greater* is in error: It misinterprets the Bible; misses the purpose of physical healing; and brings the Gospel down to a mere physical fishes-and-loaves level. We conclude that there must be a proper understanding of the Scriptures in order to do greater things for God, otherwise we will go off on tangents, get out of the center of God's will, seek that which is not His will, and end up being frustrated because the emotional high drains us. Why, it is impossible even for a drunk man to stay high all the time!

July 19

Most assuredly, I say to you, he who believes in Me, the works that I do he will do also, and greater works than these he will do, because I go to My Father. (John 14:12)

To Do Greater Things for God Involves Getting People Converted: See the "greater" in its numerical aspect. In the days of His flesh the Lord Jesus was in one place at one time. Restricted by the Incarnation the God who became Man was a Jew in Palestine; and all toll, His followers were not that many. But now the believers would soon take the Gospel out of Jerusalem into all Judea and Samaria, and into the uttermost part of the earth.

See the "greater" also in its spiritual aspect, that of conversion. Preaching the Gospel of the shed blood of the resurrected Savior would result in releasing into the marvelous light of salvation folks imprisoned in darkness. To insure that this greater work be done, the Lord Jesus ascended into Heaven in order to send down the Holy Spirit. It is the ministry of the Holy Spirit that is the basis for the greater works! The miracles the disciples performed backed up their preaching, but now the Bible is complete and is our sole authority for what we preach.

Furthermore, those physical healings do not hold a candlestick to the light of conversion, that is, souls being saved for all eternity. There is no greater work possible than that of winning souls. To reach the North Pole, swim the English Channel, descend to the depths of the Pacific Ocean with Jacques Cousteau, climb Mount Everest, perform heart transplants, break down the walls of racial segregation, etc., none of those achievements compare with being an instrument in the hands of the Holy Spirit to win souls to the Lord Jesus Christ.

I am the vine, you are the branches. He who abides in Me, and I in him, bears much fruit; for without Me you can do nothing. (John 15:5)

It is absolutely necessary to stick close with Jesus Christ in order to produce fruit and avoid the fire of chastisement. It is necessary to stay in communion with Him in order to enjoy the fellowship. The highest joy on earth is to be in close fellowship with Christ. Those in union with Him must be careful, however, lest their communion with Him is hindered, and the much fruit dwindles down to no fruit.

There are many enemies and bad situations which affect our fruit. Thus great diligence and alertness are required. As the Song of Solomon states (2:15), "Catch us the foxes, the little foxes that spoil the vines, for our vines have tender grapes." Did you see the icicles hanging on the oranges in Florida last winter? Well, if you did not see them, surely by now you have paid for the damage done.

Not only are there cold waves of worldly cares that spoil the fruit, but there are molds of malice, hijackers of hypocrisy, caterpillars of covetousness, beetles of boasting, the drought of deceit, worms of wickedness, squirrels of selfishness, the monkeys of materialism, bats of unbelief, fruit flies of fornication, foxes of foolishness, gnats of ingratitude, crows of carelessness and bugs of bitterness.

All of these are enemies of fruit. And we Christians must be on our guard. Only in staying close to Christ are we able to survive and bring forth fruit, more fruit and much fruit in the face of so much opposition and the evil circumstances of life.

The key is closeness to Christ. The vitalizing sap comes from the True Vine alone. If we are growing in Christ and becoming more like Him every day, then thank God for the fruit of life.

For without Me you can do nothing. (John 15:5)

Jesus Christ the True Vine spoke those words to saints who are likened unto branches in Him. Christ's purpose was to help His disciples understand their spiritual relationship to Him. And to help them understand that such a connection showed itself in fruit bearing. Relationships are extremely important. By them we understand our goals, purposes, reasons for being or existence, our job or task in life, how to treat others, our attitudes, functions, philosophies, etc.

It is important to know such associations. For example, if God is our Father, it is only because we are given the right, the authority, or power to become children of God through faith in Jesus Christ. As His children, our Father protects us and supplies all of our needs. If He is God then He should be worshiped in spirit and truth. If Jesus is Lord then He owns us to do with us as He pleases. If He is a Man, one of us, it is important to know that He was born of a virgin; and that He took on Him the seed of Abraham and thus after the flesh is a Jew. Such knowledge guards against anti-Semitism.

You can see that the various names of God give us some idea of our relationship to Him and with Him. Even the popular title, Lord of Hosts, lets us know that all things are at His disposal to help us. Unfortunately, some people have no connection with Christ.

Not connected with the Light of the World, they grope in darkness. Not fed by that Bread that comes down from Heaven, they go soul-hungry. Not saved by the Savior, they know not the joy of salvation. And not really connected with the Head of the Church, they are not really in His Body. That's sad, isn't it? To be without Christ is eternally dangerous. I repeat: Relationships are important. They are important not only for salvation but also for service.

July 22

For without Me you can do nothing. (John 15:5)

Understand that a child born into a family is a part of that family and always will be. He may be disowned but blood ties, genes (DNA), names and physiognomy tell the story. That child's behavior may be bad and certainly will affect his relationships. He is not however made a nonentity, disinherited or cast out for eternal punishment.

Now disobedience *does* have an effect on the quality of life lived by the believer who breaks the fellowship. You see, there are two kinds of branches: fruitless and fruitful. Both are related to and connected with the True Vine: both are in Christ. An *"in-me-not-bearing fruit"* disciple is an unproductive disciple, one who has missed the purpose of being allowed to remain on this earth after having been converted. A fruitless believer is a miserable person. Indeed, failure to produce fruit calls for some very strong action on God's part.

Note the consequences of not abiding. But first let me define the key word, "abide", for its use is at the very heart of the text. Already secured through faith in the shed blood of Jesus Christ, the abiding saint is not concerned with salvation, but with the blessings of service and the joy of bearing fruit. What does it mean then to abide?

The Greek word (*meno*) means to remain, continue; in a special sense it means to live, dwell or lodge. Figuratively, it is used of someone who does not leave the realm or sphere in which he finds himself. What does it mean to abide? It means to maintain unbroken fellowship, to be constantly present, and to be knitted to, joined or united.

"To abide" is a favorite phrase used by John, denoting an inward, enduring personal communion. By such abiding, fellowship, and communion, the fruitful branch, wholly dependent upon the vine, assimilates the sap and is nourished, quickened, and made fruitful.

July 23

For without Me you can do nothing. (John 15:5)

Fruitlessness is caused by the failure to abide in or depend upon Jesus Christ. Note we speak of service and not salvation; of communion, not union. As for salvation true believers are in union with Christ; nothing can separate us. As for service the fellowship can be broken, and the branches which bear no fruit taken away, thrown out, withered, gathered and thrown into the fire and burned. This strong language is not an abandonment of the soul to eternal destruction, but a burning judgment on fruitlessness.

The branch therefore represents the potential of possible fruit-bearing. Paul put it this way: "If anyone's work is burned, he will suffer loss; but he himself will be saved, yet so as through fire" (1 Corinthians 3:15). True fellowship then is an organic relationship. It is not based upon outward stuff like skin color, denomination, titles, uniforms, common causes, secret societies, etc. Rather, this fellowship, this communion is an abiding conscious dependence upon the Lord Jesus.

True fellowship then is based negatively upon the words, "for without Me you can do nothing," and positively upon the words, "I can do all things through Christ who strengthens me" (Philippians 4:13), for "he that abides in Me and I in him, the same brings forth much fruit." Without such organic fellowship, we cannot produce any fruit.

Many good things are covered by the word "fruit": souls won to Christ; good deeds done to help widows, the poor, orphans, and strangers; the execution of justice, etc. Fruit also is the propagation of the Gospel, praise to God, strengthening or edifying other saints, liberal giving and support, church attendance, and of course, the fruit of the Holy Spirit: love, joy, peace, longsuffering, gentleness, goodness, faith, meekness, self-control—and a thousand other aspects of becoming more like the Lord Jesus.

July 24

For without Me you can do nothing. (John 15:5)

The language and grammar of this text are intriguing. Without Me, severed from Me, apart from Me, separated from Me, having no association or connection with Me, making no use of My power, My presence—you can do nothing! You are powerless. Perhaps this is difficult to understand because we *are* able to accomplish things on our own, by ourselves. What I mean is, when I don't pray and ask God's guidance, but proceed to do things on my own, and succeed, it makes me feel good; it exhilarates.

When I play the game of *Monopoly* with my life I feel rich, like singing, "I did it my way!" Then later on, I find myself all tied up, involved, complicated and in a mess. Yes, we can do things *without* Christ, but within the context of this verse the results are not fruit, unless it is a rotten banana or a wormy apple, results of the intrusion of self-will.

"Can do" is literally continuously able to do and keep on doing. You cannot be a doer, a producer of fruit without this intimate fellowship with Jesus Christ. Use of the present tense teaches us it is at all times impossible to please God without Christ. Emphasis is not upon a here-and-there some time kind of fruit, but more fruit becoming much fruit. We must realize that we have no power within ourselves to bring forth fruit, much less produce it bountifully. The sole efficient cause is union with Christ. May this truth dawn upon us and bring us to our senses.

I need Thee ev'ry hour, Most gracious Lord;
No tender voice like Thine can peace afford.
I need Thee ev'ry hour, Stay Thou near by;
Temptations lose their power when Thou art nigh.
I need Thee, O I need Thee; Ev'ry hour I need Thee!
O bless me now, my Savior, I come to Thee.
(Annie S. Hawks)

July 25

For without Me you can do nothing. (John 15:5)

Even when we are in the Lord's will and producing fruit, the Lord still works on us to purge, cleanse literally by pruning. I don't know if my two rose bushes near my garage holler "ouch!" when I prune them. But God's plan includes the removal of whatever remains that is hindering us from producing more fruit. The old man is still in me, and never will be eradicated this side of glory. But God is working and sometimes allows us to go through trials and suffering in order to increase the fruit.

Sometimes He uses His Word to prune us. He cleanses us through the Word He has spoken. He also uses circumstances. So that in defeat or triumph, valley or mountain top, sickness or health, poverty or wealth, cursing or blessing, idle or employed, young or old, God uses all things to work together for our good, enabling us to bring forth more fruit.

A double negative is used in the original language; this is for emphasis. Literally we read; "For apart from Me you cannot habitually do nothing!" In English it is improper to say, "I don't not!" But it is certainly emphatic! The point is: We humans are *absolutely* helpless apart from Christ to bring forth good fruit.

Since you believe this verse, what then is your desire? Do you want to be a saint full of sap? And in union with Christ in such a way that your life is quickened, made fruitful? Since we cannot possibly repay Him for the blood shed for our sins, our attitude should be: "Lord, use me. I am Your disciple. Get glory out of my life. See to it that I bear more fruit and then much fruit—through Jesus Christ my Lord. Amen."

July 26

He will glorify Me. (John 16:14)

The One God of the Bible exists as Father, Son and Holy Spirit at the same time. In the Godhead, within His essential and divine nature, within Deity, in the state of being God, there is a ranking; there is an order of operation which is invariable. The Father sends the Son and He sends the Spirit, and works through Them. And you see that the Son sends the Spirit and works through Him. **This order is never reversed—the Spirit never sends the Father; the Spirit never commands the Son.**

Their subordination is not of Person but of office or function; it is a division of labor which is in the interest of economy and efficiency. So do not think for one moment that there is a division of mind or lack of harmony within the Godhead simply because there is a division of labor.

Realize that the Holy Spirit living in our bodies is the Master Teacher. He speaks what He hears from Jesus Christ, and moves in us according to the Word of God. The Lord Jesus knows what we need to hear and to learn. Because we belong to Him through faith, He looks after us.

The Holy Spirit receives the things of Christ. What are these things? They are things past, present, and future; things which He reveals to His own. He said, "All things that the Father has are Mine. What I have the Holy Spirit receives from Me. What He gets from Me, He will show to you!"

Put it this way: Christ says, "I have everything the Father has; the Spirit then draws upon what I have, and reveals, shows, declares, discloses, transmits, shares or gives it to you." Thus within the Godhead one function of the blessed Holy Spirit is to focus our attention, to help our minds zero in upon the character of Jesus Christ. He wants us to know more about our Lord. And I have discovered that the more I know about Him, the more I love Him!

July 27

He will glorify Me. (John 16:14)

To the unsaved, the non-Christian, this text means nothing. The Holy Spirit does not live in unbelievers. Indeed, one reason the teaching ministry of the Holy Spirit is hindered and there is little spiritual growth in some churches is the presence of carnal members and unsaved members.

The depository of truth, the Bible, is made clear to believers only by the Spirit of Truth. This glorifies Christ who is the Truth. No ministry that is based upon falsehood, error, fads and fashions, the philosophies, speculations, and ideologies of men can glorify the Lord Jesus Christ. The Lord has fully provided for our growth. He has made known all things to the Holy Spirit and given the Spirit to us. It is then the task of the Spirit of God to expand our knowledge, increase our ability to apprehend, yea, our desire to learn.

Since the Holy Spirit is the Chief Executive Officer in the Church doing the will of the Head of the Church, it is obvious that our concern ought to be about the Lord Jesus Christ. If our goal is to let the Holy Spirit glorify the Lord Jesus in us, it will keep down all that is dishonoring to Him: such things as the money-raising gimmicks, the power struggles, the prayerlessness, the worldliness and carnality, and all the junk to be found these days in our lives.

The Holy Spirit's duty ought to be our duty. We should do what he does by letting Him do what He wants to do in us! So that "I, yet not I" becomes a reality. And there is no big "I" and little "you", there is just the Lord Jesus Christ. Are you growing in Him? Am I? Are we better Christians today than we were yesterday or two months ago? Surely we Christians should be making steady, uninterrupted, transforming progress in the knowledge of the "all things" of Jesus Christ.

July 28

He will glorify Me. (John 16:14)

When in the proper relationship with the Holy Spirit we make good progress in Christlikeness, in the study of the Bible, and in learning spiritual truths. Oh, the Spirit has so much to tell us, so much to teach us; we will never reach the point He has no more to say to us or to share with us. No matter how many degrees we have, how long we have been in the church, how much money we have raised or what positions we hold, there are more of the rich treasures of knowledge to be imparted. We are moved to thank Him for all the things He has shown us of His glory: Thank Him for:
-- the breaking of shackling habits
-- the open door to His throne
-- the peace that passes all understanding
-- the sense of fulfillment
-- the citizenship in Heaven
-- the light that dispels darkness
-- the assurance of glory
-- that nothing can separate us from the love of God
-- the awareness of His Presence
-- the strong grasp of His hand
-- the fellowship of His Spirit
-- the goodness of His heart
-- the sweetness of His Word
-- the depth of His love
-- the pleasure of His company
-- the freedom of His liberty
-- the joy of His salvation
-- the cleansing of His blood
-- the grace whereby we are saved
-- and the blessed hope of His return

Thank Him for all that He shall reveal to us, enabling us to glorify the Lord Jesus today in a very special way.

He will glorify Me. (John 16:14)

This text points to the very reason for our existence, for we read, "You are worthy, O Lord, *to receive glory* and honor and power; for You created all things, and by Your will they exist and were created" (Revelation 4:11). A man who does not know why he is living is a sad, miserable man. Out of God's will, he substitutes his own will and thereby lines up with Satan. People who do not know the Lord seek to glorify themselves or fall into the trap of glorifying other human beings or even worshiping things, especially things which they themselves have created.

Failure to glorify God by letting the Holy Spirit exalt Christ in us makes us easy prey for the unholy hucksters, hoodwinkers and hellish hoodlums, the prophets of profit and prosperity. People who miss life's goal are deceived; they do all kinds of things to satisfy their souls' hunger. They make rich the religious rascals they respect, and grant success to the most scurrilous scoundrels. Hollywood stars are idolized; jazz artists deified; night club performers worshiped; super athletes adulated—and all of them paid fantastic salaries which in no way are commensurate with any actual, permanent *spiritual* good contributed to society.

The world loves its own (John 15:19). Churches glorify tradition; the self-indulgent glorify pornography; the homosexual glorifies sex; Russia glorifies the state; America glorifies the dollar; fools glorify ignorance; and the Devil glorifies himself. But since the goal of the Holy Spirit is to glorify Jesus Christ, then that ought to be our goal also, for the Spirit lives in us. The more we know about Christ the more we come to love Him and joyfully sing:

Glory to His name, Glory to His name;
There to my heart was the Blood applied,
Glory to His name. (Elisha A. Hoffman)

July 30

For these things were done that the Scripture should be fulfilled, "Not one of His bones shall be broken." (John 19:36)

"He guards all his bones; not one of them is broken" (Psalm 34:20). This psalm speaks of God delivering His own. The keeping or guarding all the bones is a figure of speech that means complete preservation; it is a general reference to the manner in which the Lord watches over those who belong to Him. The righteous are kept by the Lord. Regardless of what happens to us physically, nothing separates us from the love of God shown in Jesus Christ.

Although Christ died on the cross, God prevented His bones from being broken, indicating the enemy can go only so far! Breaking bones is a strong metaphor for the torture of pain that racks the frame-work of the body. Knowing this helps us to understand Psalm 51:8 "Make me hear joy and gladness, that the bones You have broken may rejoice."

When King Hezekiah was sick and God healed him, he said, "Like a lion, so He breaks all my bones; from day until night You make an end of me" (Isaiah 38:13). In Micah 3:3, God describes faithless leaders as men who "eat the flesh of My people, flay their skin from them, break their bones, and chop them in pieces like meat for the pot."

Our bones represent us; indeed, the whole body is represented by the bones, for what happens to our bones happens to our entire person. This is called *synecdoche* (to receive jointly), for a part is equal to the whole. David cried out that even the solid framework of his body, his bones which are the seat of the strength and solidity of the body, even they were racked and shaken (Psalms 6:2; 22:14, 17; 31:10; 35:10; 42:10; Proverbs 16:24). When we think of the pain, distress, weakness and broken-heartedness of our Lord's suffering, we come to appreciate Him even more. Today: Remember Calvary!

July 31

For these things were done that the Scripture should be fulfilled, "Not one of His bones shall be broken." (John 19:36)

The Passover is a memorial of redemption from Egypt. One instruction for eating the Passover lamb includes prohibiting breaking any of its bones, thus enabling Israel to maintain symbolically its unity and unbroken fellowship with Jehovah (Numbers 9:12). While commemorative, it is also an offering (oblation) up of thanksgiving and worship to God. The sacrifice was required to be perfect; there are to be no mutilated or broken bones in our service to the Lord!

Unfortunately, there are "Broken-Bone-Baptists" who offer God their leftovers. Instead of remembering our Creator in the days of our youth, some of us have done everything under the sun we wanted to do, and then crawled back, broken bones and all, promising to serve the Lord, and singing, "I promised Him that I, would serve Him till I die"—knowing we don't have too much longer to live. We pay our bills, buy what we want or think we need, and then what's left give to the Lord's work. The Lord desires commitment and dedication, not a broken bones approach in His service. We become set in our ways early in life and if steeped in tradition, nurtured in churchianity, and ignorant of the Bible, it is difficult to change.

Of course, the Passover lamb of Moses' day pointed to Jesus Christ, the true Passover Lamb that takes away the sin of the world. Paul said to the indifferent Corinthians, "Therefore purge out the old leaven, that you may be a new lump, since you truly are unleavened. For indeed Christ, our Passover, was sacrificed for us" (1 Corinthians 5:7). Like the Passover lamb of old, our Lord also was without blemish, tested, tried, slain, and His blood applied. He was the perfect protection from condemnation to Hell. Thank God, not a bone of Him was broken!

August 1

For these things were done that the Scripture should be fulfilled, "Not one of His bones shall be broken." (John 19:36)

We have seen the background of what happened at Calvary. *Crucifragium* or the breaking of limbs was indeed an ancient custom calculated to hasten death. A heavy mallet was used to end the torture of a lingering death by crucifixion, one of the cruelest forms of capital punishment invented by mankind.

The victim found only slight ease of pain and strain on the arms and chest in the fact that some of the body weight was put on the legs. However, in breaking the legs, even this support was removed and the consequent, subsequent greater constriction of the chest caused death to come more quickly.

So now look at the scene. At this point a delegation of the Jews went to Pilate. Here is the last action of this group recorded in John's Gospel. Note their hypocrisy, for there is no hypocrisy like the hypocrisy of *religious* hypocrites! Having unjustly caused the death of an innocent man, their hands stained red with the blood of Jesus Christ, they were more concerned about physical ceremonial defilement than about their own spiritual defilement.

Because it was the eve of the Sabbath the Jewish leaders wanted the bodies taken down. Had it been up to the Romans they would have left the bodies there to decompose, although the body of the Lord did not rot or see corruption (Acts 2:27; Psalm 16:10). Yea, God watched over His Son, and as John pointed out, the Scripture was fulfilled.

There were two Sabbaths that week (John 19:31) on separate days, and the one that was soon to take place was a high occasion. As it was, Jewish Law forbade leaving a dead body hanging on a "tree" overnight, for this was defilement of the land (Deuteronomy 21:23). But God thwarted the intention of the evildoers. Surely you can trust Him today to carry out His purpose in your life!

August 2

For these things were done that the Scripture should be fulfilled, "Not one of His bones shall be broken." (John 19:36)

See now the cruel Roman soldiers approach the three victims. Because the Lord Jesus hangs between the robbers, the soldiers go to one of the robbers first, whether to the penitent or the impenitent, we do not know. They swing a heavy mallet, and the awful crunch of breaking bones is heard, but the callous soldiers are unmoved. They come then to our Lord, but lo and behold, He is dead already.

This is strange, because one purpose of crucifixion was to make an example of the criminal, causing his death to linger for two or three days. At this point one soldier, not content to pass by one already dead, brutally thrust home what he thought was the *coup de grace,* piercing the Lord's body with a spear. Even this forceful thrust did no bone damage, and God's Word was fulfilled.

Immediately there came out blood and water. Not a bone of Him was broken teaches us that nothing can destroy the wholeness of Christ and those who are in Him. Not all the powers of the Devil or of his demons can break the unity, the harmony so jealously guarded. The Church, the Bride of Christ, like Eve to Adam, is bone of His bone, and flesh of His flesh. If in death He was preserved, how much more now that He rose from the grave!

The fact that not a bone of Him was broken means we too shall be kept by the power divine. All of the attempts to destroy the Church fail, whether external persecution or internal strife and corruption, and the bones of the body of Christ remain unbroken. So the Church which is His body shall be preserved, and when the trumpet sounds, not a soul shall be lost, but all who belong to the body will be snatched up to meet the Lord Jesus and be with Him throughout the ceaseless ages of eternity. How can we not rejoice today!

August 3

Because they have taken away my Lord, and I do not know where they have laid Him. (John 20:13)

Ignorance is not always bliss. What you do not know *can* hurt you. And Mary Magdalene in her ignorance was miserable. Having spoken to the angels, she turned around and saw a man standing there. It was the Lord Jesus but she did not know it. "Woman, why are you weeping? Whom are you seeking?" Thinking He was the gardener, she said, "Sir, if you have carried Him away, tell me where you have laid Him, and I will take Him away."

To this the Lord simply said, "Mary!" One word—this is all that was needed. His first word spoken to any human being on earth after the resurrection included the one word, her name, Mary. How precious was the sound! This was not the voice of a gardener, but that of the Shepherd who said, "My sheep hear My voice."

One word and ignorance became knowledge. One word proved love's labor was not lost. One word and tears of sorrow were wiped away. One word and despair beat a hasty retreat. One word and the sorrow of the evening gave place to the joy of the morning. One word and the shadows fled, reality stepped forth; and faith crushed to the ground was revived again. One word!

Christian, how is it with you today? Do you find yourself in Mary's shoes? Is there despair, disappointment, sorrow, pain, grief, heart-break, or loneliness? Are you tired of the chaos, contention and confusion? Well, the Lord Jesus is alive. Therefore let the scales of ignorance fall from your eyes. Let the wax of indifference and disobedience fall from your ears. Christ knows your name; He is aware of your problems. Yea, He is the solution. Hear Him call your name. Then reach out and touch Him, make Him yours and join that innumerable host which raises its voice in one united paean of praise and shouts, "My Lord!"

August 4

Simon . . . Feed My lambs . . . Tend My sheep . . . Feed My sheep. (John 21:15-17)

The biographical sketch of Simon Peter shows him to be emotional, impulsive, volatile, impetuous and unpredictable. He had to learn the hard way that devotion is superior to emotion. See Simon walking on the sea and then sinking; hear him rebuke the Lord about His prediction of death. Listen as he puts Moses and Elijah on the same level with the Lord Jesus; watch as he refuses at first to permit the Lord to wash his feet. Witness his profession never to deny Christ. See him cut off the right ear of Malchus, servant of the high priest. Finally, see him flee only to fall prey to a deceitful heart and vigorously deny he ever knew the Lord Jesus.

After our Lord's resurrection Simon decided to go back to the fishing business; and so with six of the other disciples toiling through the night; they caught nothing. A man appears on the scene, advises them to cast their net on the right side of the boat. They obey and the catch of fish, 153 in number, is so great they have difficulty hauling it in.

"It is the Lord," says John. Upon hearing this, Peter impulsively put on his fishers' coat and cast himself into the sea. Presumably he made his way to the shore, though this is not said in so many words (Leon Morris). Later, after eating breakfast with the disciples there, the Lord Jesus spoke to Simon Peter the words of our devotion text.

The commands to feed, tend and shepherd are all present tense imperatives, or what the scholars call durative: keep on, continue to feed, tend and shepherd the lambs and sheep of the Lord. Indeed, make a habit of doing so! It was God's desire for Simon to stick to his calling, persevere in it, and let nothing change his course. Regardless of what takes place today, by the power of the resurrected Savior living in you, fulfill His will. Let the Holy Spirit demonstrate anew that devotion is superior to emotion.

August 5

And He said to them, "It is not for you to know times or seasons which the Father has put in His own authority." (Acts 1:7)

Here our Lord teaches that God the Father is in the day-fixing business. He appointed a day in which Jesus Christ was born of the virgin Mary. He fixed a day for the Root to appear out of dry ground. The Bible calls it the fullness of time, when the Father sent forth His Son. He fixed the day of the crucifixion, letting it fall in a week when there were two Sabbaths (John 19:31), so that Christ died not on a Good Friday, but was crucified on a Wednesday and was dead before sunset (the beginning of Thursday). The timing was just right. And now see the Father appointed the day when His Son would get up out of the grave!

Luke, the writer in Acts was moved by the Holy Spirit to record, and Simon Peter was moved by the Holy Spirit to transfer the day of festivity in Psalm 118 to the resurrection joy of Jesus Christ. It is then resurrection day that is intended to be celebrated with joy and gladness, a day the Father determined long ago. How wonderful then that every Sunday is the day we celebrate the resurrection of Jesus Christ—not just on Easter Sunday! Remember, we serve a risen Savior! Take each day at a time (that's all we get anyway) and realize it is the day God has given; life will be one big celebration. Joy bells will ring in our heart. There will be a spark in our eyes, a spring in our steps, praise on our tongue, a song on our lips, kindness in our deeds, mercy in our hand, generosity in our giving, the hope of glory in our soul, faith in our walk, salt in our talk, and heaven in our view.

This is the day the Lord hath made, He calls the hours His own. Let heaven rejoice, Let earth be glad, And praise surround the throne.
(Isaac Watts)

August 6

And killed the Prince of life. (Acts 3:15)

How can He who raised the dead Himself be killed? Surely if *we* had such power, no man on earth would lay a finger on us! When we are rich, we spend in luxury. Wise, display our wisdom. Educated, flaunt our knowledge. Brilliant, sell our talent. Beautiful women parade their pulchritude. Strong men perform feats of strength, and potentates demonstrate their authority.

But at Calvary the Captain of Life permits buck privates of sin to slay Him. The Author of Life permits the readers to slam shut the book upon Him. The Giver of Life lets the recipients of life murder Him. The Creator permits the creature to kill Him. The Sun of Righteousness was eclipsed there at Calvary. The Light of the World was extinguished. The Rock of Ages shattered; the Rose of Sharon plucked up. War was declared upon the Prince of Peace; the Righteous Judge was condemned; the Son was separated from His Father; and the Morning Star was hidden from view.

I cannot tell you *how* this was done. How inadequate and feeble is the description of *what* happened. In His nature, God as God cannot die. But God the Son became a Man, and by taking upon Him the form of a servant, being made in the likeness of men, and found in fashion as a man, humbled Himself, became obedient unto death, even the death of the cross. Had He been only a mere man, or even an angel who died for us, we would be lost. You see, what gives weight on the scale of eternal life is Deity.

The very heart of Calvary is found in the fact that Christ is God, the Prince or Source of life. But He had to become a man in order to die. Thanks be to the God of the Bible who is able to reverse the schemes of men, confound their plans, confuse their minds and turn the tables on their craftiness. Thank God this day that Jesus Christ the Prince of Life lives forevermore!

Ananias, with Sapphira his wife, sold a possession. And he kept back part of the proceeds. (Acts 5:1f)

There are many liars in the Bible. Foremost, of course, is the Devil who told Eve, "You shall not surely die." And folks have been dying ever since. No wonder Christ said that when Satan tells a lie, he speaks from his own resources, he does what comes naturally, for he *is* a liar, and the father of it (John 8:44). Cain lied and acted as if he did not know the whereabouts of Abel (whom he had just murdered).

Abraham lied about his wife Sarah, saying she was his sister (she was his half-sister), but implying she was *not* his wife. Isaac lied in the same way about his beautiful wife, Rebekah. Jacob lied to his father, Isaac, and claimed he was Esau. Potiphar's wife lied on Joseph and had him imprisoned. Rahab the prostitute lied about the presence of the Israelite spies. Samson lied to Delilah. Gehazi lied to Elisha and was stricken with leprosy. Soldiers lied and said the disciples stole the body of Jesus from the sepulcher.

But the lie told by Ananias and Sapphira sticks out in our minds more than the others probably because of the quick judgment inflicted by God. In those early days of the Church, and partly because of persecution, folks were of one mind, heart and soul, and they voluntarily decided to have all things in common so that no one had to suffer need. Those who had property sold whatever they desired and turned over whatever amount they pleased to the apostles. There was no pressure on them.

However, Ananias and Sapphira, apparently wealthy folks, deliberately connived to hold back a part of what they received for some of their property, and then pretended they were big-heartedly turning it *all* over. So Ananias came in singing, "*All to Jesus I Surrender, all to Him I freely give.*" And Satan, the Liar of liars gained a victory. Today, thank God for His discernment, and for enabling us to serve Him in sincerity and in truth.

August 8

But Peter said, "Ananias, why has Satan filled your heart to lie to the Holy Spirit . . . Why have you conceived this thing in your heart? You have not lied to men but to God." (Acts 5:3-4)

When Ananias brought in the money and laid it at the feet of the apostles, he got the shock of his life. Some evil-doers need to be shocked, for they think they are clever. Simon Peter, having the direct revelation of the Spirit, said, "Ananias, why has the Devil led you to cheat and lie to the Holy Spirit? It was your property to do with as you pleased. And to give what you wanted. So why have you shamefully sought to sham and scam the Spirit?"

Ananias' mouth flew open and immediately he thought to himself, "How did *he* find out? What big blabbermouth Baptist let "tabby bust the bag"? Who told him?" Within seconds upon hearing the words of the apostle Peter, Ananias fell down and breathed his last breath on these mundane shores. He could have resisted the Devil. We don't have to succumb to Satan. Too often we are motivated by fears of losing friendship, of retaliation, or loss of money.

Such fears should not be allowed to rob us of the joy of doing our duty, the joy of standing for what we know to be right. Or rob us of the privilege of being honest in our dealings with others. Ananias and Sapphira fell into the trap of trying to put something over on man without realizing they were really trying to cheat God. Failing to realize that our battle is really not against flesh and blood, we fight each other. And so Simon had to tell Anianias, "Look man, you didn't lie to me; you lied to God!" In lying to the Holy Spirit, they lied to God. It was not an indirect lie, either. The Holy Spirit is not a medium, a go-between active force, an impersonal wind blowing things around to where God wants them to be. No! Unfortunately, there are those who think so, but they are wrong. The Holy Spirit is God Almighty! And He is the One who condemned Ananias and Sapphira.

August 9

Then Peter said to her, "How is it that you have agreed together to test the Spirit of the Lord?" (Acts 5:9)

Obviously, the early church was not free of problems. In fact, the Epistles of the New Testament are in large measure answers to the problems of the members of the early Church. Reading the Church Epistles teaches us this, and we need not wring our hands in utter despair because of the evil that goes on in our churches today. Then too, the good folks in the church would realize in a better way that we are involved in a spiritual battle. Even today there are those who pretend complete consecration to God when in truth they seek to serve only themselves.

To pretend the Holy Spirit moves us to do what we do and then offer our deed to God is hypocrisy. Attempts to palm off the Devil's work as the Spirit's work and hope the deception is not detected are demonic. There is no sense hiding behind civil rights, parliamentary procedure, tradition, skin color, racism or secular humanism, all the while trying to mix in the Holy Spirit.

Satan attacks both from the outside and from the inside. He hates the church. He does not want to see it succeed in doing what God called it to do. From Satan's point of view, it is all right if we succeed in those things God did not call us to do. Many local assemblies appear outwardly successful in their programs and influential in the community. But hear the Lord saying, "I know your works, that you have a name that you are alive, but you are dead" (Revelation 3:1: Sardis).

Ananias did not have time to repent; he did not have enough breath to holler "Lord, have mercy!" He dropped dead and the Devil over in the corner laughed and said, "You poor sap, you!" Three hours later Sapphira walked in. Note the wrong kind of loyalty here—loyalty to a liar. Because of her complicity in deliberately testing the Holy Spirit, she too dropped dead!

August 10

So great fear came upon all the church and upon all who heard these things. (Acts 5:11)

The Ananias and Sapphira incident caused great fear to come upon all those who heard of it. We could use such fear in the church today. We need some members who fear the Holy Spirit, and who fear telling lies in God's church which is the pillar and ground of the truth. We need those who fear stealing God's money, who fear using God's church for their own selfish ends.

We need church members who fear sowing the seeds of dissension and strife, and fear misusing and misquoting Scriptures. We need to fear rebelling against those whom God put in authority over us; and fear violating the church covenant, fear bringing shame upon the Church of the Lord Jesus Christ who purchased the Church with His own blood.

By unmasking these two hypocrites (Ananias and Sapphira), God's attitude towards all church hypocrisy is taught. It does not matter whether His judgment strikes them immediately or later. When folks sit down and plan their evil strategy it indicates a bad conscience.

Remember, the church had just been born, and God who gave men spectacular gifts with which to authenticate their preaching and get the church kicked off, was determined to let nothing stop the growth and establishment of His church. As you well know, a lie can certainly stop some things from getting started.

There must be the realization that the church is the temple of the Holy Spirit. His presence must be so real to us that we realize anything done to one member is done to the church, and whatever is done to the church is done to the Holy Spirit. May He make Himself so authentic to us today that we will go rejoicing in the knowledge that we are not alone, but God the Holy Spirit, the Spirit of truth, resides within us!

August 11

You stiff-necked and uncircumcised in heart and ears! You always resist the Holy Spirit; as your fathers did, so do you. (Acts 7:51)

Resisting the Holy Spirit is dangerous. We resist Him when we strive against His sanctifying impulses. He alone saves, so that to withstand Him is to resist salvation. No one who fights God can win. The danger is that individual acts of resistance may fall into a fixed pattern, a hardness of the heart that signifies God has given up that person.

We learn that it is not good to resist righteousness. Jannes and Jambres, magicians in Pharaoh's court defied Moses and Aaron (2 Timothy 3:8). Evil men sought to oppose the wisdom and Spirit by which Stephen spoke (Acts 6:10). Elymas the sorcerer withstood Saul (Paul) and Barnabas (Acts 13:8). Alexander the coppersmith greatly resisted Paul's preaching (2 Timothy 4:15).

The resistance movement goes on. Unfortunately, some church folks have blindly given in to the evil forces and ideas of the world, and have brought them into the church. Satan uses tradition and custom to blind us. He uses racism to stunt our growth. He uses so-called democracy to deceive us into believing the church of Christ is a democracy (yes, I speak as a Baptist). Only when we are about our Father's business, obedient to His Word, and submissive to the leading of the Spirit and subjecting ourselves to His authority are we most free.

We should learn from history (Romans 15:4) to avoid the mistakes of the past. There is joy in obeying the Spirit whatever the cost. Stephen took a stand, and while it is not God's intention that all of us become Stephens, it is His desire that we stand up for righteousness. When led by the Spirit we do not allow friendship, money, prestige, peer pressure, and other concerns cause us to compromise our faith. Thank God for every time the Spirit speaks to our hearts and our responses please Him.

August 12

You stiff-necked and uncircumcised in heart and ears! You always resist the Holy Spirit; as your fathers did, so do you. (Acts 7:51)

Moses called the rebellious Jews an unruly stiff-necked people. Isaiah called rebellious Jerusalem a whore, and the Israelites corrupt children, laden with iniquity, a sinful nation, and a brood of evildoers. Ezekiel called them impudent children and stiff-hearted, their prophets foolish, liars, and the nation a prostitute. John the Baptist called the evil Pharisees and Sadducees a brood of vipers!

The Lord Jesus Christ called the religious leaders of His day serpents, generation of vipers, hypocrites, blind guides, fools, white-washed tombs, and sons of the killers of the prophets. Paul called Bar-Jesus (Elymas) the sorcerer, a son of the Devil, an enemy of all righteousness; and when Paul was smacked in the mouth at the command of the high priest Ananias, the apostle called him a white-washed wall.

Those two expressions, "white-washed sepulcher" and "white-washed wall" refer to the Jewish custom of white-washing the entrances to their graves or sepulchers as a warning against defilement by touching them. Each spring after the rainy season graves were white-washed so that folks would not touch them and defile themselves ceremonially. This illustrated concern with the outside but not with the inside. Imagine a wall crumbling, tottering and about to fall, but disguised with a generous coating of white wash to hide its defects. So a hypocrite conceals his malice and hatred under an outward assumption of religiosity and piety. Or even under the guise of hospitality (Proverbs 23:6-8). James called those seeking friendship with the world adulteresses. All such invectives were proper and appropriate; they were not just blowing off steam, or running off at the mouth. I don't know what makes folks angrier, calling them what they are or what they are not. May we remember today that this world is no friend to the Holy Spirit!

225

August 13

You stiff-necked and uncircumcised in heart and ears! You always resist the Holy Spirit; as your fathers did, so do you. (Acts 7:51)

Strange how some people get upset by what others call them. As merciless as we boys were, it seems that once we grew up we learned that sticks and stones may break our bones but names won't hurt us. The very light-skinned boy was called "Reds," the tall, skinny boy, "Cue-Stick," the fat boy, "Tubby" or "Fatsy," the longhead boy, "Peanut."

As far as racial epithets were concerned, being one of the few Blacks in Northeast High School in the early 40's, I was called "Tar Baby" one day and "Snowball" the next. Some of the White boys couldn't make up their minds. Perhaps they were color-blind!

All of us have had the experience of being denounced, ridiculed, disparaged, slandered, mocked or cursed at some time in life. I am surprised that my ears (I speak as a pastor) have not fallen off. But in time we learn to shrug off such nonsense with remarks like, "Call me anything, but don't call me late for dinner." Or, "It takes one to call one!"

Perhaps the denunciation that cuts most deeply is that which is true and has a religious basis. There is no one in the world "madder" than an uncovered hypocrite, a liar caught in his own lies, or a religious pretender exposed for the phony he is. Stephen used strong language; he called the Sanhedrin stiff-necked. The word *skleros* means hard; a person with a stiff neck is stubborn, obdurate, obstinate, mule-headed or headstrong. Uncircumcised in heart means even though they had the outward cutting of the flesh, a sign of the covenant between Jehovah and Israel, there was no inward obedience.

"All the house of Israel are uncircumcised in the heart" (Jeremiah 9:26). Uncircumcised ears indicate one is deaf to God's message (Jeremiah 6:10). In their heart and in their thoughts they were still heathen. What is the condition of our necks, our hearts, and our ears?

August 14

Arise therefore, go down and go with them, doubting nothing; for I have sent them. (Acts 10:20)

It is the desire of the Holy Spirit that you not be at odds or variance with yourself, wavering, doubting, hesitating, or procrastinating. Such behavior is self-destructive and self-destruction is sin. Consider then the effects of misgivings. *Doubt limits the accomplishments of faith.* For example, after the Lord said to the fig tree, "Let no fruit grow on you ever again," it withered away immediately.

Christ assured the disciples that "If you have faith and do not doubt, you will not only do what was done to the fig tree, but also if you say to this mountain, 'Be removed and be cast into the sea' it will be done. And whatever things you ask in prayer, believing, you will receive" (Matthew 21:21f).

Doubt also condemns (Romans 14:23). If you believe a thing is wrong, regardless of whether on an absolute scale it is wrong or right, then for you it is wrong; if you commit that which you believe is wrong, you stand condemned.

Doubt robs your prayer life. God is willing to give you whatever you lack, whatever you need to fill up every deficiency. But when you ask, when you pray, do it in faith, not doubting. He who doubts says James (1:6), is like a wave of the sea driven and tossed by the wind. He is double-minded, two-souled (*dipsuchos*), divided in interest. Later James (4:8) exhorts, "Purify your hearts, you double-minded." Such a person is unstable (*akatastatos*: not seated down, not settled in place) in all his ways.

You can see now what is behind the Spirit's admonition to Peter: "Arise therefore, go down and go with them, *doubting nothing.*" Doubt limits the accomplishments of faith, condemns the doubter, and robs him or her of an effective prayer life. May you this day take God at His Word!

August 15

*Your household . . . his house . . . all his family . . . his house
. . . all his household.* (Acts 16:31-34)

Metonymy (change of name) means one word may be used
for another word that it suggests. The substitution is based
upon a mental relationship and not a physical resemblance;
"house" becomes more than brick and mortar. It means also
family, all those under the authority of the head of the house:
children, slaves, servants, etc (John 4:53; Acts 11:14, 16:15).

What's going on in your *house*? Is there *Discipline of
Love* in your home? Paul believed that families which exer-
cised order in their homes put themselves in a position to be
used of God in the church. Some Christian parents need to be
convinced that discipline is an act of love; for whom the
Lord loves He spanks or chastens. Psychologists and family
counselors who do not approve of corporal punishment tread
dangerous ground; rejecting the Bible, they give bad advice
(Proverbs 22:6, 15; 23:13f). All children are not alike, so all
do not need the same kind or degree of discipline: Different
strokes for different folks, even the little folks.

Is there *Division of Labor* in your home? As a boy my
chores consisted of sweeping the front pavement, putting out
ashes, dusting furniture, scrubbing steps with Dutch Cleanser
and running errands. And I made money shining shoes,
wiping off cars, scrubbing floors, setting up pins in a
bowling alley, and collecting junk.

Is there *Devotion to the Lord* in your home? Prayer and
worship at church will mean more if there is corresponding
prayer and worship of the Lord Jesus at home. Blessed is the
house whose children are taught God's Word diligently
(Deuteronomy 6:7). Blessed is the family that meditates on
God's Word day and night (Psalm 1:2). Make it a special
point today to lift up your family in prayer that every
member might come to a saving knowledge of Jesus Christ.
For it is His will that whole families be saved.

August 16

Except that the Holy Spirit testifies in every city, saying that chains and tribulations await me. (Acts 20:23)

Life at its fullest, richest and deepest is Holy Spirit directed. Such life is not an easy one; it is not a bed of roses. But it is a good life; it is fruitful, productive; it is a good witness to the power of the Living God. Led by the Spirit of God the believer is able to wage a winning warfare and to fight a good fight.

When directed by the Spirit we are given a glimpse of the future. This is interesting because human beings are curious creatures, inquisitive, exploring, probing and experimenting. Yea, God has given us minds to investigate His world. However, we are limited to digging up the past, searching out the here and now. As for the past and the present we but know in part. The future is a mystery.

We do not know what a day may bring forth, or what will happen the next day, hour or minute. Frustrated, we chafe at the bits of such temporal restraint; we detest having to remain in darkness or wallow in the mud of ignorance. In the attempt to relieve our frustration we deal with the occult and thereby displease God. We waste time and money on astrology (horoscopes: "horriblescopes"); we consult dream books, and fortune tellers. We stand in long lottery lines lusting after lucky lucre, scratching where we don't itch.

On the other hand, the knowledgeable Christian does not strive to discover that which God alone can uncover. Paul had no crystal ball: "I go bound in the spirit to Jerusalem, not knowing the things that will happen to me there." Oh, he knew some things: He knew the world would wax worse and worse in its wickedness. He knew the Lord was coming back again. But he also heeded the words Moses spoke centuries earlier: "The secret things belong to the LORD our God, but those things which are revealed belong to us and to our children forever" (Deuteronomy 29:29).

August 17

Except that the Holy Spirit testifies in every city, saying that chains and tribulations await me. (Acts 20:23)

The Spirit-led life is one of surrenderedness. If you ask, "Lord, what do you want me to do?" and you mean it from your heart, the Spirit will make known unto you the will of God. And what He tells you to do He gives you the power to do. When you have the assurance that you are being led by the Holy Spirit it does something to you.

This text impressed upon my heart that we should *do what the Spirit of God leads us to do regardless of the consequences!* This attitude is sadly lacking in the lives of some saints. Rather than follow the leading of the Spirit, we take what we think is the easy way out. We don't want to hurt peoples' feelings, so we let them do as they wish.

We want instantaneous results, so we take the short cut. We want convenience so we join the church that is nearby, never mind the doctrine it teaches. We want the feeling of belonging—so what if the group is composed of scoundrels! We want to be entertained, not made to think. We want revenge even though the Lord says, "I will repay, vengeance is Mine!" Bonds and afflictions are not for us.

Did you know that there is joy in obedience? There is joy even in knowing about tribulation or affliction, chains or bonds. For the vision of the heavenly home leads you to hang loose here on earth. The sticks that are thrown become rungs on the ladder of success. The rocks that are tossed become restful pillows for sleep. The lies that are told illustrate the truth of your testimony.

When known enemies confront you, God raises up secret friends to help you. When some plot, others pray. When some take, others give. When some curse, others bless. When some doors close, other doors open. When some folks tear down, others build up. That's why we are able to do whatever the Holy Spirit tells us to do.

Except that the Holy Spirit testifies in every city, saying that chains and tribulations await me. (Acts 20:23)

Recall that a certain prophet named Agabus came down from Judea, and took Paul's belt, bound his own hands and feet and said, forewarning Paul, "Thus says the Holy Spirit, 'So shall the Jews at Jerusalem bind the man who owns this belt, and deliver him into the hands of the Gentiles'" (Acts 21:11).

However, the apostle considered the forewarning part of the command to go on. For him the knowledge of the future was an expression of God's will. Go Paul! There's work to be done, a walk to travel, wages to earn, a witness to make, a war to be won—go on!

Never mind the chains and tribulations. Go on. Your course has been set, your steps already numbered, the boundary already established. Run your race. Finish your course! For when you are consumed with the idea of serving Christ all obstacles are crushed.

We too are reminded that the schedule for our lives was made in Heaven. The Holy Spirit has mapped it out for us. He knows what we need, and if we come to Him with a surrendered heart, we can make it. It is wonderful to know that the Lord has given us a job in life, some goals He wants us to attain, some task to perform. He desires we have a determination to see it through no matter what the cost.

What assurance, what inner certainty to see the guidance of the Spirit of God in the force of circumstances, no matter what! It is as if Paul said, "Yes, bonds and afflictions await me. Trials and tribulations shall be my lot. But I count it all joy. Through Jesus Christ I am more than conqueror. The sufferings of this present time do not weigh enough to be compared with the glory that shall be revealed in me. None of these things move me, nor do I count my life dear to myself, so that I may finish my race with joy. And at the end hear my Savior say, 'Well done.'"

August 19

This being so, I myself always strive to have a conscience without offense toward God and men. (Acts 24:16)

Conscience is that faculty in man that sits in judgment whether an action is good or bad. All men are born with a conscience. However, conscience was ill-affected by sin when Adam disobeyed God. Thus "let your conscience be your guide" is not always the best thing to do. Because of sin it is possible for the conscience to tell you something is right when it is wrong; or tell you something is wrong when it is right; or on occasions to say nothing at all.

Some scholars teach that the conscience is the product of acquired attitudes. By early training your mental attitude is developed so that discipline enables you to discern right from wrong. This opinion is weakened by the fact that so-called uncivilized people who have not had certain morals taught them, yet regard as wrong the violation of those principles (Romans 2:14-15).

Others believe it is not so much the influence of early childhood, but the voice of God speaking directly to the human soul, and that this is conscience. But it is not likely that conscience is God's voice, for conscience may be weakened, ignored, wholly defeated and even burned out (cauterized). The possibility of such things happening to the conscience leads us to deny the conscience is God's voice.

The indwelling Holy Spirit superintends the human spirit of the Christian, and aids the conscience. He re-orders its values, realigns its standards according to the Word of God, gets rid of humanistic concepts and enables the believer not to grieve the Holy Spirit. Through Him the saint's conscience may be pricked, and the saint is enabled to say, "My conscience also bearing me witness in the Holy Spirit" (Romans 9:1). Today understand that your Holy-Spirit-directed conscience is your guide!

August 20

Therefore, having been justified by faith, we have peace with God through our Lord Jesus Christ. (Romans 5:1)

One of the basic tenets of biblical Christianity is the belief that we come into this world at enmity, at war with and antagonistic to God. Call it total depravity, original sin, the old man, the flesh, the adamic, unregenerate nature—call it what you will! The fact is, we were shaped in iniquity and in sin did our mothers conceive us (Psalm 51:5)

This is a foundational, fundamental truth. Reject it and the Christian Church may as well close its doors. For the doctor cannot help us to the best of his ability if we do not realize we are sick; he cannot help us if we will not accept his diagnosis and act accordingly. When we acknowledge we are sinners undone and accept the blood of Jesus Christ He shed for our sin, we establish a good relationship with God, a connection we call *peace*.

Satisfied with the sacrifice of Christ, God the Father is satisfied with those who find satisfaction in His Son. We call this satisfaction, *peace*. When we become Christians the war with God is over. And that is good, for we were fighting a losing battle anyway. Indeed, a man at war with God is both foolish and crazy. And we call the end of such delusion, *peace*.

Only Jesus Christ makes available this peace *with* God. When our sins are washed away by His blood, it means God is no longer angry with us, but there is a unity of purpose and mind. Positionally (in Christ) this peace is salvation! What a wonderful concept: Peace *with* God.

Praise God today for our good relationship with Him, His satisfaction with us, the end of delusion, the beginning of harmony; and thank the Prince of Peace for the gift of faith. May we enjoy conditionally that peace *of* God that passes all understanding!

August 21

For when we were still without strength. (Romans 5:6)

In what way were we helpless, without strength? *Physically?* I read about one of the world's strongest men, "Cyclone Mitchell," who for many years amazed audiences with his feats of strength. He pulled heavily loaded wagons with his teeth and allowed an automobile to roll over boards on his powerful chest. He took catnaps on a bed of nails. And he laughed as aids used a heavy mallet to smash stones on his chest. After he gave up barnstorming, he became a part-time policeman. Then he suffered a heart attack and on the way to the hospital turned to a companion and gasped in disbelief, "All this strength and I'm powerless. There's nothing I can do." He was dead on arrival.

Were we weak *intellectually?* Hear God ask Job (38:2-7), "Who is this who darkens counsel by words without knowledge . . . Where were you when I laid the foundations of the earth . . . Who laid its cornerstone, when the morning stars sang together, and all the sons of God shouted for joy?"

In what way were we weak? *Morally?* Yes, that is the main thing here. This weakness is the inability to work out any righteousness for ourselves. We are powerless to do right and incapable of not doing wrong. We are unable to resist evil and utterly impotent as far as pleasing God is concerned. So this devotion text points gently to our "guilty inability to meet the sinless claim of the Law of God" (Moule). Man is powerless to atone for sin. So the poet was correct when he wrote:

Not the labors of my hands Can fulfill Thy law's demands;
Could my zeal no respite know, Could my tears forever flow,
All for sin could not atone, Thou must save and Thou alone.
(Toplady)

August 22

In due time Christ died for the ungodly. (Romans 5:6)

I thank God that when I was yet without strength, in due time the Lord Jesus Christ died for ungodly me. I recall one day while passing by a Gospel Mission on North 12th Street in Philadelphia, that I noticed painted on the outside wall: CHRIST DIED FOR THE UNGODLY.

My eyes centered on the word "ungodly" and it occurred to me to erase the letters N, O, and D (nod), which is the thing some people do in church on Sunday mornings. Take away NOD from ungodly and what do you have? Ugly. Christ died for the ugly! The fact that man distorts, mars, spots, dirties, and sullies what he touches reflects what is wrong with his heart. His heart is unclean, and a dirty heart leads to dirty hands. A polluted heart contaminates the environment. Bad thoughts lead to bad deeds. In other words an ugly heart moves men to do ugly. This is sin's inevitable result. And God "don't like ugly."

This truth is seen early in man's history. Adam and Eve lived in a beautiful place. There was peace, harmony, beauty, no toiling fatigue and frustration as they worked there in the Garden of Eden. There was fellowship with God. Talk about a perfect environment, here was one!

Then what happened? Sin entered and messed up things. The inhabitants were thrown out into a world of thorns, weeds and thistles; the ground was cursed (Genesis 3:17-19). And so it is today. This aspect of man's nature reflects itself in the way man "uglifies" so many things he touches.

Wrecks, trash and garbage litter our streets; vermin, rats infest our homes. Prejudice and racism adversely affect our society. Strip mining, advertisement billboards, oil spills, smog and air pollution, animals driven to extinction, unsafe streets, crime, war, etc. Yes, it cannot be denied: Christ died for the ugly. What a beautiful thought!

August 23

Knowing this, that our old man was crucified with Him, that the body of sin might be done away with, that we should no longer be slaves of sin. (Romans 6:6)

The old man is the corrupt, sinful nature with which we were born. He is the sum total of our inner being before we became Christians. He is old because we humans had him first; and born old we must be reborn new. He is man (*anthropos*) because the whole person is involved. Each of us has him. Note Paul said "our old man"—that means the old man in us. Yes, he remains in Christians!

God does not seek to patch up, renovate, re-train, educate, sugar-coat, counsel, relocate or cuddle the old man, hoping he will act better. No. He must be broken up, put to death, disintegrated, mortified, made inoperative, his fangs pulled, and his sting removed.

Otherwise all of the progress we make will serve only as opportunities for the old man to express himself in new and remarkable ways. Only crucifixion destroys him and frees us from the slavery of sin, for the believer should not be in constant slavery to the dictatorship of sin.

The words "serve sin" or "slaves to sin" are in the present tense, a present infinitive, meaning to habitually be enslaved by sin. We learn then that the crucifixion of the old man is the underlying basis for sanctification. The death of Christ was the judgment stroke of God upon the power of sin. Through faith in the shed blood of Calvary we are delivered from this power.

What remains for us to do then? Believe God. Take Him at His Word. Accept what He says about our position in Him, for remember, if we died with Him we also rose with Him. And if we rose with Him then let us live the victorious resurrection life today and every day!

August 24

For what the law could not do in that it was weak through the flesh, God did by sending His own Son in the likeness of sinful flesh, on account of sin: He condemned sin in the flesh.
(Romans 8:3)

The law's inability to accomplish its goal is not a sin; it is not evil. Rather, it is a fact of life. For what messed up the law was what it had to work with: frail, weak, impotent, sinful, Hell-bound human beings. Before our conversion sin ruled and showed its dominance in our flesh: in fists that hit, palms that smack, feet that run to mischief, eyes that lust, tongues that curse, lips that lie, teeth that backbite, necks that are stiff, shoulders that shirk responsibility, mouths that mock, hearts that are bad, and heads that are hard.

Now Christ assumed our flesh, but not its sinfulness. True humanity does not necessarily include the possibility of sinning. In this we shall be superior to Adam in the Garden of Eden, for he possessed the potential for sinning and did sin. Once in heaven we shall not be able to sin, yet we shall be human beings in the truest sense, like the humanity of our Lord Jesus.

Since fleshly living is not to be our lifestyle or daily behavior pattern, we must walk by the aid of the Holy Spirit, led by the new principle of life, the indwelling Spirit of God. It is possible to live sanctified, a living-in-the-spirit kind of life because God the Son became a Man, joined Himself to the likeness of human flesh, put on a body of humiliation, and at Calvary had our sins placed upon Him.

He who knew no sin became sin, and was smitten, judged and condemned. Here was a judgment that made it righteously possible for the Holy Spirit to live in the human body and keep reins on the old adamic nature still in us. He disannulled the sin nature's power in such a way that we believers do not have to be slaves to the old man still in us. What a wonderful thing God has wrought!

August 25

And we know that all things work together for good to those who love God. (Romans 8:28)

I ignored the "idiot light" warning that the oil level in my car was extremely low. About a mile from the Walt Whitman Bridge the motor shut down, conked out. Miraculously, in the midst of heavy traffic, I maneuvered the car onto the shoulder of the road. Within thirty minutes a New Jersey State trooper came, called a tow truck, and by nightfall my wife and I were home—the immediate cost, $71.80.

But the repair to the engine came to $2,517.00. I could not help but wonder why the Lord let me do such a stupid thing as to fail to check the oil. Then I felt guilty about blaming God, the Lord who is able to make all things work together for my good! All things?

At this point I became concerned about my attitude toward the Lord Jesus. Could Job possibly have had *me* in mind (Job 5.7). What does the Lord seek to teach me? Have I repeatedly disregarded His desire in some aspect of my life that this financial ax should fall upon my neck?

Anger, disappointment, perplexity, mixed emotions surged through my heart. How easy it is for us to become despondent, discouraged, even bitter, seeking to blame the Lord for the "misfortunes" that befall us.

Sometime later I read of a class action suit brought against the car manufacturers, and I joined in the suit. Fortunately I had kept all of the service papers showing my complaints about the oil pressure "idiot-light." God saw to it that all my expenses were repaid. What excuse do I have not to believe God's Word?

August 26

Yet in all these things we are more than conquerors through Him who loved us. (Romans 8:37)

The love of Christ is vitally tied in with victorious living—that life of the Christian where there is no known sin we have not confessed. His love enables us to endure; it supplies us with the whole armor, and shows us the victory at Calvary. His love creates faith in our hearts and opens our eyes to the future. It was His love that found us when we were lost; that opened our eyes when we were blind; gave us peace when we were at war; and quickened us when we were dead.

His love enlightened us when we were ignorant; clothed us when we were naked; and replaced our sorrow with His joy. It is this love that gives us the victory! The apostle Paul wanted the world to know that nothing can separate us from the love of God shown in Jesus Christ.

Such knowledge makes us aware of the victory we have in Christ. There is no need for us to mope around as if we are defeated warriors. Like Job, who in spite of all his troubles and afflictions, we can say, "Though He slay me, yet will I trust in Him."

If your heart is cleansed in the blood of Jesus Christ it means that the Holy Spirit lives in your body. You can indeed be more than a conqueror. Through the Lord Jesus mountainous obstacles will become molehills; enemies are ensnared in their own traps; fierce wolves become as meek puppies; and snarling lions become as cuddly kittens.

O victory in Jesus, my Savior, forever!
He sought me and bought me with His redeeming blood;
He loved me ere I knew Him, and all my love is due Him,
He plunged me to victory beneath the cleansing flood.
(Eugene M. Bartlett)

August 27

But put on the Lord Jesus Christ, and make no provision for the flesh, to fulfill its lusts. (Romans 13:14)

The believer is exhorted to be sanctified, to put on the character of Christ from the crown of the head to the sole of the foot. In this way, said Paul, we Christians will not have to worry about satisfying the desires of the old nature still in us. The possibility of solving our moral problems lies in the adequacy of Jesus Christ. When we appropriate Him by faith we have the victory.

To put on Christ, to be clothed with Him, speaks of a very close, intimate relation. Think of wearing your skin—that's pretty close, isn't it? Total submerging is the idea here of the word rendered "put on" (*enduo*). "Put on the Lord Jesus Christ" and you won't be naked, you won't be in rags. You will always be in style, looking good! You will always be among the best dressed in Philadelphia, for you will look like Him. And by the power of the Holy Spirit in your life the similarity will increase.

As time goes on you grow. You reach the point you don't have to plan or pre-plan or take aforethought about providing for the flesh or satisfying the lusts and desires of the old man. Here then is an appeal to those in Christ to renew the life with which we have been clothed. Don't fall for the gimmickry used by some churches which invite you "to come as you are," (and run the risk of leaving as you came!). Inwardly this is how we come anyway.

Don't be fooled; God *does* look at our outside (Deuteronomy 22:5). In other words, live in such a way that Christ is seen. Let what is on the inside show on the outside. Don't hide the Christ *in* us with a lot of junk *on* us. Don't let what is seen on the outside make a lie out of what exists on the inside. Let Christ be seen *on* us as well as *in* us. May the fruit produced by the Holy Spirit (Galatians 5:22-23) be exhibited as our daily garment.

August 28

That you may with one mind and one mouth glorify the God and Father of our Lord Jesus Christ. (Romans 15:6)

Man is in a predicament. Sin affects the whole person, body, soul and spirit. Sin is devastatingly holistic, touching both the material and immaterial aspects of every human life. Obviously then, man's *mind* is touched by sin. But even when we say man's mind, much more is meant than meets the eye. The different words from other languages that are translated "mind" have many meanings and thereby indicate the depth of sin's impact.

For example, the Old Testament Hebrew words for heart, imagination, soul and spirit often are rendered "mind" in our King James Version. Likewise Greek words used in the New Testament which mean knowledge, intellect, thought, will or soul are translated "mind."

We suggest also then that man's mind is messed up because man himself as a total being is confused. This old earth is one big spinning insane asylum, sick with sin. Thus it should come as no surprise that the Bible describes man's mind as evil affected, reprobate, carnal, blinded, vain, hostile, fleshly, corrupt, high, defiled and perverted.

If man's mind is out of whack, loosely screwed morally speaking, it goes without saying that his mouth is also out of line. According to the Bible man's mouth is: Smoother than oil, crooked or froward, full of cursing, deceit, bitterness and flattery. Corrupt communication and filth proceed from it; and it blasphemes, speaking great swelling words.

It is significant that the mind is put before the mouth. This is as it should be. If more of us would think before we speak, things would be much better for us. We must learn it is not always beneficial for our big mouths to give out pieces of our minds, for "a fool utters all his mind" (Proverbs 29:11). By the leading of the Holy Spirit today, may our minds and our mouths glorify God.

August 29

Now may the God of hope fill you with all joy and peace in believing, that you may abound in hope by the power of the Holy Spirit. (Romans 15:13)

Paul spoke of the ministry of Christ that is designed for both the Jew and the Gentile in order that we may glorify God together. He cited 2 Samuel 22, Psalms 18 and 117, Deuteronomy 32 and Isaiah 11 to support the inclusion of the Gentiles. Indeed, the text is a prayer, an invocation, a calling upon God to assist or bless.

Paul's prayers were overwhelmingly for spiritual blessings, not at all the emphasis we hear today upon physical healing or material prosperity. Paul was no TV Happiness Huckster, Prosperity Prophet, Guarantee Guru, Wealth Wizard or Success Seer. His prayers were for things like patience, inner peace, joy, forgiveness, kindness, love, increased faith, matters calculated to make us more like the Lord Jesus. And here he expressed a sincere desire for the spiritual welfare of the saints at Rome.

The expression "God of hope" is not used of the gods of this world. There are so-called gods, but for the Christian such idols are nothing. All the gods of the nations are idols (Psalm 96:5). Yet in Bible days mention is made of Ashtareth, chief goddess of the Canaanites, and of Astarte, goddess of love. Mention is made of Baal, chief god of fertility and nature; Chemosh, god of war; Dagon, god of the earth; and Diana, goddess of the moon and hunting.

Mention is made of Jupiter, god of the state; Mercury, god of commerce, travel and thievery; Molech, Ammonite god to whom babies were sacrificed and burned. But not a one is called the god of hope.

See how many gods we humans have! But the one true living God is the God of the Bible. Unlike the heathen in their mythology and satanic delusion, who have all kinds of gods for all kinds of things, through Jesus Christ we have the one God who is all things to us.

August 30

Now may the God of hope fill you with all joy and peace in believing, that you may abound in hope by the power of the Holy Spirit. (Romans 15:13)

Instead of having many different gods, see the One God who is also the *God of Heaven, Israel and Jerusalem.* As the God of those places He operates there, does His will, has plans for, sanctifies, rules and takes care of them. He is likewise the *God of Abraham, Isaac and Jacob, of Daniel, of David, Hezekiah, and the holy prophets.* To be their God implies He watches over them, uses them for His own praise, preserves, maintains, protects and supplies their every need.

He is also the *God of all comfort, all grace, judgment, knowledge, love, peace, mercy, patience, consolation, recompense, salvation and truth.* This means He is their Source; they are qualities that a sovereign God imparts to whom He pleases. Next we learn that He is the *God of hope*; hope is the expectation of good. To be the God of hope means He is the Source of hope, out of Him hope comes. Because of Him we have hope. He bestows hope, supplies hope, fills us with hope; instead of singing the blues we can sing the Hallelujah Chorus. Instead of crying poormouth, we thank Him for our riches in Christ Jesus.

Paul prays for the God of hope to fill the believer with all joy and peace, qualities that compose God's kingdom (Romans 14:17). God wants to do this, but some of us won't let Him. Our unholy ambitions get in the way; our desire for power blocks Him. Our bad habits shackle Him; twisted values make it hard for Him to get through. Stingy, balled up fists make it impossible for Him to put anything in our hands. Bad company keeps Him off at a distance.

Ingratitude inhibits, and hypocrisy hinders. Surely there is no need for us to live beneath our heritage, below our privilege—not when our God is the God of hope, and "our hope is built on nothing less than Jesus' blood and righteousness."

August 31

And so I have made it my aim to preach the gospel. (Romans 15:20)

"To make it my aim" is literally to esteem as an honor. It came to mean to strive earnestly to bring something to pass, and so to have as your ambition because you consider it an honor. Paul's constant ambition was to preach the Gospel. Because he knew this was his charge, his commission, he put all he had into it. He pushed; he was bold; he pursued; he traveled, suffered, labored and endured. Indeed, he regarded his apostleship to the Gentiles as a priestly ministry, a divine commission.

He said, "Therefore we make it our aim (we labor, KJV) whether present or absent, to be well pleasing to Him" (2 Corinthians 5:9). Here is an ambition to work on earth that is not adversely affected by our desire to go to heaven. Contemplation, thinking about heaven should not hinder us from doing on earth what is right. If anything, our desire for heaven should help us properly work on earth with the right motives and methods.

A third place this word is used is 1 Thessalonians 4:11: "You also *aspire* to lead a quiet life, to mind your own business, and to work with your own hands." Be ambitious to be quiet, to play it cool. Seek honor in being quiet, not noisy, loud, screaming or part of some mob scene marching on Washington, or parading around City Hall or tossing stones at the Board of Education building.

Make it your business to attend to your business. Your priority of business, of course, is your spiritual relationship with the Lord Jesus. Here then in summary is what Holy Ambition is: It is a wholehearted and energetic pursuit of the will of God, whether to preach the Gospel, please the Lord, or live a quiet life. The Lord is looking for some folks who will show that they have a goal in life, that they have holy ambition, a heavenly aim, and a spiritual purpose. For this is what life is all about.

September 1

God is faithful, by whom you were called into the fellowship of His Son, Jesus Christ our Lord. (1 Corinthians 1:9)

Paul wanted the saints at Corinth to know that God had called them to communion with Christ. The word *koinonia* rendered fellowship also means communion, partnership, agreement, sharing or participation. The fellowship with Christ is not established like membership in a club, fraternity or secret society. Place of residence, economic status, political party, skin color—such matters mean nothing here.

In Christ there is no East or West,
In Him no South or North;
But one great fellowship of love
Throughout the whole wide earth. (John Oxenham)

A church requiring members to wear the same color suit or dress each Sunday would have uniformity but not necessarily fellowship. This communion is not created by human effort or based upon loyalty to any mere man.

There is a scene where spirits blend,
Where friend holds fellowship with friend;
Tho' sundered far, by faith they meet
Around one common mercy-seat. (H. Stowell)

In a world growing increasingly mean-spirited, hard, callous and impersonal, what a joy to meet true Christians and receive a smile, a warm handshake, and feel their genuine interest in you. Indeed, people in fellowship with Christ have fellowship with one another. To be in partnership with Christ is both a present responsibility and a future honor. Fellow laborers on earth now, and joint-heirs with Christ, we shall share in His glory later. As right-now partners with Christ, remember today you're not alone, as you sing, "What a fellowship, what a joy divine."

September 2

God is faithful, by whom you were called into the fellowship of His Son, Jesus Christ our Lord. (1 Corinthians 1:9)

This faithful God whom we characterize as constant, consistent and changeless is also the One who calls, who extends an invitation to the children of men. And the call is efficacious; it is effective, accomplishing its goal. God's persuasion is sufficient to guarantee that the one called will come. God inclines the heart and mind to gladly accept the invitation. He calls and man accepts; God inclines, draws, and man believes, accepts and comes. Praise God for His gracious and effective invitation.

In some form or fashion the Lord has called all men. But if men do not respond to His general call, God cannot be blamed for not extending to them His effective call. If I offer you a brand new shiny penny and you refuse it, you should not get angry with me if I give a new, crisp one-hundred dollar bill to all those who accepted the penny.

There is some cooperation on our part, some response we are to make to this call. If we had no part in this, what would be the sense in extending an invitation? The mystery is that God is able to so move in us, even imparting faith that we respond favorably, not coerced or forced, but responding willingly because the Holy Spirit in us has enlightened and persuaded.

Some who have been called effectively and are positionally secure don't always show it practically. Called saints (Romans 1:7), sometimes we act like sinners. Called sheep (John 10:3), sometimes we behave like goats. Called to suffer because of Christ (1 Peter 2:21), some are at ease in Zion. Called to glory and virtue (2 Peter 1:3), some flirt with pigs in the pen. Called out of darkness (1 Peter 2:9), some still play around in the shadows. But praise God today that we realize we have been called with a Holy, High, and Heavenly calling (2 Timothy 1:9; Philippians 3:14; Hebrews 3:1).

God is faithful, by whom you were called into the fellowship of His Son, Jesus Christ our Lord. (1 Corinthians 1:9)

Paul was greatly troubled by what he heard concerning the church at Corinth. Divisions were there, each group contending to outdo the other, each with its favorite preacher put into competition with the other. Not only did their wrong concept of true wisdom lead them into parties and factions or cliques, but their carnality manifested itself in various other ways: Strife, immorality, indifference to evil in the church, going to court one against the other, disorder at the Lord's Table, disruption of services by tongues-speakers, etc.

Now to encourage their hearts, to instruct them in the way of truth, to admonish them, Paul wrote, "I thank my God always concerning you . . . and know that you will not come short in any gifts, waiting for the revelation of our Lord." Paul spoke thus because of God's faithfulness, because God is trustworthy, reliable. Man often proves unfaithful, but the God of the Bible is always faithful.

Years ago it was customary to give to our Sunday School students little picture cards with Bible verses. One little girl received just such a card and upon it was imprinted the text, "Have Faith in God" (Mark 11:22). While riding home on the bus, a gust of wind blew the treasured text out of her hand and through the bus window. In distress she shouted to the bus driver, "Stop the bus! I've lost my 'Faith in God'!" It seems that the slogan, "Keep the faith, baby!" was not enough to help her.

Men are fickle, up and down, in and out; if we had to depend upon ourselves to keep ourselves saved what a fearful religion we would have. Thank God He did not save us then put us on the race track of life to run on our own steam. Today trust God's trustworthiness; have faith in God's faithfulness. He cannot deny Himself (2 Timothy 2:13). Great is His faithfulness (Lamentations 3:23).

September 4

For Christ did not send me to baptize, but to preach the gospel. (1 Corinthians 1:17)

Paul does not here belittle baptism. He wants it known that baptism is important, but Christ did not commission Paul to be a baptizer (present infinitive, *baptizein*). His task was not to ritualize but evangelize. His calling was to indoctrinate, not to dip; to preach, not plunge; to instruct, not immerse.

We Baptists pride ourselves on the method of baptism, but we do well to remember that water baptism saves no one. We have a saying, "Dry devil, Wet devil"; it means to go in dry and come up wet. Without faith in the shed blood of Jesus Christ water baptism means nothing.

Paul was not like a preacher who regardless of the text always managed to make of it a sermon on baptism. Some friends conspired to get him to use a text which would not lend itself to the defense of water immersion and so requested that he preach on Genesis 1:1.

The next Sunday the preacher introduced his sermon as follows: "In the beginning God created the heavens and the earth. He made the earth one-fourth land and three-fourths water, which is conclusive evidence to my mind, that without doubt immersion is the correct mode of baptism." And so he was off again to a running start on his favorite theme.

Thank God for the gospel, and for all who preach it and live it. Rejoice today that you heard it, believed it, and publicly acknowledged it through baptism. But remember the possibility: "Dry devil, wet devil."

September 5

. . . not with wisdom of words, lest the cross of Christ should be made of no effect. (1 Corinthians 1:17)

Paul was grateful that in God's providence he baptized so few there at Corinth. No one could say he was out trying to make converts for himself. His primary task was to preach Christ, and he was not about to embellish the plain truth with flowery language, bedazzling his hearers to the point they enjoyed listening to him but did not know or remember what he said after he preached.

Dr. J. H. Robinson told how during the early months of his ministry he felt frustrated because the older folks seemed silently to ask, "Well, young man, what are you going to tell us this morning?" Faculty members from Columbia University and Union Seminary usually were in the audience, so he decided to preach on a series of profound theological topics.

One Sunday, after preaching on "The Ontological Argument for the Proof of the Existence of God", a deacon invited him to supper. After supper the deacon's wife said, kindly, "You know, Pastor, you are a young preacher and we all love you, but for goodness sake, if you take us step by step and begin where we are, we'll follow you. They taught you theology, psychology, and philosophy in the seminary, but you haven't learned any 'peopleology.'

"You've been trying to give us in three weeks what you learned in three years. Next Sunday morning, preach about something that *we* know something about, and give us just a little something new." Then smiling, her face half turned away, she added, "It would be well if you preached on something *you* knew about, too."

When you tell the story to someone today, tell it because you know Him who loved you and gave Himself for *you.*

September 6

. . . lest the cross of Christ should be made of no effect. (1 Corinthians 1:17)

Paul was concerned lest the cross of Christ be emptied, nullified, made void, deprived, divested, and robbed of its power and meaning, and made of no effect. For the central theme in his preaching was the cross. The cross story is not philosophical; it does not fit well with man's logic or concept of things. It is nonsense. Sneering, the world asks, "How can the ignominious, common-criminal death of a man named Jesus affect me?"

Sin looms large at the cross. Man's inherent disposition is to minimize sin and its consequences. Since *sin* is not so bad, why accept the cross? To tell an unbeliever that he is right now perishing sounds silly to him, especially if he has a good job, fringe benefits, a strong union, beautiful home with wall to wall carpeting, color television, late model car; and if he is a good citizen, moral, never arrested, votes at every election, contributes to charity, never beats his wife, kicks his dog, or curses his neighbor.

However, if there were some other way or method whereby men might be saved, then the cross of Christ would be unnecessary. If rhetoric and eloquence could save; if education, job training, social revolution, racial betterment societies, politics, personality, charisma could save! But no, it is only at the cross of Christ where His precious blood was shed that we find guilt and love vitally integrated, and man's sinful guilt and God's matchless love intimately associated.

When I survey the wondrous cross, On which the Prince of glory died, My richest gain I count but loss, And pour contempt on all my pride. Forbid it, Lord, that I should boast, Save in the death of Christ, my God; All the vain things that charm me most, I sacrifice them to His blood. (Isaac Watts)

September 7

For since, in the wisdom of God, the world through wisdom did not know God, it pleased God through the foolishness of the message preached to save those who believe. (1 Corinthians 1:21)

Perhaps the very simplicity of the gospel offends some people. They like to think there is something they can add to it to help God out. It is at this point you see one characteristic of the lost. Because he thinks he is smart, he labels Christianity as dumb, illogical, irrational and silly. Such an unfavorable judgment labels that man as lost. And unless he changes his attitude towards the cross of Christ he will die and go to Hell. So it is natural, it is human, for man's wisdom to see the cross as futile.

False prophets are correct as far as worldly wisdom is concerned. Christ **was** a failure from the world's point of view. What else could He be? And it is not new for men to dogmatically state that the cross is foolishness, that there is no sense to it. What folly for human beings to call gospel preaching foolishness!

We learn that by using His "foolishness" in contending with the world's wisdom, God makes a joke of the world and its lofty wisdom, and in spite of their criticism people are saved by this gospel; lives are changed dramatically, effectively and eternally. What men need to learn is this: God works paradoxically. What sounds like contradiction really is not. Through death there is life. The humble is exalted. By way of the cross comes the crown. God's strength shows itself in weakness. God's gift of wisdom manifests itself in folly.

In other words, the fool for Christ is the wise person. Christians are destined to share in and have fellowship in the sufferings of Christ. And humiliation is a part of the suffering; being called a fool by the world is a part of that humiliation. Be a fool for Christ today! (1 Corinthians 3.18)

September 8

And my speech and my preaching were not with persuasive words of human wisdom, but in demonstration of the Spirit and of power. (1 Corinthians 2:4)

Without Holy Spirit power our speaking is no more than hot air; there is no depth of conviction that saves, illumines or sanctifies, and our speaking cannot supply peace, love, joy or hope. Mere human philosophy may dazzle, overwhelm and mesmerize, but then fail to penetrate the soul of the hearer and move him to change his lifestyle to please God.

D. L. Moody said, "My friends, we have too many orators in the pulpit. I am tired and sick of your 'silver-tongued orators'. I used to mourn because I couldn't be an orator. I thought, oh, if I could only have the gift of speech like some men! I have heard men with a smooth flow of language take the audience captive; but they came and they went. Their voice was like the air—there wasn't any power back of it; they trusted in their eloquence and their fine speeches."

Perhaps an old Indian chief put it better. After listening to a high-powered orator, a man who used a lot of big, high sounding, flowery language the old chief gave this estimate of the speaker: "High wind, big thunder, no rain!" There is no Holy Spirit power where the message is not biblical or Christ-centered. Some men preach politics, making the pulpit a spring board to launch great economic enterprises or schemes of racial advancement. Some preach a humanistic moralism, do-goodism and a be-goodism, but there is no power to change lives for the better.

Preaching power is tied in with the cross of Calvary. There is power in the blood. In the cross is seen the intimate association of guilt and love. In the cross is Heaven come down to suffer Hell. In the cross man's sinful guilt and God's matchless love are vitally integrated and combined, so that no matter who or what you are, this gospel can save you.

September 9

And my speech and my preaching were not with persuasive words of human wisdom, but in demonstration of the Spirit and of power. (1 Corinthians 2:4)

One basic misconception held by the saints at Corinth concerned the matter of wisdom. There is a true wisdom and there is a false wisdom: God's wisdom and man's wisdom. Human wisdom leads to arrogance; God's wisdom stresses humility. Man's wisdom causes puffed-up-ness; God's wisdom keeps you level-headed. Man's wisdom leads to wrong ideas about the Christian ministry; God's wisdom gives the right perspective.

Man's wisdom divides the Church, the body of Christ; God's wisdom unites. And so cliques, factions, parties, and schisms existed in the church at Corinth; and Paul gave no encouragement whatever to the divisions at Corinth. He came to the city with a made-up mind to preach Christ and Him alone, knowing that the foolishness of God is wiser than the wisdom of men.

There was no ostentatious display of oratory, for there was not in him a spirit bent upon impressing his audience with eloquence. Paul would never have to be prayed for as one preacher had to pray concerning a guest minister who used such flowery language and big words that practically no one understood what he had preached. At the end of the guest minister's sermon, the host pastor prayed, "We thank Thee, O Lord, for our brother and for his ministry. But oh, Lord, help him to take a few feathers out of the wings of his imagination and stick them in the tail of his judgment."

The Greeks loved good public speaking. They had schools of oratory, special lecturers on rhetoric traveled from city to city. But Paul did not rely upon the wisdom of words, for he knew there was the danger of people becoming attracted more to the speaker than to Christ. And after all, it was Christ alone who gave His life for us at Calvary! He's the Main Attraction!

September 10

And my speech and my preaching were not with persuasive words of human wisdom, but in demonstration of the Spirit and of power. (1 Corinthians 2:4)

We are to speak the truth in love (Ephesians 4:15), but in order to speak the truth we have to know the truth. We must believe God's Word is truth (John 17:17), and so we must be taught. Instead of conferring with flesh and blood, Paul went into the desert of Arabia to be taught of the Lord. So must we study if we expect to speak with Holy Spirit power!

Nothing in the head means the Holy Spirit has nothing to work with. We may huff and puff, and try to get by on a gift of gab, but folks too lazy to study the Bible and do their homework are of little service to the God of the Bible who would not have us to be ignorant. Error is not blessed; truth is; and that truth must be spoken in love.

Without love for those who hear us, our speech becomes like sounding brass, tinkling cymbals or the cacophony created by squealing pigs running on paved streets with tin cans tied to their tails. Paul's preaching then was not in man's wisdom but in the wisdom of God. He knew that no matter how sophisticates ridiculed Calvary, only the cross of Christ could conquer the carnality in the church at Corinth.

The Greeks had their own criteria for good public speaking. Adornment and embellishment were important to them. It was not so much *what* you said but *how* you said it that counted; they were moved by flowery language, worldly show, elocution, display of knowledge, brilliance of delivery and philosophic speculation.

But Paul preached a simple message: Jesus Christ crucified, buried, risen and coming again. What a beautiful Word! What a powerful Word!

September 11

That none of you may be puffed up on behalf of one against the other. (1 Corinthians 4:6)

Purse your lips against your upper front teeth and say, "Phooey!" You are well on your way to pronouncing the Greek word (*phusioo*) rendered "puffed up." "Phooey" expresses disgust, disbelief, contempt, scorn or impatience. Likewise one who is puffed up expresses conceit or swellings (2 Corinthians 12:20). One with a swelled head is conceited; he has an unduly high opinion of himself.

Puffed-up people are very difficult to deal with and often make the most noise in our churches [letting out hot air!]. A false feeling of superiority is always a by-product of the spirit of self-inflation, and often it leads to hostility. Anyone who is not in their camp following their leader is regarded as inferior.

The fundamental cause of the divisions in the church at Corinth was the wrong concept of true wisdom. Quarreling among themselves, they formed different parties, causing all kinds of problems in the church. One cure for puffed-up-ness (inflated ego) is obedience to the Word of God (Deuteronomy 17.19-20). Another cure for puffed-up-ness is love (1 Corinthians 13.4). A third cure is Christ Himself (Matthew 23.11-12; Philippians 2.5-8). Schisms have no place in the body of Jesus Christ. He is One, and we are one in Him.

First Corinthians 4.7 is a wonderful verse to prick the balloon of pride, for everything we have has been given to us: Our physical strength, skin color, intellect, wealth, talents, looks, position, job, salvation, the Holy Spirit, etc. The basic point of this most humbling verse is **God** gave us all that we have. And if *all* was given to us, what are we bragging about? You worked hard? Good for you, but who gave you the know-how, the strength, eyesight, opportunity, etc.? Grant that what the saints at Corinth needed to learn, we have learned already.

And such were some of you. (1 Corinthians 6:11)

<u>*The Past Condition:*</u> Many times God's people are reminded of their past. Israel was told, "You shall remember that you were a slave in the land of Egypt, and the Lord your God redeemed you." Likewise the saints at Rome, at Ephesus and Colosse are reminded of their past life (Deuteronomy 15:15; Romans 5:6-10; Ephesians 2:12; and Colossians 1:21).

    <u>*The Present Contrast:*</u> But now the past has passed. Former slaves are now free. In darkness before, now we walk in the light; where there was weakness, strength now prevails, and hatred is displaced by love. Alienation is now nearness; hopelessness is now a blessed hope, for we are washed in the blood of Jesus Christ.

    <u>*The Purpose of Christ:*</u> What is the purpose of Christ in reminding us of our past? It is to fight self-righteousness. The old nature still in us does not like to be reminded of its weaknesses and depravity, for such is a blow to the Old Man's pride. We do not like to hear anyone say, "I knew you when . . ." We attempt to obliterate the past, and forget about the clay from whence we were dug.

    But knowing the depth from which we came serves to encourage us to higher heights; it also creates an impetus, a motivation, and a desire to reach the zenith. Not content to dwell on past progress, and not feeling that we have attained already, we press on toward the goal for the prize of the upward call of God in Christ (Philippians 3:13-14).

    We are moved to run, and to keep on running to see what the end will be. Another purpose in reminding us of our past is to restore our sensitivity to the grace of God. How soon we forget the magnitude of God's grace shown at Calvary! Reminding us what we were reveals what it took to put us where we are. May we be so reminded today!

September 13

Or do you not know that your body is the temple of the Holy Spirit who is in you? (1 Corinthians 6:19)

The omnipresent God dwells in each true believer. Yet God is not cut up into pieces nor is there more of Him in me than in you. The moment we accept the shed blood of Jesus Christ the Holy Spirit, who is God, comes to live in our bodies. No "tongues speaking" is required. It does not matter how we feel or what we experience.

It is a fact and we are to believe it. God in us is rich. It cost Him the precious blood of Christ, more valuable than silver or gold. God in us means we don't have to travel to Mecca or to Rome. God in us means we are special to the Lord, His possession, and His responsibility. We are never alone. Father and mother may die and leave us; children grow up, strike out on their own, but the Lord is still in us.

A spouse may abandon us; church members and friends turn their backs upon us, and exclude us from their inner circle; God is still in us. This means there is no waiting list, no standing in a long line to have a talk with Him. He is in us and there's no receptionist or secretary to put us off, lie to us, ask embarrassing questions, or have us fill out a ten-page questionnaire before an interview is granted.

God in us means instantaneous contact and intimate fellowship. Even before we speak, He knows our thoughts, and He moves before our request is uttered. No one has cornered the market on Him.

God in us is proof that we have been born again, that we are His children. Otherwise, if we have not the Spirit of Christ in us we are none of His. Yea, God in us is the down payment of a guaranteed purchase. God in us means that what the Lord started He is going to finish. What a wonderful truth—God in us!

For you were bought at a price. (1 Corinthians 6:20; 7:23)

When I was a paratrooper (555) stationed in Fort Bragg, N.C., I visited Fayetteville and saw an old slave market that had been erected in the middle of the street back in antebellum days. God knows how many people were sold from that place of auction. Thoughts of the inhumanity associated with the heinous slave trade sadden the heart.

The verb *bought* emphasizes ownership. In what was considered "sacral manumission," a slave could save his money and then deposit the price of his freedom with the priest of the temple. Supposedly, the god of that temple would protect the former slave from any future attempts to return him to slavery. The owner received the price of the slave; and the legal papers were drawn up. In actuality the religious phase was not that important.

Sin enslaves: "His own iniquities entrap the wicked man, and he is caught in the cords of his sin" (Proverbs 5:22). Christ said, "Whoever commits sin is a slave of sin" (John 8:34). So strong is sin in the soul, so deep its roots, and its shackling power, and so detrimental its influence, so deadly its results that man cannot free himself.

He cannot purchase himself from the slave market. "Having been bought" is passive; an outside force made the purchase. In the spiritual realm you cannot purchase yourself. Born in slavery because born in sin, we have to be born again. There is nothing in us capable of affecting a ransom; a sinner dying for another sinner is of no avail. The purchase must be made by Someone else, Someone without sin.

Sing, oh, sing of my Redeemer,
With His blood He purchased me;
On the cross He sealed my pardon,
Paid the debt and made me free.
(P. P. Bliss)

September 15

For you were bought at a price. (1 Corinthians 6:20, 7:23)

We were purchased with a price for a definite reason and purpose, namely that God might be glorified in us, in our body and spirit. Christians are bought people. We are not free to do as we please, but free to please Him in all that we do. Paradoxically, the slave of Christ is the person most free. Since we are His property, He owns us; therefore He owns all we possess: our body, soul and spirit. Yea, our home, pocketbook or wallet, bank account, and car are His.

All our possessions are His. Well, not quite all—the cans of beer, cigarettes, state lottery tickets, jazz records and tapes, trash-back novels and certain pills—these belong to us, not to God. Surely all that we have should reflect the truth that we are not our own.

Ephesians 4:27 warns, "Nor give place to the Devil." The world should know that your property is not for rent. When Satan comes looking for a room or place to stay, ask the Lord for strength to see to it that Satan keeps on moving! God is glorified when you take care of your (His) property for Him. If you need a hearing aid, get one.

Take care of your eyes and teeth. Get rid of that bay window! Beware of burglars. Watch out for the graffiti artists who seek to deface and spoil your witness. In other words, don't let the outside make a lie of your inside; you have been ransomed from the slave market. Live like it!

"Poor-mouth" Christians, always crying the blues, see only a garbage-can level of things; they live on the city dump, play in the back alleys and are miserable. God says, "You've been redeemed, stay out of the pawn shops. You've been delivered, stay out of Egypt. You've been cleansed, stay out of the trash pile. You've been set free; become no man's slave. You've been paid for, stay out of debt." Remember this today and live like one who has been purchased with a price.

September 16

For you were bought at a price. (1 Corinthians 6:20, 7:23)

There are some things money cannot buy. Who has money enough to stop the devastating winds of a hurricane, or to bribe an earthquake to stop its shaking? If God tells the sun to stay in its chamber, not to board its flaming golden chariot and travel across the heavens, who can pay the sun to rise and shine? Who can buy true love? Who can buy heart worship? The price cannot be estimated in terms of dollars and cents. You cannot value your redemption from slavery.

The price paid to purchase us from the slave market of sin was the blood of Jesus Christ. We were not redeemed with corruptible things like silver and gold. The word *precious* has the same root as the word *price*. Precious because it was the blood of God who became Man, priceless because of its uniqueness, His blood does something that nothing else can do. "For it is not possible that the blood of bulls and goats could take away sins" (Hebrews 10:4).

What can wash away my sin?
What can make me whole again?
Nothing but the blood of Jesus.
(Robert Lowry)

Precious then because it alone can cleanse from sin, and precious because of its expression of love, His blood is also precious because it manifests grace. May you sing joyfully today:

Savior, more than life to me,
I am clinging, clinging close to Thee;
Let Thy precious blood applied,
Keep me ever, ever near Thy side.
(Fanny Crosby)

September 17

Knowledge puffs up, but love edifies. (1 Corinthians 8:1)

An attractive teenager walked through the library turnstile and immediately the alarm went off. Stopped by the guard, she was made to pull out the books from her knap-sack. She owned a library card but claimed she had forgotten about the books. The guard took her bag, waved it in front of the detector, and then made her go back through it. This time there was no sound. When the young lady protested, the guard answered, "Do you mind if I do my job?"

After I left the library, I thought to myself, "What good is knowledge and book learning if we steal the books that give us the knowledge?" It is obvious that knowledge is not necessarily power. This is why it is sad to hear of people who deliberately leave God out of their lives. For no matter what you may know, if Jesus Christ is not in your heart, spiritually you are a dumbbell, an ignoramus.

Knowledge is a wonderful thing. We need it, in reality we cannot do without it. For ignorance is not bliss; ignorance is a handicap. What you do *not* know *can* hurt you. The God of the Bible does not want us to be ignorant. Paul repeatedly expresses God's will when he says, "I would not have you to be ignorant, brethren" (Romans 1:13, 11:25; 1 Corinthians 10:1, 12:1; 1 Thessalonians 4:13). This is why the Lord gave us brains, the Bible, the Holy Spirit, and pastors who are also teachers.

Unfortunately, sometimes knowledge goes to our heads! We become know-it-alls! We know we know and we let others know we know. Puffed up with pride, arrogant, we are blind to what is right and what is wrong. Knowledge needs love. With love to guide us, we will use our knowledge to help others. With love in our hearts, the knowledge in our heads will be used aright. True love does not puff us up (1 Corinthians 13:4); it is not arrogant, rude or full of pride. True love builds up.

September 18

Love . . . bears all things. (1 Corinthians 13:7)

The verb translated *bears* means to cover, pass over in silence, keep confidential, thus to suffer or endure. The noun form is rendered *roof* in Mark 2:4, where men brought one sick of the palsy and because the crowd was so heavy, they could not get into the house. They uncovered the roof and let down the bed to the place where the Lord Jesus was.

Love is a roof for all things. It shelters us in the time of storm. The first 32 days I spent in Liberia it rained; then there was one dry day, followed by 12 more days of downpour. Some people may not appreciate having a roof overhead until sleeping outdoors or getting soaked in a downpour is experienced.

Years ago we sang "Into each life some rain must fall." Well, precipitation comes in varied forms. It may be oppressive humidity; or rain that soaks and overflows; or hail that pelts us. It may be snow that unobtrusively, silently falls and blankets us, shutting us in. In each case it is good to have a roof that does not leak, that will not cave in, one that protects and shelters. Love is just such a roof.

Seemingly the "bearing all things" characteristic of love is despised today. Rather than demonstrate such love with a spirit of giving-in and not pushing for our rights, we would rather fight than switch, strike than negotiate, and protest rather than pray. Love is like a roof which covers us, throwing a cloak of silence over its object. This does not mean love is blind. It sees faults, failings, foibles, failures and follies. It sees shortcomings, weaknesses, idiosyncrasies and peculiarities in those we love. But rather than show annoyance, displeasure or open rebuke, love cloaks, and "roofs" them in silence. Love says, "I've got you covered!" This in turn is a sign of Christlikeness. For it was the Lord Jesus who silently passed over our evil against Him; He never said "a mumbalin word" as He died on the cross for us.

September 19

Love . . . believes all things. (1 Corinthians 13:7)

A young blade spied a beautiful girl on the high road and followed her deliberately for a mile. Finally, she wheeled and demanded, "Why do you dog my footsteps?" "Because," he declared fervently, "you are the loveliest thing I ever have seen, and I have fallen madly in love with you at first sight. Be mine!"

"But you have merely to look behind you," said the maiden, "to see my younger sister who is ten times more beautiful than I am." The gallant cavalier wheeled about and his gaze fell on the ugliest woman that ever drew breath. "What mockery is this?" he demanded. "You lied to me!" he said. She replied, "So did you. If you were so madly in love with me, why did you turn around?"

Love which believes all things is not gullibility; it is not naiveté. It has discernment and believes all that *ought* to be believed. This love does not believe a lie just to "keep peace." It has no pipe dreams or dope or alcohol trips. It is not soft on sin or deluded by an easy optimism. It looks life full in the face, and sees beyond outward appearances.

This love that believes all things is a love which dispels suspicion and goes to work, believing in laboring. It is not mere intellectual assent. The belief of love is not just in the head, it is also in the heart and in the hands. Instead of yielding to suspicions or doubts, instead of displaying a willingness to believe the evil that is heard, love offers its hand to help. It seeks to win sinners to Christ and to build up the saints.

In these days of credibility and generation gaps, political corruption (and "correctness"), misleading advertisements, when so much is false, and so many are phonies putting on a front, it is no easy task to believe all things. But the same Lord who saw through us, yet gave Himself for us, enables us to manifest this love that believes all things.

September 20

Love . . . hopes all things. (1 Corinthians 13:7)

The Bible definition of hope is the expectation of good. Paul spoke of our hope *for* the world, not our hope *in* the world. Our hope is Jesus Christ; our expectation of good is in Him. Love's hope is that which holds out in the face of adversities, without pessimism, despair and disappointment smashing it into hopelessness.

Holy optimism does not fade away because of bad circumstances. Love's hope has the assurance of final victory even when it seems there is no adequate ground for such hope. That is why Paul spoke of "all things" meaning every given situation is made by God to work out for our good.

Love's hope is not only directed vertically to God, but horizontally to man. It is a hope that expects what is best from others. Without it we would stop praying for others, shut down our Sunday Schools, cease giving to missions, and no longer support evangelism.

Like the rest of the world we would become pessimists, skeptics, cynics, agnostics, fatalists and atheists. We would become sad-sack saints in the sanctuary, overwhelmed by man's inhumanity to man. Hope then is the expectation of love to conquer, to win out in spite of what appear to be insurmountable odds against it. With such hope we continue to live the life when others live the lie.

We live a clean life in a dirty age. We continue to bless those who curse us, and pray for those who prey upon us. All this is not mere human natural optimism; rather, it is that which is born of God. We are hoping all things because we remember that the Lord Jesus kept on working with us, in spite of our hard heads and cold hearts.

Do not forget that God did not give up on us. Remember that He came through and love conquered our souls. If there was hope for you and for me, there is hope for others. Such hope, born of love, does not give up.

September 21

Love . . . endures all things. (1 Corinthians 13:7)

To endure means literally to remain under, the opposite of running away or giving up in fear and defeat. Love holds on when loaded down with burdens. It takes abuse. Taunts, gibes and persecutions of life are never returned with an unloving spirit. Enduring love is a remarkable quality today in a nation of crybabies and protesters, eaten up with pride, materialism, and the love of things, self and pleasure, rather than the love of Christ and concern for the other person.

Enduring love is not fly-by-night, here today and gone tomorrow, fresh today and stale tomorrow, or sweet today and bitter tomorrow. It is easy for some of us to become cynical over the race issue and bitter over the hypocrisy of the prejudiced; to get weary in well-doing and even decide to do nothing. But this love is no quitter; it sticks it out. Love is not a friend who says, "I'm with you to the end," and when trouble comes, says, "Well, old buddy, this is the end!"

Love does not thin out when things become too thick. Love is patient; it remains under the load, outlasting the times of trials and trouble. If love is on the bottom of your priority list, you do not see love as a way of life, a solution to problems or a key to success. Perhaps you would rather have money, political clout, a high office, prestigious title, guaranteed job security, physical strength, flower of youth, regained health, etc.

But all these will fail eventually, while love continues to march on! Surely there is power in such love. Our love for Christ shows itself in love for other saints, and overflows to touch folks who are not Christians. Love which bears all things, says, "I've got you covered"; love that believes all things says, "Don't be so suspicious"; love which hopes all things says, "We're on the winning side"; love which endures all things says, "Stick with it!" Yea, this is the love that points to Jesus Christ who in love cleansed us with His own blood.

September 22

Pursue love (NKJV) – Follow love (KJV). (1 Corinthians 14:1)

Do not let the price, the preciousness of love lead you to believe love is weak. There is power in love. Without love, oratory is sounding brass, tinkling cymbals and cacophony. Power without love is tyranny. Without love zeal becomes fanaticism. Truth without love can be harsh. Mountain-moving faith without love is nothing. Good works without love profit nothing. Yes, there is power in love.

Love works no ill to its neighbor; fulfills the law; casts out all fear and covers a multitude of faults. Love constrains us to tell others, "Jesus saves!" Knowledge may puff up, but love builds up. Love of the brethren and sisters is a sign of discipleship and salvation. Love is greater than faith and hope. Love melts the heart of stone.

Love prevented Joseph from seeking revenge upon his brothers after Jacob their father died. It was love that cured the cursing wild demoniac of Gadara and stopped him from running wild and naked among the tombstones. Love put him in his right mind, clothed him, and placed him in peace at the feet of the Lord Jesus. It was love that brought a zealous Pharisee—a blasphemer, injurious, persecuting the church—to his senses one day there on the Damascan road. It was love that cried from the cross, "It is finished!"

Follow after love; make up your mind today to pursue it and to chase after it. And you will discover that you are walking in the footsteps of Jesus Christ.

See, from His head, His hands, His feet,
Sorrow and love flow mingled down;
Did e'er such love and sorrow meet,
Or thorns compose so rich a crown?
(Isaac Watts)

September 23

Let all things be done for edification. (1 Corinthians 14:26)

A friend of mine enjoyed telling me, "Bill, we have a saying in our church that there are three ways of doing things--one, the right way--two, the wrong way. And three, the way *we* do it." Well, there's nothing new under the sun, for over 1,900 years ago the folks in Corinth were also having troubles in their church. Some people there got up in the worship service and expressed themselves all at the same time, rather than one at a time.

The result was sheer chaos. No doubt there were those who complained that the Spirit was quenched when they were told to stop. Then, as now, some people mistake their own human spirit's promptings for the will of the Holy Spirit. We should keep this in mind: The Holy Spirit will not lead us to disobey God's will. He cannot! He is God.

Far too many people disobey the plain teaching of the Bible and then blame it on the Holy Spirit. That is, they claim to have been moved by Him, at which point they would make Him the unholy Spirit. They never realize that the Holy Spirit also humbles and leads us to give in and be obedient; and if He wants us to express what is in our hearts He will open doors and opportunities to do so without our attempts to force Him.

The point of our text is clear: The people at Corinth felt they were free to exercise their gifts in the worship service as they felt moved by the Spirit. Paul argued: Is it the Holy Spirit or the human spirit? And how would anyone know? Is there indeed not a very real danger of quenching the Spirit?

Paul answered: The Holy Spirit is not the Spirit of confusion. In corporate worship we must be mindful of others; we must consider the welfare of the entire group. What helps the entire congregation matters most; mutual edification is important. Let all things be done unto building up, improving and strengthening the true church. Nothing should go on in the assembly that does not make us better Christians.

September 24

Let all things be done for edification. (1 Corinthians 14:26)

Here is another word about how to act in church. This exhortation was one sorely needed at Corinth, for there had been much confusion in the church services. Some of the saints, eager to show off their spiritual gifts or desirous of proving they possessed such gifts, paid little attention to the rules of common courtesy and order.

One saint would stand up to preach while another would at the same time break out in song; at the same time, another would commence to speak in tongues (gibberish); each would become louder in order to be heard. Whoever had the strongest voice prevailed. Imagine the confusion!

The word *decently* is elsewhere translated "honestly, properly, comely, honorably or seemly." The church, then, is to conduct its services with honor. This does not mean a cold ceremony, a ritualistic service full of God's frozen people. But it does mean to avoid extravagances, those emotional excesses which do not edify.

Next we see that all things are to be done in order, that is, in an orderly, arranged manner. Here is the Greek word that has given us the word *taxi.* It means arrangement, or division. A taximeter is an instrument for use in a hired vehicle, as a taxicab, for automatically showing the fare due on a pre-arranged basis. So much to get in, so much per mile or part of a mile—and so much to get out!

Since it is God's desire that all things be done decently and in order, and since the Holy Spirit is God, it follows that emotional excesses and disorder and confusion cannot be blamed on the Spirit. Greater is He that is in us than he that is in the world. And if we rely upon His power, strength, and guidance we will do all things decently and in order. May we do all things this day well-pleasing to the Lord in appreciation for what He did at Calvary for us!

September 25

Stand fast in the faith. (1 Corinthians 16:13)

A Command for Christians: This verse is not written to non-Christians or unbelievers. Indeed, infidels are not *in the faith.* They are outside of the faith, and stand on sinking sand; they tread the broad way to destruction. As unbelievers they are not citizens of Heaven. Their sins are still on them. Consequently, their stand is one of instability; their ground is a pit that is at the very mouth of Hell. The wrath of God abides (present tense) on them (John 3:36).

And so it makes no sense whatever to exhort unbelievers to live right until first they come to the Lord and are declared right. The declaration must come before the manifestation; you cannot *do* right until God declares you *are* right. Otherwise, it is like talking to a dead man; you will get no response whatever.

That this is a command directed to Christians is seen in the opening verses of this Epistle. Paul wrote to the Church of God which is at Corinth, to them that are sanctified in Christ Jesus, called saints. And what a church it was! There were factions and dissension; tolerance of immorality; saints taking saints to court; abuse of Christian liberty, doctrinal disputes, and the counterfeiting of the gift of tongues. Such troubles indicated an immaturity and carnality.

Many of the saints there were unable to cope with the fiery darts of the Devil *and* the dictates of their own sinful hearts. And so, many succumbed to this awesome combination and sinned grievously. Having written in answer to their many needs, Paul exhorted: Be alert. Stand fast. Act like men. Be strong! Yes, these are commands for Christians. Without the power of the Holy Spirit, no one can obey such imperatives. Without faith in the shed blood of Jesus Christ, no one has the Holy Spirit. But what God commands He empowers us to do. Whatever confronts you today—stand firm in the faith!

September 26

Stand fast in the faith. (1 Corinthians 16:13)

<u>A Call for Consistency</u>: To stand fast means to stand firm, to persevere. The text echoes the command of Moses to the Israelites. Jehovah had visited Egypt with plagues, and then redeemed the Jews by blood. For as the death angel flew by, those houses with door posts sprinkled with the blood of the Passover lamb escaped having their first-born slain. Then Jehovah redeemed the Israelites by power.

See them standing there immobilized by fear. The Red Sea stood before them, natural barriers on each side; and the Egyptians in hot pursuit at their back. "Moses, why did you bring us out here to die? We told you to let us stay in Egypt!" Moses replied, "Do not be afraid. Stand still, and see the salvation of the LORD, which He will accomplish for you today!" (Exodus 14:13).

The tense of the verb "to stand fast" supports the point of consistency. Paul used a present tense command, one that expresses action that is continuous, durative. Stand firm and keep on standing firm is the idea. I remember when I first tried to do the "dead-man's float" at Camp Streamside. Each time I would sink and would give up trying until Brother Sacher told me to hold it a second longer and I would float up again. So I did and it worked. Today I can lie on top of the water as long as I desire.

Perseverance, holding on, is much needed these days. We have so little patience; we are all in a hurry. There are quickie divorces, instant replays, push-button computer speed controls, fast food restaurants, micro-wave quick-heat ovens. And with instant soup, instant coffee, instant rice, and instant potatoes, we have instant indigestion.

Such a lifestyle makes consistency difficult. But the Holy Spirit always gives us power to do whatever the Lord commands. In His strength then, resolve today to respond to the call for consistency. Stick with it!

September 27

Stand fast in the faith. (1 Corinthians 16:13)

<u>A Choice of Christlikeness</u>: The person who stands firm or fast in the faith demonstrates Christlikeness. Christ Jesus came to die on Calvary and would let nothing move Him from His goal. Satan tempted, scribes tried to trick Him, and His own brothers did not believe in Him.

The crowds laughed at Him, folks falsely accused Him, Judas betrayed Him, the disciples deserted Him, Simon Peter denied Him, the Pharisees plotted, and Pilate interrogated. Wicked men beat, cursed, spat upon Him, then drove cruel spikes through His hands and feet. But the Lord remained steadfast; He had come to die and nothing could turn Him around until He would cry triumphantly, "It is finished!"

It is in faith that we are given the steadfastness that leads to Christlikeness. Faith comes by hearing and hearing by the Word of God. Reliance upon anything else results in error and instability. Faith here is not just a body of beliefs or creeds. This faith is something subjective, something on the inside, an inner confidence that God is able.

So let Absalom conspire, Amalek snipe, Balaam curse, Cain kill, demons oppress, Delilah entice, Demas go his way, and Diotrephes have the pre-eminence! Let Esau despise spiritual things, let the gays live in Gomorrah, let Gehazi tell lies and Goliath boast of his prowess. Let Haman build the gallows, and let Herodias have the head of John the Baptist.

Let Jannes and Jambres practice their magic, Jezebel curse and threaten, Judas betray, the lions roar at Daniel, Lot's wife linger, lust and look! Let Nebuchadnezzar heat his fiery furnace seven times hotter, Pharaoh pursue, the Pharisees plot, the people complain, and Pontius Pilate play politics. Let Salome dance to her doom, Sanballat scheme to sabotage, Satan seek to devour, Saul cast his spears, and Rehoboam split the kingdom! You stand fast and firm in the faith. And God will use every situation, every circumstance to make you more like the Lord Jesus Christ.

September 28

Let all that you do be done with love. (1 Corinthians 16:14)

Here is one more thing to be done; and like the other ways of doing all things, a present tense command is used signifying we *continue* to do them in love. Note the Old English word "charity" is changed to "love." The importance of love in the life of the believer can never be emphasized enough. God loved us and sent His Son to die for us. Now we love Him. And one way to show our love for the Lord is to obey Him.

Another way is to love other Christians. Our love of the brethren and sisters impresses unbelievers and may be used by God to win them to Christ. First Corinthians 13 makes the power of love abundantly clear. Here was the solution that had escaped the Corinthians. Their twisted concepts of knowledge had caused strife, contention and dissension.

Look at this command within its context. In First Corinthians 16:13 there is the exhortation, Watch! Alertness without love degenerates into suspicion. It is not difficult for us to be suspicious of others. To stand fast in the faith, untempered by love is to fall into obstinacy, and to be muleheaded. We then become unteachable, arrogant, ultra, super-duper self-righteous saints. To stress manliness and strength without love opens up the danger of becoming brutal and cruel, believing man's wrath works God's righteousness.

"Christianity never appears to so much advantage as when the love of Christians is most conspicuous, when they can bear with their mistaken brethren, and oppose the open enemies of their holy faith in love, when everything is done in love, when they behave toward one another, and towards all men, with a spirit of meekness and good will" (Matthew Henry). Here then are the three ways to do all things: Let *all things* be done for edification; do *all things* properly and in an orderly manner; let *all things* that you do be done in love (1 Corinthians 14:26, 40; 16:14). Edification, decent order, and love; these three, but the greatest of these is love.

September 29

For all the promises of God in Him are Yes. (2 Corinthians 1:20)

Christ is the answer to every question, the cure for every sickness, the ark of safety for every flood, a city of refuge for every fugitive, and an oasis for every straggler in the desert. Christ is the order for every chaos, light for every darkness, and conqueror over death and the grave. He is the settler of every controversy, Savior of the Hell-bound, landlord of Heaven, the peaceful end to every war, and the solution to every problem.

God, who at various times in the past, in many portions and in many different ways spoke unto the fathers by the prophets, has in these last days spoken unto us by His Son (*Son-wise*; Hebrews 1:1-2). Thus Jesus Christ is the final word in any matter. To Him our hearts can say, Amen.

He is the giver of every perfect gift; source of all truth; and bestower of every blessing. He is the joy of all salvation, Friend of friends, regulator of minds, fixer of every heart, Sin-bearer, guilt eliminator, wisest of counselors, healer of backsliders, deliverer from afflictions, bed-maker in sickness and a spring of water in time of drought.

Christ promised when you pass through the waters of adversity the rivers will not overflow you; when you walk through the fire you will not be burned; and when you walk through the valley of the shadow of death, He will be right there with you. He said that those who seek Him early would find Him. And He has kept all His promises.

He promised that although weeping may endure for a night, joy comes in the morning. He promised life eternal for all washed in His blood. When He rose from the grave with all power in His hands, He promised, "Lo, I am with you always, even unto the end of the age." He has kept every promise thus far, and my heart is assured that all the promises of God in Him are yea and amen. I believe God, don't you?

September 30

For all the promises of God in Him are Yes. (2 Corinthians 1:20)

The apostle planned to visit the saints in Corinth but did not go. Because he changed his travel plans there were those who accused him of being a "yes and no man." This interesting expression means he was wavering, unreliable, double-tongued, false, faithless, irresponsible, vacillating, untrustworthy, unstable or wishy-washy.

Such was the wave of distrust that swept through the church that some folks were persuaded Paul was indeed fickle. But the preacher protested. He argued that his *Conscience* was clear. He had acted in holiness and sincerity, and could rejoice in the testimony of his conscience. An enlightened conscience that is clear and not condemnatory is indeed an asset.

He believed there was meaning in the *Circumstances* which prevented him from going to Corinth. There are things in life over which we have no control. We say we are going to do a certain thing, then something happens and we don't do it, leaving us open to criticism, but the critics do not see God's hand. Not knowing His mind, like the friends of Job they see only the outward change. We don't know what is behind the change in circumstances, and we should believe that our God is the Sovereign of circumstances, able to make all things work together for our good.

Attention is directed to the *Converts* at Corinth. Paul said, "If I am a 'yes and no man,' then you have ignored the fruit of my ministry. If I had preached a 'yes and no' gospel, where would you be? My message has always been affirmative and positive. You who were converted under my ministry must know this!" Paul's point was: Yes and No preachers do not preach a consistent gospel. This brings us to the fourth point, *Christ.* Never mind the fickleness of man. Today, keep your eyes on Christ in whom there is no yes and no. He is the Amen of God. In Him Yes is realized.

While we do not look at the things which are seen, but at the things which are not seen. (2 Corinthians 4:18)

Set your gaze; fix your eyes on things *not* seen. Look ahead at the eternal, and do it now! The eternal has right-now roots. Build your hope on things eternal; hold to God's steady, unchanging, unvarying, powerful and immutable hand. Don't let the Devil's presence in the Garden cause you to get kicked out and miss a blessing. Don't allow Esau's anger move you to flee in fear and get out of God's will.

Don't get so upset by Jezebel's threats that you stop trusting God. Don't permit the beautiful picture of the Jordan Valley persuade you to pitch your tent near Sodom. Don't let the treasures of Gomorrah cause you to linger and be turned into a pillar of salt.

Don't let the bright lights of so-called good times bring you to a low level of life, to a pig pen feeding hogs. Don't let the visible things of earth blind you to the invisible things of heaven. Don't permit an emphasis upon the right-now block out the reality of the hereafter.

Don't let the temporal eradicate the eternal in your thinking. Don't let Gehazi's greed afflict you with Naaman's leprosy. Don't allow Pharaoh's wrath stop you from leaving Egypt land. Don't let the riches of Egypt's treasury blind you to the right-now blessings of the Promised Land. Look ahead! See the joys that await you when you've gone the last mile of the way, and sing, "Soon ah will be done wid de troubles of de world—goin' home to live with God!"

Looking at things unseen develops a proper perspective of life which in turn helps you to live a lifestyle pleasing to God. Moreover, you become like Him who looked beyond the temporal and saw you and me saved; the joy of seeing us helped Him to endure the cross, despising the shame. Today, if you will keep looking at the invisible you will experience right now some aspect of the eternal.

October 2

While we are at home in the body we are absent from the Lord. (2 Corinthians 5:6)

<u>*No Stopping of Life*</u>: To die is not to cease to exist, nor is living mere existence. Figuratively speaking, some people who are physically alive are spiritually dead. Without faith in the shed blood of Jesus Christ there is no true life. Real life, life with a purpose is to have Christ enthroned upon your heart. When He is there death becomes but a portal to a greater experience of that life already begun.

<u>*No Separation from Love*</u>: Of course, there is separation from loved ones on earth; there is separation from family, relatives, friends, neighbors, and co-workers. But this is made up, so far as the deceased saint is concerned, by meeting those old friends and loved ones who preceded in death and who wait to greet us on the other side. Death does not separate us from the love of God which is in Christ Jesus our Lord (Romans 8:38f). Indeed, there is no time gap—for to be absent is to be present with Christ.

<u>*No Sorrow with the Lord:*</u> Remember the words of this text. We saints have no business fearing death, no business sorrowing as those who are not Christians—scared to death of death. For the believer death is no stopping of life, no separation from love, and no sorrowing with the Lord.

Come, ye disconsolate, where'er ye languish;
Come to the mercy seat, fervently kneel;
Here bring your wounded hearts; here tell your anguish,
Earth has no sorrow that heav'n cannot heal.

Joy of the desolate, Light of the straying,
Hope of the penitent, fadeless and pure;
Here speaks the Comforter, tenderly saying,
"Earth has no sorrow that heav'n cannot cure."
(Thomas Moore)

October 3

While we are at home in the body we are absent from the Lord. (2 Corinthians 5:6)

In recent weeks the deaths of two close friends stayed on my mind. I found myself wondering more and more, "What is Heaven like?" As C. A. Tindley wrote:

> I am thinking of friends whom I used to know,
> Who lived and suffered in this world below;
> They've gone up to heaven; but I want to know,
> What they are doing now?

> What are they doing in heaven today?
> Where sin and sorrow are all done away,
> And peace abounds like a river, they say;
> O what are they doing there now?

Perhaps this curiosity is in all of us. Have you found yourself thinking about death, and the life hereafter? What happens that split second when you breathe out your last breath, when you close your eyes in time and open them in eternity? Books have been written by people claiming to have died; and now **brought back to life**, write of their experiences.

I don't bother to read them, for the Bible is the only valid, authentic, knowledgeable book on this subject. And God in His wisdom never allowed those brought from the dead to describe their experience. Incidentally, I am not convinced that Jonah was dead while in the belly of the great fish. No doubt folks asked Lazarus what it was like, and the others raised from the dead by our Lord were probably questioned. But no definite information is given, so that man cannot speak with any authority about the event called death. Praise God the day is coming when we shall be at home with Christ in bodies of glory!

October 4

Therefore, if anyone is in Christ, he is a new creation; old things have passed away; behold, all things have become new. (2 Corinthians 5:17)

The word *new* (*kainos*) is qualitative; difference is the thing stressed. It is in contrast to our former old sinful being and state. Once hooked up in Christ, in union with Him, the old loses its hold, its grip, or its dominion. The new covenant of Christ calls for a new man or woman, a new creature or creation, with a new name, a new robe, observing a new commandment, singing a new song, and with a citizenship in the New Jerusalem where all things are new.

This verse is basically a *positional truth.* It tells how God sees us in Christ, saved, born again. Our position or standing in God's sight is the issue here. However, doctrine is not divorced from deeds; position is not unconnected from practice; standing is not separated from state.

To act like somebody we should know we *are* somebody. And before we know we *are* somebody, we have to *be* somebody. And *being* comes only in Christ. Hear then the jubilant cry of the apostle: "Behold!"

Christ, who was Somebody, became a Nobody. From man's point of view, at Calvary He had no comeliness or form, no beauty that we should desire Him; He was despised and rejected of men. He who was in heaven came to earth; He who owned all the silver, gold, and cattle upon a thousand hills, had no place to rest His head (Matthew 8:20).

He made the oceans, rivers, lakes and creeks, but asked the Samaritan woman at the well for a drink of water. He cried out on the cross, "I thirst." Because of what He suffered we Nobodies have become Somebodies. In Him we are free, the sons and daughters of God. In Christ we are heirs and joint-heirs, citizens of heaven. We have passed from darkness into light, from death unto life; and from oldness into newness. Praise God!

October 5

Therefore, if anyone is in Christ, he is a new creation; old things have passed away; behold, all things have become new. (2 Corinthians 5:17)

Without Christ a man has missed his purpose in life. Without Christ a woman remains on a "soulish" level like the animals of her environment. Sin has so vitiated man's gifts and distorted his values, marred his image, darkened his reasoning and twisted his thinking that he calls good evil, sweet bitter, and light darkness.

Sin is so deeply rooted in our hearts that only the new birth can clear up things. "Social gospelers" are very naïve at this point about the depth of the seriousness of sin. More than mouth is needed, and shouting slogans like "I am Somebody!" is wasted breath.

The attempts of a nobody to become somebody in his own strength and efforts are fraught with danger (Romans 12:3; 2 Corinthians 10:12; Galatians 6:3). Only in Christ are we Somebody. A man who is not in Christ, who is not a Christian is a Nobody in the sense that he has no purpose in life that is realistic or wholesome.

He is a spiritual sad-sack, a Hell-bound hobo, a vision-less vagabond, and a purposeless punk. Paul admitted that before the Damascan road experience, before the Lord Jesus straightened him out, that Christ to him was just another mere man. When spiritual insight through faith in the shed blood of Jesus Christ was granted to the apostle his attitudes changed. He was not impressed by university degrees, wealth, physical strength, IQ, political power, position or authority, nationality, skin color, race or culture—the things so many of us get hung up on these days. Indeed, newness is characteristic of "somebodiness". The things we loved, felt we had to have, indulged in legally and illegally—the good for nothings of the old life which prevented us from being Somebody have been cast aside. Christ's love controls us now and in Him we *are* Somebody!

October 6

For you know the grace of our Lord Jesus Christ, that though He was rich, yet for your sakes He became poor, that you through His poverty might become rich. (2 Corinthians 8:9)

<u>Riches</u>: Before the world was (John 17:5), Jesus Christ was rich in glory. Our word "doxology" is derived from the word *doxa* which means glory, majesty, radiance, brilliance, brightness, effulgence, splendor, praise, magnificence, honor, grace, pre-eminence, dignity and absolute perfection.

He was rich because He is God the Son in the Father's bosom. He was rich in material possessions, for the silver and the gold were His; so were the cattle upon a thousand hills and the hills also. He was rich in power, for legions of angels who worshiped Him were His servants. He was rich in creation, for by Him were all things made; without Him was not anything made that was made.

<u>Rags</u>: With an immeasurable impoverishment, what the theologians call the "exinanition of His glory," an "emptying out" of whatever was necessary to accomplish His goal, He began His riches to rags saga with His incarnation, making Himself of no reputation (Philippians 2:7). What a leap—from heaven to earth!

For the Child born (Son given) there was no room in the inn, so He was laid in a manger. Foxes had holes and birds of the air had nests, but the Son of Man had nowhere to lay His head. He had no earthly riches to renounce as did Moses who lived in Pharaoh's palace. His temple tax was paid with a coin taken from the mouth of a fish.

<u>Reason:</u> Why riches to rags? He did it for us. He came to enrich us spiritually; to share with us the same wealth He Himself had originally—this was His goal. He became poor that we through His poverty might be rich. And so we are. Indeed, all who have faith in the shed blood of Jesus Christ are rich!

October 7

So let each one give as he purposes in his heart, not grudgingly or of necessity; for God loves a cheerful giver. (2 Corinthians 9:7)

Christians are to give *without show*. In Matthew 6:1-4, our Lord rebukes religious ostentation or showiness. There is no need for singling out tithers to come up first to put their shekels in a tithing box. Motives are important in giving, and we want to avoid the very appearance of giving to be seen. He commands that our charitable deeds be done in secret.

Christians are to give *without self or stinginess*. He who sows sparingly, holding back, and is miserly is both stingy and skinny. A stingy saint is a skinny, string bean, sad sack sight who does not realize how much more blessed it is to give than to receive (Acts 20:35).

Christians are to give *without sorrow*. "Give until it hurts" is not biblical. Grudgingly means literally *from grief;* and cheerful in the Greek is *hilarion,* the word from which we have derived "hilarious," uproarious merriment, gladly, and graciously. God loves the lighthearted, joyous, happy giver!

A church was raising funds to repair the ceiling and the minister was calling on members for subscription. One of the pillars of the church rose and said, "I will give five dollars." Just at that instant a piece of plaster fell on his head. Half stunned, he mumbled, "Fifty dollars!" And then the minister prayed, "Oh Lord, hit him again." Is this an example of "giving until it hurts"?

Surely as Christians we remember that our sins were washed away by the blood of Jesus Christ, and we are precious in His sight. We are heirs and joint-heirs with Him who owns all of the silver and gold in this world. Our Lord who owns us owns all we possess.

October 8

But I fear, lest somehow, as the serpent deceived Eve by his craftiness, so your minds may be corrupted from the simplicity that is in Christ. (2 Corinthians 11:3)

Listen to the humanistic philosophies of the "liberation" theologians. They say that what counts are jobs, elimination of slums, racism, poverty, etc. Of course, Christians desire the best for everyone. But Paul would say, "Aha, I see the false teachers have gotten hold of you. That whiff of their pot smoke has messed up your minds. Christ alone used to be uppermost in your thoughts, but now you hanker after the things the world loves most. You are more interested in security than in a Savior. Your loyalty to Christ has become lust after someone else."

In his seduction efforts Satan promises all kinds of emoluments and rewards for disloyalty and disobedience to God: such things as a second blessing, deeper experience, financial blessing plans, special insight, and an unforgettable emotional sensation, indiscriminant faith healing, freedom of expression, ability to speak in tongues, guaranteed success, health and wealth, etc. And Satan whispers, "Worship me and all this shall be yours" (Luke 4:6-7).

However, the secret of biblical Christianity is the pure, sincere, wholesome-hearted, simple-minded devotion to the Person of Jesus Christ, who desires honesty of purpose, not mixed motives for following Him. If we are honest in seeking to serve Him, His grace will suffice. Let no one tamper with your whole-hearted devotion to the Lord.

Let nothing supplant the true faith. Make it up in your mind to follow Him all the way. By the strength of the Holy Spirit redouble your determination to keep your mind stayed on Jesus Christ—a mind not entangled by plans which others make. A mind not influenced by church charlatans and ecclesiastical quacks; a mind that desires to see Christ and Him alone. For in the simplicity of Christ there is beauty, there is joy, there is peace, and there is hope.

October 9

But I fear, lest somehow, as the serpent deceived Eve by his craftiness, so your minds may be corrupted from the simplicity that is in Christ. (2 Corinthians 11:3)

Why not take the story in Genesis chapter three literally? If you reduce the players in the arena to symbolism, what do you make of the garden, the trees, the fruit, the serpent, the man, the woman, or of the God mentioned there? What or who do they represent? And why should I believe the explanation that you then give to me?

Really, there is no indication Paul did not take the events there as literal, historical truth. He spoke of Adam being a living soul (1 Corinthians 15:45); and stated Adam was formed first, then Eve (1 Timothy 2:13); and he spoke of the similitude of Adam's transgression (Romans 5:14). You could suggest Paul was a Jew steeped in Old Testament tradition and did not know any better. Unenlightened, he accepted uncritically the teachings of Judaism. You *could* say that! But you still would not prove that what he believed was not accurate or that it was not historical.

How far do we push the so-called mythological character of the early Genesis account? If Adam and Eve were not real, was there a real Cain or Abel? Can you adequately explain the evil in this world apart from the existence of Satan? Why do men still die? What happens to the doctrine of verbal inspiration, the belief that in the original manuscripts each word was breathed out by God, and therefore the Bible is without error of any kind— geographical, historical, psychological *or* scientific?

No, I submit to you that the Adam and Eve story is to be taken literally. Satan took advantage of Eve's unsuspecting innocence. Paul wanted the Corinthians to understand that Satan's methods and purposes have not changed. And this is information the Christian still needs to know. Be careful!

October 10

But I fear, lest somehow, as the serpent deceived Eve by his craftiness, so your minds may be corrupted from the simplicity that is in Christ. (2 Corinthians 11:3)

Satan picked his spot, his candidate, and his time. He went to Eve not Adam. For some things he works on women, for some things he works on man; and for many things both men and women are attacked. Satan recognizes there are psychological differences between the sexes.

Unisex-minded people ignore God's division of labor and functional purposes. To make money, they change fashions, seek acceptance of homosexuality, create confusion and cause chaos (Acting Up!). Satan knows the differences and desires to use the diversity for his program whether men accept those differences or not. In other words, while some men hem and haw about him and her, they are headed for Hell.

Satan sowed suspicion in his attempt to seduce. God had commanded the **man** not to eat of the tree of the knowledge of good and evil (Genesis 2:16). The order was simple, clear, unequivocal, unmuddled, consistent, straightforward, and not open to misinterpretation; it was unmistakable in purpose, explicit in thrust, and exact in goal. But you see Satan loves to complicate things.

He told a half truth, which as you know is still a lie. "You shall not surely die." Adam and Eve did not drop dead the very second they reached out for the forbidden fruit or sank their teeth into it. Not physically. But their good relationship with God died immediately. This was a type of spiritual death which resulted in physical death. And so it remains today—we come into the world as the offspring of Adam spiritually dead, unable on our own to please God, and in time we reap the inevitable consequence—physical death. This is why we must be born again through faith in the shed blood of the Lord Jesus Christ. Rejoice today that through the Second Adam you have life eternal and abundant.

October 11

My grace is sufficient for you. (2 Corinthians 12:9)

Testing and trials are permitted so that we may learn better that God is able to undertake for us. We can count on Him. Our attempts to eliminate the cause of the trouble may be rebellion against God's will. Whatever your lot, your way, your portion—whatever part God has assigned you to play, however difficult it may be—do it!

Whatever task He gave you to do, you can do it, but you will need the help of Him who keeps the earth in orbit, causes the sun to rise every morning, commands the rain and snow to fall and hurls thunderbolts and flashes lightning; surely He is able to sustain us. He who established the boundaries of the seas, the courses of the rivers, the migration patterns of birds, whales and even insects; whose eye is upon the sparrow, who provides for the ant and the bear to face winter—He can sustain you and me.

Count then on His *sustaining* grace, even as Elijah did (1 Kings 17:9). Remember too, how Jehovah took care of the Israelites. The Lord sustained them forty years in the wilderness; they lacked nothing; their clothes did not wear out and their feet did not swell" (Nehemiah 9:21).

Count on His *safeguarding* grace. You never know how He is going to work things out. As Lord of hosts He has illimitable resources at His disposal. In drought He opens rain clouds; in hunger, He sends manna from heaven; in trouble, He cools the flames; ravens do His bidding; and enemies are destroyed.

Count on His *supporting* grace. He may not remove the burden, but He gives strength to bear it. He may not remove the mountain, but He will tunnel through, take you around it, lift you over it, or make you turn back and retrace your steps. He may leave the thorn in your side to teach you that His sustaining grace is all sufficient. May we show today that we believe that God's grace is more than enough!

October 12

Stand fast therefore in the liberty by which Christ has made us free, and do not be entangled again with a yoke of bondage. (Galatians 5:1)

Liberty is a great word in American history. In the harbor of NYC, on Ellis Island there is a statue of a woman with a torch upraised in one hand and a book under the other arm. Beneath this Statue of Liberty are the words by Emma Lazarus:

"Give me your tired, your poor,
Your huddled masses yearning to breathe free,
The wretched refuse of your teeming shore.
Send these, the homeless, tempest-tost to me,
I lift my lamp beside the golden door!"

In Philadelphia these words are inscribed upon the Liberty Bell: "Proclaim liberty throughout the land to all its inhabitants" (Leviticus 25:10). Men value highly their political freedom. In fact, it is recorded that one man said, "Give me liberty or give me death!" But now the great slave master of mankind is sin. All around us is sad evidence that men are not really free.

The phony is a slave to his vanity. The deceiver is a slave to his own deceit. The smoker is a slave to nicotine; the racist is a slave to skin color and culture; the immoral man is a slave to self-indulgence. The gambler is a slave to the cards and dice; the drunkard is a slave to alcohol. The dope addict is a slave to cocaine. The homosexual is a slave to his acquired narcissistic lifestyle. Sin is a tyrant in whatever way it shows itself. True freedom is to have our sins forgiven, our wickedness washed away! Biblical freedom is true liberty. True freedom comes in knowing Jesus Christ; and it is primarily emancipation from the slavery to sin. Today, freely walk in that freedom with which Christ has made you free!

October 13

Nor give place to the Devil (NKJV). *And do not give the Devil an opportunity* (NASB). (Ephesians 4:27)

If you are truly a Christian, then by virtue of your faith in Jesus Christ the Holy Spirit lives in you. Your body is His home, His temple (1 Corinthians 6:19); it is impossible for demons to dispossess Him. Satan cannot possess (a word that means literally, "sit down in as owner or boss") you. Perhaps some of us need to lead the Spirit on a tour of the whole house, and each time we get to a room, say, "Spirit of God, come on in. Make Yourself at home."

We could open up closets and let Him look in. No harm in opening secret closets to the Holy Spirit, is there? Let Him see the money room, the bed room (Hebrews 13:4), the kitchen and the guest room. Let Him into our library so He can see what kinds of books and magazines we read. And do not forget the room where the television is, especially Cable! Then show Him the room of our heart, and say, "Sir, this is *Your* room!"

There is no better resident than the Holy Spirit. He can fill your life with unspeakable joy, and with a peace that passes all understanding. If you love the Lord Jesus, then take down the FOR RENT sign that invites evil thoughts into your life. And Christ will clean up your house; He will give you clean hands, a pure heart, a sweet tongue, bent knees, soft neck and a surrendered will.

He will keep you from falling into the pernicious trap of homosexuality; and guard you from promiscuous immoral heterosexuality! And while the house is deteriorating on the outside, it will be refurbished on the inside. So wonderful will life be that you will find yourself shouting, "All this and heaven too!" Yes, because Christ came to give us not only life eternal, but also life abundant through the Presence of the indwelling Holy Spirit.

October 14

He humbled Himself and became obedient to the point of death, even the death of the cross. (Philippians 2:8)

That humility begun in the Incarnation continued at Calvary. The God-Man could not do anything contrary to His moral nature, but His inherent, essential righteousness was no barrier to being humbled. The sacrifice at Golgotha contained a large measure of Isaiah's prediction of the brokenness of divine discipline, "Surely He has borne our griefs and carried our sorrows; yet we esteemed Him stricken, smitten by God, and afflicted" (Isaiah 53:4)

To allow roughneck heathen soldiers and blasphemous temple guards, led by a traitor, to come with sticks and swords to arrest Him like a common criminal took humility. To stand before a weak-kneed politician and be interrogated as if He were a lunatic visionary, a religious fanatic, or a synagogue quack took humility.

To be slapped and buffeted by hands that He as Creator had fashioned with His own hands; for Him who created oceans and rivers, who controls the rain that falls from the skies and the dew that covers the grass in the mornings—for Him to be spat upon, for Him to cry out, "I thirst"—took humbleness. To hear mockery, curses, insults, vituperation, reviling, and blasphemies from a shouting, clamoring, screaming mob surely required humility.

For Christ who was accustomed to hearing angelic beings in symphonic exaltation cause the heavens to ring and reverberate with the praise of His glory, to hear men cursing Him called for deep humility. To lie down upon a cross made of wood, cut from a tree, which as any fool knows, only God can make; to have cruel spikes of iron, drawn from the ore God put in the ground; to have those spikes driven through His hands and feet took humility. Surely His humbleness paid off, for on the third day He rose triumphantly from the grave; and today we serve a living Savior!

October 15

For our citizenship is in heaven. (Philippians 3:20)

There is a land of pure delight, Where saints immortal reign; Eternal day excludes the night, And pleasures banish pain.
(Isaac Watts)

We don't hear much said about Heaven these days. Could it be that we have been too much influenced by the enemies of the cross of whom Paul spoke? Their end is destruction because their **belly** is their god; their **boast** is their shame, and their **brains** are earthly minded. How we need to be reminded that we are citizens of Heaven! For the trend of the times, the emphasis of the age is terrestrial, and earthbound.

Look, how we grovel here below, Fond of these earthly toys; Our souls, how heavily they go, To reach eternal joys.
(Isaac Watts)

Materialism seeks to remove from our souls all thoughts about the life hereafter. Unless we resist this humanist approach there will be no joy in our hearts and we shall not experience the thrill that comes from contemplating being in glory with the Lord Jesus. You see, through faith in the shed blood of Christ we sinners are declared saints. Realization of what God says we are helps us to become what He says we are. Our home-land exists in Heaven. The claim we make is not that of usurpers. We are not wetbacks, fence climbers, squatters, illegal aliens, stowaways or spies. No. Having been born again we are right now citizens of God's heaven.

I never talked to God, Nor visited in heaven; Yet certain am I of the spot As if the chart were given.
(Emily Dickinson)

October 16

For our citizenship is in heaven. (Philippians 3:20)

It's too bad we don't hear much serious talk about heaven these days. What is worse, some churches are partly responsible; some preachers are to blame also. So much emphasis is put on the here and now, that our eyes are easily directed to the mundane, the secular, and the temporal.

Race advancement is needed, but its thrust is necessarily earthbound. Politics is interesting, but the political kingdom some men seek first is earthbound. And, of course, if you want to really specialize in the earthbound, then you ought to talk about Hell. The Bible teaches that Hell is beneath, down, below; it is the nether world. Logically, if there is no Hell there is no Heaven.

And if there is no Heaven, there is no need of a translation or rapture of the saints. So that when you are dead, you are done; and as Ecclesiastes (9:4) says, "A living dog is better than a dead lion." So you may as well do before you get done. Indeed, eat, drink and be merry, for tomorrow we die! And when you're dead, you're done!

However, there *is* a Heaven; it *is* a place, not the figment of man's imagination or the extension of wishful thinking. Enoch was translated there. Jacob's ladder ascended there. Elijah was transported there in a sweet chariot that swung low and carried him home. The psalmist said Heaven is God's throne. Furthermore, God's Word is settled in Heaven. It is the place from which Lucifer fell and became the Devil. Yea, Heaven is where Christ went after shedding His blood for you and for me. And there He now prepares a place for all who love Him. Yes, my citizenship, my hope and my inheritance are there. I believe in Heaven, don't you? And as I have gotten older, I don't mind telling you: Heaven is on my mind! Are you Heaven-minded, too?

October 17

I can do all things through Christ who strengthens me.
(Philippians 4:13)

The essential thrust of the phrase "all things" is the will of Christ. Paul does not say, "Whatever I want to do, Christ gives me the strength to do it!" No such idle boast is made here. What Christ wills for my life, states the apostle is that which can be done, for Christ is the spring of all my strength, the source of all my power.

It is patently impossible for a man to be empowered by God in that which God has not called him to do. The "all things" here are the "all things" God called, equipped and sent us to do in His will. The power is supplied within the division of labor for which He has called us.

He does not ask us to do what *we* can do. Sometimes you hear people say, "If you take the first step, God will take the second step." This is akin to the saying, "God helps them who help themselves." They are not biblical sayings; they are false. Walk out of the jungle of fleshly striving into the cultivated land of spirituality, and depend upon the strength of Christ living in you.

This way you will discover the joy of victory in Christ; you will see the reality of accomplishment in Him; there is satisfaction in knowing God in you is moving, working, and blessing. Stay in touch with the Source of all power, Jesus Christ in you. In Him there is no energy crisis.

He is your Dynamo. Connected with Him you can fight the good fight, run the race with patience, cross the burning sands of the desert of despair, lift up your bowed-down head, catch a gleam of glory bright, run through troops and leap over walls, worship God in spirit and truth, and like Samson, hoist the city gates upon your shoulders and spoil the schemes of Satan and unscrupulous sinners! Do it today in His strength!

Because of the hope which is laid up for you in heaven.
(Colossians 1:5)

Paul wrote the above introductory words to the saints in the city of Colosse while he was a prisoner in Rome. Our attention is drawn quickly to the value he gave to spiritual gifts. Praise for these came first, and this truth, this way of teaching sets the priority for the New Testament church of today. Unfortunately there are those who see value in the church only as it relates to what they consider is socially relevant, or has political clout, or potential economic power.

The New Testament is much more interested in the development of Christian character or Christlikeness. Thanks -giving is made repeatedly for such graces as their faith in Christ; their love towards all the believers; and for hope that is stored up in heaven.

True hope must be grounded in truth. Sincerity is not enough, for a man may be sincerely wrong. Hope based upon falsehood is false hope. Satan's hope is false, for he is determined to be like the Most High God (Isaiah 14:12-14). His expectation, desire and anticipation are absurd, an impossibility; for his deluded mind and for such a goal he shall be brought down to Hell.

Bildad said the hypocrite's hope shall perish, whose confidence shall be cut off, and whose trust shall be a spider's web. Zophar said the hope of the wicked shall be as one dying (Job 8:13; 11:20). Solomon said that there is more hope of a fool than a man wise in his own conceit or of a man that is hasty in his words (Proverbs 26:12; 29:20). Thus, from a negative point of view hope may be classified as evil, false, satanic, hypocritical, wicked and foolish. Only through Christ do we value the spiritualities of life more than the materiality. The hope held by the Colossian saints came to them through the Good News preached to them. When they heard, they believed. That hope is none other than the pre-eminent Christ; He is our hope of glory.

October 19

Because of the hope which is laid up for you in heaven.
(Colossians 1:5)

There are different kinds of hope. One is a *living hope* by the resurrection of the Lord Jesus Christ from the dead (1 Peter 1:3), a hope that gives life because as long as He lives our hope shall live. As long as Christ lives our inheritance reserved in heaven shall be incorruptible, undefiled and fadeless. Hallelujah, what a Savior! What assurance!

The writer of Hebrews (6:18-19) said *the hope set before us is* as an *anchor of the soul*, sure, steadfast, safe and firm. As Christ is in the very presence of God the Father, so are we, because we are in Christ. Our confidence holds fast within the unseen depths of the sea. There is nothing surer in this world than the promise of the Lord. And we who for refuge have fled to God in Christ have it made. We shall not be moved from His Presence.

Note also there is a helmet described as the *hope of salvation* (1 Thessalonians 5:8). The Christian soldier has his head wrapped (literally, an "around the head" helmet, *perikephalaia*) with the assurance of salvation. God wants us to know we are saved. Such assurance is not presumptuous, but factual, and the Christian soldier who is not sure of salvation is ill equipped to fight.

Hope then is a helmet (Ephesians 6:17). If you know you are a Christian, no cult, no "ism," schism or "centrism" (Afro or Euro), no reverend, doctor, prophet, preacher, pope, priest, guru, bishop, apostle, witness, or messenger can rob you of that certainty.

Finally, there is the *blessed hope* (Titus 2:13) of the second coming of the great God and our Savior, Jesus Christ, who gave Himself for us and is coming back again for His purchased property. *My hope is built on nothing less, Than Jesus' blood and righteousness.* Even so, come, Lord Jesus!

October 20

Because of the hope which is laid up for you in heaven.
(Colossians 1:5)

Some folks with Bibles under their arms live in a dream world. Their goals are unrealistic, phantasmic projections of perverted pipe-dreams, lustful longings, and Christless aspirations. But just because some people are religious and not realistic is no reason for relegating this text to regions of irrationality. Do not throw out the baby with the dirty water. A laid-up-in-heaven hope does not necessarily make us unaware of earthly needs.

But what are our priorities? What comes first? What do we feed the most? Who is in charge? Which aspect of life weighs the most for us? What are our values? We must not let our concept of the whole man blind us to the importance of the spirit. For only when the spirit is right with God, that is, superintended by the indwelling Holy Spirit, can a man or woman be a better off whole being.

It must be understood then that the Christian's priorities are different from those of the world. We used to have the same values but the Holy Spirit changed our minds. We now know that a beautiful environment does not automatically solve the sin problem. Ask Adam and Eve. We know too that blood ties won't necessarily solve the sin problem. Ask Cain and Abel. Neither is earthly wisdom the cure. Ask Solomon. Wealth does not supply the answer to all of life's problems. Ask the rich man who died and in Hell lifted up his eyes.

Physical strength is no match for spiritual wickedness and chicanery. Ask Samson. Love of this present world does not solve the perplexities created by sin and sinners. Ask Demas (2 Timothy 4:10). And the same goes for integration, civil rights, welfare, job training, etc, for when all these things in this life on earth are done away with, then what? There is still a laid-up-in-heaven hope. Praise God today that this hope belongs to you, and to all who are cleansed in the precious blood of Jesus Christ.

October 21

Because of the hope which is laid up for you in heaven.
(Colossians 1:5)

There is a saying attributed to Socrates: "A ship is not to be held by one anchor or life by one hope." We Christians have a living hope, the soul-anchoring hope, the helmet of salvation hope, the blessed hope, and also a laid-up kind of hope. "Laid up" means reserved, preserved, in store, awaiting in such a way that it can be counted on. The literal meaning is seen (Luke 19:20) where a certain nobleman gave his servants some money and ordered them to see what they could earn while he was gone. One man earned about $160; another nearly $80; and they were praised and promoted.

A third servant said, "Sir, here is your money which I have kept **laid up** in a handkerchief." He was punished for failing to put the money to use to gain interest. Again, in 2 Timothy 4:8, "Finally, there is **laid up** for me the crown of righteousness." Paul spoke with great certainty, avowing that this laid-up crown was for all who love the appearing of Jesus Christ.

For the unsaved church member nothing is laid up but a strap. As boys we played a game called, "Hot Beans and Butter." A strap was hid and we searched for it. Whoever found it would whip everybody he could catch until all of us reached home base. Do some Christians get strapped here on earth only to receive no crown in heaven!

Finally, "it is appointed (**laid up**) for men to die once" (Hebrews 9:27). Spiritualize this verse, for we all died in Adam. Now physical death awaits us. However, we shall not all sleep (die physically). God gave evidence of this in the translations of Enoch and Elijah. When the Lord Jesus Christ returns He shall find some believers alive, change them (1 Corinthians 15:51), and shall rapture or translate them. This is our blessed hope!

October 22

Because of the hope which is laid up for you in heaven.
(Colossians 1:5)

We have seen this hope we have is laid away, reserved, preserved, put in store, hidden away, and waiting in an appointed place. Where then is this depository, this place of safekeeping, this repository? It is in heaven. But is that a safe place? Does not Satan have access there to accuse believers (by telling the truth on us, not just telling lies on us!)? Yes, the Devil seeks to turn our hope into a perhaps. But he cannot touch the hope laid up in heaven.

God's Word is settled there; no thieves can break through there. No rust corrodes or moth larvae eat there. There the angels of God live, and seraphim and cherubim dwell. God's throne is there, where He sits high and looks low. Heaven! What a depository! It cannot be measured by man, who while probing space, has set foot on the moon, but still has not plumbed the deepest part of the Pacific Ocean.

Our citizenship is in heaven where King Jesus is seated at the right hand of the Father making intercession for us. What a place to have a laid up hope—where no unscrupulous lawyer can defraud; no racist politician can gerrymander it out; and no phony preacher can rob with false doctrine. Our hope is untouchable there; it is unsullied.

No treachery can betray such a hope; no conspiracy can upset such a hope; no demon can possess or dispossess this hope. No disease germs can affect it; no parasites infest it; and no aches or pains cause this hope agony. No paralysis immobilizes; no strokes or sicknesses incapacitate; and no death can destroy this hope.

No chilling winds nor pois'nous breath
Can reach that healthful shore;
Sickness and sorrow, pain and death
Are felt and feared no more. (Samuel Stennett)

October 23

As you therefore have received Christ Jesus the Lord, so walk in Him, rooted and built up in Him and established in the faith, as you have been taught, abounding in it with thanksgiving. (Colossians 2:6-7)

When we were unbelievers, lost and on our way to Hell, we walked in the vanity of our minds, disorderly; after the flesh, in the lust of uncleanness, in darkness, in craftiness, in lusts, lasciviousness, excess of wine, revelries, carousing, partying, abominable idolatries and according to the course of the Devil who is the prince of the power of the air (Romans 8:1; 2 Corinthians 4:2; Ephesians 2:2; 4:17; 2 Thessalonians 3:11; I Peter 4:3, 2 Peter 2:10; and 1 John 1:6).

We *should* walk in love, in newness of life, in honesty; by faith, and not by sight, in the Holy Spirit; in good works; worthy of the calling to which we are called. Walk as children of light, circumspectly; pleasing to the Lord, worthy of God, in honesty and in wisdom toward non-Christians; in the light, as He is in the light, after His commandments, as He walked and in truth (Romans 6:4, 13:13, 14:15; 2 Corinthians 5:7; Galatians 5:16, 25; Ephesians 2:10; 4:1, 5:2, 8, 15; Colossians 1:10, 4:5; 1 Thessalonians 2:12, 4:12; 1 John 1:7, 2:6; 2 John 6; 3 John 4).

You see from a Bible standpoint the importance of behavior. How else can it be known that we are Christians except by our walk? What other way is there to show fruit? Well, talk is one way, for the fruit of the lips (Hebrews 13:15) is acceptable to God. Talk is good, but without walk talk is a word without work. Our walk is our witness. Our walk is our work.

Our walk includes what we do with our wages and wallet; how we wait on the Lord, wag our tongues, waste time, and war against sin; what we weep, whine or get weary about. All of these help make up our walk. And the successful walk lies in the Holy Spirit. It is not to be a struggle of the flesh; our source of power is His power!

As you therefore have received Christ Jesus the Lord, so walk in Him, rooted and built up in Him and established in the faith, as you have been taught, abounding in it with thanksgiving. (Colossians 2:6-7)

Understand that our walk is our conduct, our behavior, our lifestyle. The Bible has much to say about our walk. Enoch walked with God and was taken up to heaven (Genesis 5:22, 24). Noah walked with God and was delivered from the Flood (Genesis 6:9). Abraham was commanded by Jehovah, "Walk before Me, and be blameless" (Genesis 17:1).

Repeatedly the children of Israel were commanded not to walk after other gods (Deuteronomy 8:19) or walk contrary to Jehovah (Leviticus 26:21), but walk in the laws, ordinances and ways of God (Leviticus 18:4). The psalmist had this to say about the walk of the wicked: They walk in darkness (82:5), in their own counsels (81:12); and in a vain show (39:6). Concerning the righteous the psalmist said: They walk in integrity (26:11), not in the counsel of the ungodly (1:1); in God's truth (86:11); in the light of God's countenance (89:15), and at liberty (119:45). The result of such a walk: No good thing is withheld from them.

From the prophets we learn: The wicked walk to go down into Egypt, not trusting God, but the righteous walk in the light of the Lord; and they that wait upon Him shall walk and not faint (Isaiah 30:2; 2:5; 40:31). Evildoers walk after vanity, after things that do not profit, and after the imaginations of their evil hearts. As for false prophets, they walk in lies (Jeremiah 2:5, 8; 3:17; 23:14). The ways of the Lord are right, and the just shall walk in them (Hosea 14:9).

The believer walks in the name of the Lord, and our duty is to do justly, love mercy, and walk humbly with our God (Micah 4:5; 6:8). Malachi spoke of walking with the Lord in peace and equity; and mournfully before the Lord of hosts (2:6; 3:14). It is through faith in the shed blood of the Lord Jesus Christ that we are enabled to walk in Him.

October 25

And you are complete in Him. (Colossians 2:10)

False teachers in the city of Colosse taught that since the very nature of God forbade man's direct contact with Deity, there had to be a series of intermediaries or go-betweens. Christ was considered to be but one stepping stone to God, one of many other spirits, angels, and divine beings to be worshiped and recognized as rungs in the glorious ladder to God. They also said it was necessary to perform ritual circumcision, practice asceticism, and observe special days like the new moon or the Sabbaths. They said Christ was not enough; something more had to be added.

Moved by the Spirit of God, Paul wrote: In Christ you have your fullness, your perfection and your completeness. In Christ there is no deficiency. This message is much needed today because there are saints living beneath their privilege, playing God cheap like prodigal children sleeping in pigpens. They do not enjoy knowing whose they are or what they have by virtue of their union with Christ.

Sometimes we read of eccentric misers who live in filthy, vermin-infested houses, without available modern conveniences and utilities. They live on meager diets, suffer malnutrition, and their warped minds drive them further into seclusion. They die and in their homes police discover large sums of money stuffed in tin cans, shoe boxes, coat linings, as well as in bank deposit books.

What do you think of people like that? Well, through ignorance, lack of Bible study, failure to pray, deceit of the Devil, some Christians live like misers, religious recluses, and ecclesiastical eccentrics, crying poor-mouth and living in the lowlands of self-made and self-inflicted misery. This ought not to be, for all that we need is in Jesus Christ. He satisfies. Yea, in Him we are filled full, and He desires that we live accordingly.

October 26

And whatever you do in word or deed, do all in the name of the Lord Jesus, giving thanks to God the Father through Him. (Colossians 3:17)

As usual in his letters the apostle puts doctrine first. Then, after telling us what to believe, he deals with how to act. The first part of Colossians concerns the exalted nature of the Lord Jesus Christ. He is God in the flesh, the fullness of the Godhead dwelling in Him bodily. He is the Head of the Church, and we are complete in Him.

All that we need is in Christ. Such truths should have practical effect upon all who are washed in the blood of the Lamb. His Lordship in our lives should be manifest to all who meet us. This is the setting of our text. We are to let what we believe show itself in how we act. The Lordship of Christ covers the whole of life; see this in the phrase, "whatever you do in word or deed."

The two disciples on the road to Emmaus described Christ as "mighty in *deed and word* before God and all the people" (Luke 24:19). In his sermon to the Sanhedrin recounting Israel's unbelief, Stephen described Moses as "mighty in *words and deeds*" (Acts 7:22). In defending his apostleship, Paul pointed out to the saints at Corinth that his detractors should not fall into the trap of believing he made up for his weak presence by writing strong letters.

No, said Paul: "What we are *in word* by letters when we are absent, such we will also be *in deed* when we are present" (2 Corinthians 10:11). In his letter to the Romans (15:18), the apostle boasted in what Christ had accomplished through him in *word and deed*. Finally, Paul prayed for the Thessalonians, asking God to strengthen, comfort their hearts, and establish them in "every good *word and work*" (2 Thessalonians 2:17). "Word and deed" is a combination that speaks of the total life. And today's text declares that both are required as means whereby the Gospel is heard. May we praise Him today in *word and deed*!

October 27

And whatever you do in word or deed, do all in the name of the Lord Jesus, giving thanks to God the Father through Him. (Colossians 3:17)

This verse warns us that God is concerned not only with *what* we do, but *how* we do it, and *why* we do it. Harsh as it may sound, unless Jesus Christ is at the very center of our do-gooding (or is it good-doing?) we are at best no-goodniks. And we receive no blessing from the Lord. See then that we are to serve in the name of the Lord Jesus.

What does this mean? Well, let's see what it does *not* mean first. It is not a bit of magic. Some people think that by tacking on the words "in Jesus' name" that automatically something supernatural happens, as if those words constitute some magical formula, some abracadabra or "open sesame."

Frequently we hear folks use "in Jesus' name" like a tail to wag the dog, to force God to bless them, or compel the Devil to cry, or make his demons flee in fright. Listening to a preacher on the radio some nights ago, I was shocked when a lady called in and asked him to pray for her arthritis.

He told her that she did not have arthritis, but that it was the Devil's arthritis. And so "in Jesus' name" he proceeded to rebuke Satan. And I thought to myself, if it is the Devil's arthritis, *he* sure has a strange way of feeling it.

No, it is not just the saying of the name. Doing things in His name speaks of a lifestyle, an attitude toward life. External rules, however good, are replaced by inward motivation. Our "doing" is with a consciousness of the will of Christ born of the presence of the indwelling Holy Spirit.

You know that He is present with you. "In His name" means in Him, through Him, in union with Him, in connection with Him, in His strength, in His power, authorized by Him, and motivated by Him. His very presence and being give character to the deed. Whether we eat or drink, or whatever we do, we are to do all things in harmony with what we know about Jesus Christ.

October 28

And whatever you do in word or deed, do all in the name of the Lord Jesus, giving thanks to God the Father through Him. (Colossians 3:17)

Our third devotional message from this text concerns thanksgiving. The element of gratitude looms large in biblical Christianity. Because God has done so much for us, whatever we do for Him should be in profound gratitude, and heartfelt thanksgiving. Somehow this attitude of gratitude lifts even the most menial work to the level of worship. I am learning this. How about you? What a wonderful philosophy of life—do all that you do because you love the Lord Jesus. Do it in His name, giving thanks. Do this and you will follow in the footsteps of the saints of old. Ask them.

Noah, why do you give thanks: Because He saved me from the Flood waters. Abraham? He made of me a great nation, as He promised. Job? He blessed my latter days more than my beginning. Jacob? He changed my name. Joseph? He lifted me out of a pit, out of a prison and put me into Pharaoh's palace. Moses? When I stood there at the banks of the Red Sea, I saw the salvation of the Lord.

How about you, Joshua? He kept His promise to be with me as He was with Moses. David? He was my Shepherd and I lacked nothing. Elijah? He answered my prayer with fire on Mount Carmel, and when my work was over He sent a chariot to swing low and carry me home. Hezekiah? He gave me fifteen more years of life.

Isaiah? He gave me a vision of His holiness. Jeremiah? He pulled me out of a muddy dungeon. Bartimaeus? He opened my eyes. Zacchaeus? I was up a tree, out on a limb and He rescued me. Simon Peter? I was sinking in the water and He stretched forth His hand and lifted me up. Repentant robber on the cross? He had mercy on me and opened the gates of Paradise for me. Paul? Although a blasphemer and persecutor of the Church, I obtained mercy. Surely today you too have reason to praise Him in all that you say or do!

And whatever you do, do it heartily, as to the Lord and not to men. (Colossians 3:23)

A motive is defined as an emotion, desire, physiological need, or similar impulse acting as an incitement to action. To motivate is to stimulate to action, to provide with a reason or incentive; to impel or incite. One basic, foundational truth of biblical Christianity is that it is a heart faith. God judges not only the deeds we do, but the basis for our conduct.

Is fear then a valid motive for the saint? Does fear have its place in moving us to do what we know is right? Some people do not think so; they see fear as debasing, a sign of weakness. Yet our God is a consuming fire (Hebrews 12:29), and we have every cause for fearing the judgment of God.

He cast Adam and Eve out of the Garden; put a mark upon Cain; put a curse upon Canaan; flooded the entire world; burned Sodom and Gomorrah to ashes; and brought plagues upon Egypt. He moved snakes to bite the Israelites; opened the earth to swallow Korah and his family in their rebellion; stoned Achan; broke down the walls of Jericho; and dashed Jezebel to the ground to be eaten of the dogs.

He put Naaman's leprosy upon Gehazi for lying; and struck Zacharias dumb for doubting. And whereas I have no fear of losing my salvation and going to Hell, I think there is some disciplinary value for the believer in fear, especially what is defined as reverential awe.

Men need to fear going to Hell in this day and age when it is fashionable to deny such a place exists. There *is* a Hell; and it was made for the Devil and his angels. There is a Hell just as sure as there is a Heaven. But Hell will become the home of all who ignore the claims of the Lord Jesus Christ. I believe in judgment preaching because the Bible teaches it (Romans 1:18). Warning men of the coming wrath of God is in itself an act of love and grace.

October 30

You turned to God from idols to serve the living and true God, and to wait for His Son from heaven. (1 Thessalonians 1:9-10)

Turn: Pure and simple, this is conversion, and means to turn around. We were on our way to Hell when the gospel of the shed blood of Jesus Christ turned us around and pointed our feet towards Heaven. What a change! And when there is a real change, there is a genuine Christian. Paul reminds the church of its beginnings, how the members were "converted" to God from idols. And the first thing that is true of the ideal local assembly is that it is composed of people genuinely converted or turned around.

Serve: The second characteristic of the ideal church concerns service. The tense of the verb translated "serve" signifies to serve habitually, constantly; in short, to be a bond slave, one in complete subjection. Now if we ask, "To whom are we slaves," Paul answers: slaves to the living and true God.

What is needed, however, is a fresh vision of God-approved service, of doing God's will, God's way, according to God's Word. There is the sign of the ideal church—a church made up of folks who sing: *I promised Him that I Would serve Him till I die, I'm on the battle field for my Lord.* (Sylvania Bell; E. V. Banks)

Wait: Here is the third verb characterizing the ideal church. Its tense suggests habitual, constant waiting, to be a waiter, thus on the lookout, watching, ever alert. It means to await one whose coming is foreseen, with the added notion of patience and trust. In other words, the church at Thessalonica was composed of people who patiently, confidently, expectantly waited. May these characteristics of the ideal church become ours personally, as today we turn to God in Christ, serve Him and wait for His return.

You turned to God from idols to serve the living and true God, and to wait for His Son from heaven. (1 Thessalonians 1:9-10)

Have you ever waited for something to happen, and when it happened it was not what you expected? Disappointment mildly describes what you experienced. Often what we wait for is not worth waiting for. Some folks have been waiting for their ship to come in and do not know their ship never left the dock. Or as one of our members suggested, "When their ship did come in, they were down at the bus station." Others are waiting until they straighten out a few things in their lives before giving themselves to Christ, or coming back to church. They run the risk of having the undertaker straighten them out and bringing them in.

Thank God there are some "waits" that will not break down the wagon. *Job*: All the days of my appointed time will I wait, until my change comes (14:14). *David*: Let none that wait on the Lord be ashamed . . . wait on the Lord, be of good courage; He shall strengthen your heart; wait, I say, on the Lord (Psalms 25:3; 27:14).

Solomon: Wait on the Lord and He will save you (Proverbs 20:22). *Isaiah:* Blessed are all they that wait for Him . . . they shall renew their strength (30:18; 40:31). *Jeremiah*: The Lord is good to those who wait for Him (Lamentations 3:25). *Hosea*: Wait on your God continually (12:6). *Micah*: I will wait for the God of my salvation (7:7).

Paul exhorts: Wait for God's Son (Deity); wait for God's Son from Heaven (Ascension); wait for God's Son from Heaven whom the Father raised (Resurrection); wait for God's Son from Heaven whom the Father raised from the dead whose name is Jesus (Humanity); wait for God's Son from Heaven whom the Father raised from the dead whose name is Jesus who delivers us from the wrath to come (Salvation). I repeat: There are some "waits" that will not break down your wagon.

November 1

Rejoice always. (1 Thessalonians 5:16)

The God of the Bible wants you to experience the joy of your salvation. So cheer up! Rejoice: Not in man's strength, but in God's power. Not in man's science, but in God's omniscience. Not in man's knowledge, but in God's wisdom. Not in man's humanitarianism, but in God's everlasting kindness. Not in man's money and materialism, but in God's mercy. Not in man's reason, but in God's truth.

Not man's lust, but God's love. Not man's concept of life, but in God's reality. Not in man's goodness, but in God's righteousness. Not in man's works, but in God's grace. Cheer up! For whatever the project, the Lord will finish it. Whatever the purpose, the Lord will succeed. Whatever the promise, the Lord will keep it.

Whatever the provision, the Lord will supply it. Whatever the protection, the Lord will grant it. Whatever the plan, the Lord will perfect it! Cheer up! We may not look like much now; indeed, we are poor resemblances of the Perfect Model, Jesus Christ. But hold on a little longer. We shall bear the image of the heavenly. God the Father planned it long time ago and predestined us to be conformed to the image of His Son. He is working it out right now. And soon we shall see Him as He is. And when we do, we will be made just like Him.

When we see Jesus coming in glory,
When He comes from His home in the sky;
Then we shall meet Him in that bright mansion,
We'll understand it all by and by.
Farther along we'll know all about it.
Farther along we'll understand why;
Cheer up my brother, live in the sunshine,
We'll understand it all by and by.
(W. B. Stevens)

November 2

In everything give thanks; for this is the will of God in Christ Jesus for you. (1 Thessalonians 5:18)

This is a command, so that not to give thanks in everything is an act of disobedience. Ingratitude is sin. Some people disobey because their values are twisted; and their values are twisted because they have little spirituality. Thus, some folks do not appreciate what God works out for them. When the Lord does not give them that which they demand or desire of Him, they are disappointed and often become bitter.

They remind me of Naaman who wanted the prophet Elisha to cure him the way he, Naaman, wanted it done (2 Kings 5:11-12). There are those who believe they know better than God does what they need. So what the Lord holds high they hold in low esteem. Naturally, they are not prone to give thanks for that which they do not honor.

Others disobey this command because they succumb to persecution. There are those of us who cannot take too much. Accidents, sickness, pain, and tragedy overwhelm us and so in the midst of a bad situation we cannot find it in ourselves to give thanks. Instead, we often grumble and question God: "Why me, why did this happen to me?"

The tense of the verb "give thanks" does not permit spotty gratitude. It does not suggest we give thanks sometimes in some situations, and then withhold it at other times. When we were boys we played "rings" at marbles. We would put the marbles in a large circle and take turns trying to shoot them out. If the boy who owned the marbles became angry because he was losing, he would pick up all of the agates and go home.

Some folks are like that. As long as they are on the winning side, or in charge, or in the majority, or have their own way, they appear to be grateful, to have much for which to thank God. But we are exhorted to give continual thanks in *all* circumstances. Say now within your heart: No matter what happens today, I will be thankful.

November 3

In everything give thanks; for this is the will of God in Christ Jesus for you. (1 Thessalonians 5:18)

Paul said "in everything," not all the time or every time, for the reference is not temporal. Give thanks *in* all circumstances, whatever they may be, whatever happens—this is the idea. It is somewhat broader than any emphasis upon time. If you join the times together—the minutes, hours and days—you have a basis for talking about being thankful in the circumstances of life, for some events do not come and go; some situations come and stay.

The history of the church at Thessalonica suggests some of the "everythings" are bad. Paul met violent persecution there because of his preaching. He was forced to leave town for his own good (Acts 17). Saints at Thessalonica suffered for their faith: They were persecuted, afflicted and assaulted. So the command is: Give thanks in bad circumstances.

But we should give thanks also in good circumstances, when things are peaceful, going our way, and in times of material blessing. Ordinary men and women cannot obey this command. It takes superhuman strength, and Holy Spirit presence of mind. Thus the command to give thanks in all matters is addressed to Christians, not to unbelievers.

Jesus Christ guarantees ability to do what the Word says. Because we are in Christ and He is in us, it is possible for us to manifest an attitude of gratitude in every circumstance. This is God's will in Christ. If the Lord Jesus did not empower us we would succumb easily to the evil spirit of ingratitude so prevalent in our society today.

Children are not grateful to their parents; politicians laugh at the voters who put them in office; and the more we get the more we want. You can see why it is absolutely necessary that Christ stimulate us to thanksgiving. May we do the will of God in Christ today! Whatever your situation or condition, give thanks!

November 4

In everything give thanks; for this is the will of God in Christ Jesus for you. (1 Thessalonians 5:18)

We have learned that God empowers the believer to give thanks in all situations. Ingratitude is injurious and detrimental. Inevitably, the sin of omitting good soon leads to committing wrong. Ingratitude makes for miserable living. Ingrates are often also stingy, suspicious, and hard to get along with. Ingratitude leads to idolatry. It is disobedience, for we are commanded to give Him thanks. Furthermore, disobedience reaps its own reward.

"Unthankful" is one of the evils of the last days. It is a failure to glorify God. Ingratitude shuts off future rewards and causes us to misuse present blessings. It reveals a heart out of touch with the Lord, estranged from God. People who are ungrateful to God are usually ungrateful to men.

Admittedly, what we believe is an advantage may not be what God deems advantageous. Our good may not be what God calls "good." Evil trends, opinions, speculations, and non-biblical philosophies and methods, foolish fads and fancies, all combine to cause us to lose sight of God's will to bless us with His beneficial care.

If anybody knows what is good for us He knows. When saints are full of thanksgiving they appreciate what they own, and take better care of their possessions. With gratitude comes humbleness and obedience to the Bible, honoring God's Word. The thankful believer keeps things in their proper places and puts the right values upon them.

I thank God for the mountains,
And I thank Him for the valleys,
I thank Him for the storms He brought me through;
For if I'd never had a problem,
I wouldn't know that He could solve them,
I'd never know what faith in God could do. (Andraé Crouch)

November 5

Do not quench the Spirit. (1 Thessalonians 5:19)

"Quench", an Old English word means (1) put out, or extinguish (2) suppress, subdue (3) put an end to, destroy (4) slake, satisfy. The verb is used literally and figuratively (1) of goat's milk drying up (2) "Quenched the violence of fire" (Hebrews 11:34) alludes to the three Hebrew young men in Nebuchadnezzar's furnace (3) of a lamp being extinguished, put out. The five foolish virgins said, "Our lamps are going out!" (Matthew 25:8). (4) Quench is used of judgment fire: "Neither shall their fire be quenched" combined with "their worm shall not die" depicts the dread torments of Hell (5) The "Shield of faith" enables us to quench all the fiery darts of the wicked one" (Ephesians 6:16).

Kittel says, "Arrows encased in blazing tow [*coarse broken flax or hemp fiber*] and pitch [*tar*] strike against the shield and fall to the ground, where they go out ineffectively . . . expresses the victorious superiority of God's power, which is appropriated in faith, against all the onslaughts of the Devil."

Squelch is also a good word for quench. A Perfect Squelch story tells of a sister who made it her business to criticize preachers. They were too young or too old; too liberal or too conservative; too quiet or too talkative. And if they were none of these, she always managed to invent a few things to criticize. Once after listening to a fine sermon by their new pastor, she cornered a fellow worshiper and after giving a lengthy explanation of just what was wrong with him, finally said: "You know, I just don't get anything from his sermons that I can carry home with me." Her weary listener replied, "Perhaps, Sister, you don't bring anything to put it in." God's Spirit lives in the bodies of all who have been cleansed by the blood of the Lord Jesus Christ. Let us determine today, "I will not smother, stifle, or squelch the holy promptings of the Holy Spirit who lives in me."

November 6

Do not quench the Spirit. (1 Thessalonians 5:19)

The word "quench" cannot be applied literally to the Holy Spirit. He is not a fire that can be put out, or a cheating student that can be expelled from school. He is not the mayor seated in the City Hall of your heart who can be impeached, deposed or recalled. Indeed, He is that other Comforter who came to abide forever (John 14:16).

Paul dealt with the believer's relationship with the Holy Spirit. He was concerned here not so much with grieving the Spirit (Ephesians 4:30) through slothfulness and dirty living, but with deliberate suppression, restraining the Spirit. It is a saying "No" to Him.

When we resist or reject the known will of God for our lives we quench the Spirit. To know His will on any point and resist, neglect, suppress, or act indifferent toward that will is to quench the Spirit. Once that will is revealed—through Bible study, prayer, circumstances, events, an inner perception—there is to be no debate, no equivocation, no hesitation, no procrastination, no fence-walking. Just do it!

God uses our wills as instruments of His will. He stirs up holy desires within us, enlightens us, and through these stirrings and illumination our wills are motivated to respond. Yet this work of the Spirit cannot be labeled force or coercion. When you respond, *you* respond; when I answer, *I* answer. God's effective call to my heart moves me to do that which He determined I should do, yet it is my will which chooses to do it. My integrity is not violated. Paradoxical, yes: "I, yet not I" is what the Bible teaches.

It goes without saying then that the failure to surrender to God's will is fraught with danger. But God in you helps you to do God's will, "For it is God who works in you both to will and to do for His good pleasure" (Philippians 2:13). Empowered by Him, you can do His will. You can say "Yes" to the Spirit of God.

November 7

Do not quench the Spirit. (1 Thessalonians 5:19)

Spirit here is the Holy Spirit, not the human spirit. This is not to say the human spirit is not quenched. Once a visiting minister sat behind me and raised so much noise that I could not hear my own sermon. So I stopped preaching, walked over to him, asked him to be quiet, and resumed preaching. After the service he angrily informed me that I "had quenched his spirit." He probably was right; it was *his* spirit. Yes, it is certainly possible for noble, generous impulses to be extinguished.

Some people are squelchers! There appears to be a snake in every garden; a Cain who hates his brother; an Esau who despises spiritual things; and a Balaam for hire if the price is right. There is a pharaoh who does not want God's people to be free; a Sanballat to discourage those building the wall and paying for the renovation; a greedy Gehazi telling lies in order to line his own pockets.

There is in every group a Demas in love with this present world; a Goliath who depends upon his physical size and strength, and loses his head. In every congregation there is a Judas who is disloyal; a Sapphira and Ananias cheating on God; a Diotrephes who seeks to have the pre-eminence.

All kinds of folks are in our churches. Some are self-righteous Pharisees and Levites who ignore those in need and cross over to the other side. There are fearful folks who bury their talents. There are rich folks who count their money but do not count on God. There are unwise people with lamps, the profession of faith, but no oil in their lamps. There are cleansed lepers who fail to give God thanks; and there are foolish folks who build their houses on sand. There are killers of the dream, who would sell the dreamer into slavery. There are those who squelch the spirits of those who want to do right. Be careful today! Do not let those who would quench your human spirit lead you to quench the Holy Spirit living in you. Continue to say "Yes" to Him!

November 8

Test all things; hold fast what is good. (1 Thessalonians 5:21)

The Christian's life is set under the divine scrutiny, the searching holy eyes of a righteous God. He wants us to exercise our faculties, use the spirit of discernment He gives us through the Holy Spirit, so that we may practice examining everything carefully, holding fast that which is good. Such testing is serious business; and is made all the more so by the presence of the Devil, the great enemy of our souls, the master masquerader, the peerless phony, the consummate counterfeiter.

Satan wants over the world to reign, and unruly man to tame. He seeks our Lord to defame; and puts upon God the blame. Leads the careless into shame, thus he causes mortals pain. He searches for minds to maim, for destruction is his aim. Being like God is his claim. Notorious is his fame. Surely deceit is his name, and fooling folks is his game.

In other words, the very presence of the Devil and demons, as well as oppression, persecution, and wickedness call for testing. We should not be ignorant of the devices and wiles (methods) of Satan, nor be unrealistic about the world's attitude toward the church and true believers. Prove, test, examine, scrutinize and pray over all things. Study your Bible so that you will have a standard whereby to judge, and you will have some knowledge of God's will.

Christ gives us a light that shows up dark schemes; a hammer to smash rocks of opposition, a fire to foil the flimflammers, a satisfaction that will help keep down the lust of something for nothing; and a lamp that will light up the path we tread. He who commands we examine all things gives us the standard whereby all things might be examined—His Word. Make it up in your mind today to walk circumspectly, prove what is acceptable unto the Lord (Ephesians 5:10, 15), and hold fast that which is good.

November 9

Test all things; hold fast what is good. (1 Thessalonians 5:21)

What is good? In Genesis all that God made is good. In Ezra and Nehemiah, His hand is good; in the Psalms God Himself is good. We can taste and see this is true. His name is good, and to be praised; so are His loving kindnesses, mercy, judgments and His Spirit. Yea, it is a good thing to give thanks unto the Lord, to sing praises unto His holy name. It is good for brethren to dwell together in unity.

What is good? Proverbs teaches that a word spoken in due season is good! And to find a wife is good (it is "gooder" when God finds her for you). In Isaiah, King Hezekiah told the prophet, "Good is the word of the Lord which you have spoken." Jeremiah said the Lord is good who will cause the captivity of the land to return. According to Nahum the Lord is good, a stronghold in the day of trouble.

In Matthew Christ said the fruit of a good tree is good; forgiveness of sin brings good cheer. John spoke of the Good Shepherd and of all the good works He did. Paul wrote that God makes all things work together for the good of the saint. Good is that which the believer ought to cleave to; God's pleasure is good; the purpose of our creation in Christ is good. The will to work as unto the Lord; the Law; the warfare we wage; every creature of God is good for food.

The once-for-all delivered doctrine is good; the fight of faith; our profession and confessions in the shed blood of Christ, these all are good. According to Hebrews, God's Word is good; things to come are good; it is good for the heart to be established with grace. James said that every gift from God is good!

What then are you doing with so much goodness all about you? Today when the Spirit gives you discernment and you see the good, try it out, taste it, eat it, digest it, assimilate it, and hold on to it. If you hold fast to the good, the bad will never overpower you. For we serve a good God!

[This is] manifest evidence of the righteous judgment of God, that you may be counted worthy of the kingdom of God, for which you also suffer. (2 Thessalonians 1:5)

Emphasis here centers upon the ***suffering*** that is connected with witnessing for Christ, reminding us that Christians should expect tribulation (John 16:33), for all who desire to live godly in Christ shall suffer persecution (2 Timothy 3:12). Our Lord would remind us that the world has not changed for the better since Calvary!

Can it be that we have become so soft, so in love with ease and luxury, so tolerant and broadminded, so full of soap operas and Hollywood that we have become gospel-hardened? Have we forgotten that God uses suffering to bring us to perfection? Imagine being taught that finding comfort in persecution, holding the proper attitude and outlook about suffering can be evidence that we are indeed members of God's spiritual kingdom that exists in the hearts of believers.

We reject the idea that being counted or declared worthy is based upon human merit; we do not *earn* the right to enter the Kingdom. While endurance is noteworthy, attainment to the kingdom of God is purely, solely by the grace of God through faith in the shed blood of Calvary.

We receive guaranteed, positive evidence of the fact that we have been declared worthy of God's kingdom, and that what others may do to harm us cannot undo what the Lord has done. No foe can pull us out of the kingdom. Realize then that there is no such thing as needless hardship for the saint. Experiencing trouble because we strive to please God in our lives is not in vain. The Thessalonians saints were encouraged when told that their unshaken faith moved God to adjudge them as folks worthy of His kingdom! May those of us who are first seeking the kingdom also demonstrate that we are willing to suffer for the kingdom!

November 11

[This is] manifest evidence of the righteous judgment of God, that you may be counted worthy of the kingdom of God, for which you also suffer. (2 Thessalonians 1:5)

The word "kingdom" is mentioned only once in Second Thessalonians, but occurs more than 150 times elsewhere in the New Testament. It is not easy to interpret the phrase "Kingdom of God," one of the most important concepts of the Bible. Sometimes it means (1) the universal and eternal aspect (2) an earthly kingdom promised to David and realized by Christ who will rule in Jerusalem in the age of the Millennial Kingdom (3) that which we call Christendom, the kingdom in mystery (4) that final kingdom which God the Son gives back to God the Father.

Our present text deals with that spiritual kingdom existing in the hearts of men and women for which they have suffered persecutions and tribulations. Three things are said about this kingdom; in addition to *suffering* there is the matter of *seeing* it: "Unless one is born again (from above), he cannot see the kingdom of God" (John 3:3). The tense means he cannot see it at any time. Only a spiritual renewal will open blind eyes, a step called regeneration, a creative act performed by God in the soul of the man, woman, boy or girl who accepts the shed blood of Jesus Christ.

There is no other way! Education, culture, good works, money—will not help a man to see God's kingdom. Flesh and blood, man in his natural state, cannot see, let alone inherit God's kingdom. He has no idea what God's kingdom is like. No one automatically knows the things of God. They must be revealed by the Holy Spirit. To *see* means to understand by sharing, to have a conception. It is not superficial, but a deep inward change of heart based upon faith in the finished work of the Lord Jesus. Have you had a preview of the Kingdom of God?

November 12

[This is] manifest evidence of the righteous judgment of God, that you may be counted worthy of the kingdom of God, for which you also suffer. (2 Thessalonians 1:5)

Not only is there ***suffering*** and ***seeing*** connected with this kingdom of God, but thirdly there is the emphasis on ***seeking*** the kingdom. We read, "But seek first the kingdom of God and His righteousness" (Matthew 6:33). The tense of the verb translated *to seek* (require, desire, question) demands continued action.

To seek *first* means make this your great object, your number one reason, subjecting everything to this first cause. This yearning, hungering, striving involves clean living (1 Corinthians 6:9-10). To seek then means to strive to become more like the Lord Jesus, for holiness of heart and purity of life are required by God of all those who profess to be subjects of this spiritual kingdom.

"His righteousness" is connected with the seeking first of the kingdom, meaning spiritual purity is a part of such seeking. The necessities of life—food, clothing, shelter are important, but if we are not careful we become preoccupied with them. And as a nation we become overly concerned with automobiles, fashions, beautiful homes, jobs, skin color, political office, prestige, sex and money. But the kingdom of God is not eating and drinking, but righteousness, and peace and joy in the Holy Spirit (Romans 14:17).

The Church must keep this ever in mind, for if we fail who will put first God's kingdom? Will secret societies or race advancement organizations or political parties? No. The body of Christ must seek first God's kingdom, and do it by actually putting spiritual things first, by living a clean life, by witnessing and telling the story of the finished work of the Lord Jesus Christ at Calvary.

November 13

It is a righteous thing with God to repay with tribulation those who trouble you, and to give you who are troubled rest with us when the Lord Jesus is revealed from heaven with His mighty angels. (2 Thessalonians 1:6-7)

Rascality from the Synagogue: When Paul visited a city he would go first to the synagogue to preach. In Thessalonica the unbelievers became so angry with jealousy that they hired some ruffians and rascals to start a riot in the town. Jason's house was assaulted in the search for Paul, but friends had slipped him and Silas out of the city. The apostle then went on to Berea where the noble folks there more readily received the Good News. When it was discovered he was in Berea, his enemies came even there to stir up strife. The Devil is a busy person, isn't he? And of all wicked people the religious wicked are the worst.

Recompense for the Sinner: Paul wrote back to the saints at Thessalonica who were being persecuted, and commended them for their patience and faith. He pointed out to them that retribution is righteous. God knew their troubles and He would eventually trouble those who were troublesome.

Rest for the Saved: The Lord is going to give rest to the suffering saints. Originally the word translated "relief" signified the slackening of a taut bow string. It is like stretching a large rubber band. While stretched it is under tension; release it and it is at rest. So the rest promised is relief from tension, the very opposite of affliction.

Revelation of the Savior: When shall we receive this rest, this relief? When will the wicked cease from troubling? The time element is wrapped up in the unveiling of Jesus Christ, at present hidden from the world's view. But He is coming back: First to snatch up His Church; later, after Tribulation on this earth, He is coming from heaven to this earth with angels, in flaming fire, and with trumpet blast. Be assured today that Jesus Christ is a righteous Judge.

Now may the Lord of peace Himself give you peace always in every way. The Lord be with you all. (2 Thessalonians 3:16)

I once preached from this text the following outline: (1) The Church must Proclaim Its Definition of Peace (2) The Church Must Preach Christ the Dispenser of Peace (3) The Church Must Practice the Demonstration of Peace. At the time I was impressed by the words "in every way" (in all ways, in every circumstance, by all means, whatever comes).

We ought to have His peace *wherever we go and under all circumstances.* His peace is unchanging, no matter how bad things seem, and my, what terrible situations believers sometimes encounter: Despised by Cain, seduced by the Potiphar's wife, deceived by the king of Sodom, sold into slavery by jealous brothers, chased after by the Pharaoh's army, murmured against by ingrates, and tricked by Jannes and Jambres, and spears thrown at us by king Saul.

We are conspired against by Absalom, challenged by giants like Goliath, enticed by Delilah, lied to by Gehazi, captured by cruel Chaldeans, mocked by the Rabshakeh, falsely accused by Irijah, held in contempt by Amaziah, and schemed against by Haman. We are threatened by Jezebel, cursed by Shimei, plotted against by Sanballat, cast into a fiery furnace and into the lions' den by envious idolaters.

We flee murderous Herod; suffer the controversy of hypocritical Pharisees, hated by Herodias, persecuted by Alexander the coppersmith, betrayed by Judas, disdained by Diotrephes, made a laughing stock and spectacle by the world, imprisoned by the unbelieving, spat upon and jeered by the faithless, oppressed by demons, and attacked by Satan! In every adversity of life, the Lord's peace is ours for the taking. The Prince of Peace stands with nail-pierced hands pleading with us to partake of that peace that passes all understanding. Take it! And show the world that the Lord *in* you is indeed *with* you.

November 15

Pray . . . without wrath and doubting. (1 Timothy 2:8)

Let your prayer be without wrath, apart from anger. Some people misuse their privilege of prayer. They have a grudge or want to tell somebody off. Sometimes they even forewarn you with, "I'm going to *pray* for you!" They remind me of a little boy who had misbehaved, and was spanked and sent to his room without dinner. His parents relented, and let him eat in the kitchen. They requested he say grace, and he said, "Lord, I thank Thee for preparing a table before me in the presence of mine enemies."

There is such a thing as righteous indignation. If we don't hate sin there is something amiss in our lives. Paul was moved to write: "Be angry and do not sin. Do not let the sun go down on your wrath" (Ephesians 4:26). The anger in today's text is not that sudden, explosive outburst which is more or less temporary, like a straw-fire quick to blaze up and quick to die out. No. Here it is settled, a habit of mind, what we call the "slow burn."

With this anger comes the spirit of vindictiveness, wanting to get even, pay back, revenge, seeking vengeance, maintaining an unforgiving spirit, the kind that says, "I'll get you if it's the last thing I do!" And sometimes it is the last thing. "So then, my beloved brethren, let every man be swift to hear, slow to speak, slow to wrath; for the wrath of man does not produce the righteousness of God" (James 1:19-20). Our prayers should be without doubting and free of all irritation towards others.

From the original language the word *dialogue* is translated "doubting." Literally, it means a conversation, a colloquy between two or more persons. Doubting here means the thinking of a man deliberating with himself. Praying in this manner, we hesitate and show a lack of confidence in God. May our prayer life be strengthened today. And remember: "To say my prayers is not to pray, unless I mean the words I say."

November 16

He will manifest in His own time, He who is the blessed and only Potentate, the King of kings and Lord of lords.
(1 Timothy 6:15)

Schedule: The expression "in His own time" means "proper time" and is identical with "in due time" (1 Timothy 2:6; Titus 1:3). The writer of Ecclesiastes says, "To everything there is a season, a time for every purpose under heaven" (3:1-8). God's sure purpose, His certain goal, points to what is called the fullness of time. When the fullness of time was come, God sent forth His Son (Galatians 4:4). In His own good time God will move, not pressured by men or coerced by the Devil. He shall make known whatever it is He desires and when it is manifested we will joyfully say, "God was right on time!"

Sovereign: The word *Sovereign* or Potentate (*dunastes*) means one who can do something; who has a sense of power, might, or dominion. He who is powerful exercising authority and rule is the potentate, Almighty God, the blessed Controller and Ruler of all things.

Supreme: In Revelation 17:14, it is definitely Christ who is described as "the Lamb" who shall overcome them, "for He is Lord of lords, and King of kings." Revelation 19:16 states, "And He has on His robe and on His thigh a name written: KING OF KINGS, AND LORD OF LORDS." This interesting expression speaks of Christ's supremacy over all earthly rulers.

Look at it this way: Suppose someone called you a mule of mules, how would you feel? You would resent it, wouldn't you? If someone called me a fool of fools, I would know that it is an expression of the superlative. So it is here. Jesus Christ is King of all others who act as kings; He is Lord of all others who act as lords. He is infinitely superior and supreme. There is none greater than He.

November 17

For I know whom I have believed and am persuaded that He is able to keep what I have committed to Him until that Day. (2 Timothy 1:12)

Throughout the centuries God has expressed His desire that He wants us to know that He is the God who would not have us to be ignorant. In many different ways He gave believers assurance: For ***Noah*** He put a rainbow in the sky; He made ***Joseph's*** dreams come true, and convinced ***Jacob*** by wrestling with him and crippling him; for ***Moses***, He turned the rod into a snake.

He assured the ***Israelites*** and rained down manna and quail from heaven; for ***Joshua*** He made the sun stand still upon Gibeon, and the moon in the valley of Aijalon; ***Gideon's*** fleece was first wet and then dry. ***Samson's*** strength was restored; ***Solomon*** was granted great wisdom; and fire came down from heaven for ***Elijah.***

He told the ***Samaritan Woman*** at the well about her past life; to ***Thomas*** He said, "Reach here your finger and touch Me." ***Paul*** was assured by his Damascus Road experience. All the saints throughout the ages received assurance. Let us too accept what God has offered. May we too come out of the dark shadows of doubt, ignorance and uncertainty, and walk in the bright assurance of God's awareness, authority and assurance. Begin this day with the positive knowledge that with faith in Christ you are on good terms with God.

I know not why God's wondrous grace
To me He hath made known,
Nor why, unworthy, Christ in love
Redeemed me for His own.
But "I know whom I have believed,
And am persuaded that He is able
To keep that which I've committed
Unto Him against that day." (Daniel W. Whittle)

322

November 18

You therefore must endure hardship as a good soldier of Jesus Christ. (2 Timothy 2:3)

Equipment: In 1946 I was a member of the all-Black 555th Infantry Paratroop Battalion. If I had had to pay for my own parachutes I never would have jumped. But Uncle Sam was my Supply Sergeant. So it is in the spiritual battle of life. The Captain of our Salvation supplies us with the necessary armor enabling us to be well-equipped.

Along with the belt of truth, we are given the breastplate of righteousness, gospel shoes, the shield of faith, the helmet of salvation, and the sword of the Spirit, the Bible. Because the battle is primarily spiritual, we need those pieces of armor (Ephesians 6:12-17).

Entanglement: In Second Timothy 2:4, we are warned that no man that wars entangles himself with the affairs of this life, that he may please Him who has chosen him to be a soldier. Caught up in civilian affairs, some church members merely tip their hats to God *when* they come to church. They are too busy for their own spiritual good.

Endurance: In Second Timothy 2:3 we are exhorted to endure hardness as good soldiers of Jesus Christ, to suffer hardships together with one another. Whatever the affliction, whatever the wounds suffered in battle, Christian soldiers are to endure. We are to hold on, persevere, and stick it out; for this, all of us need more patience.

When we endure we strike fear into the hearts of the enemy. When they throw their best at us and we keep on fighting, it disheartens them. What kind of Christian soldier will you be today? Remember, there are battles to fight, enemies to vanquish, foes to capture, castles to bring down, evil plans to disrupt, and territory to claim for Christ. There is a blood-stained banner to be lifted high, for we are on the battlefield for our Lord!

November 19

. . . that he may please Him who enlisted him as a soldier. (2 Timothy 2:4)

Crowns and thrones may perish, Kingdoms rise and wane,
But the Church of Jesus Constant will remain;
Gates of hell can never 'Gainst that Church prevail;
We have Christ's own promise, And that cannot fail.
Onward, Christian soldiers, marching as to war,
With the cross of Jesus going on before!
(S. Baring-Gould)

Our ability as Christians to suffer hardship yet keep on fighting the good fight demoralizes the enemy, takes the wind out of his sails, and is an evident token of the righteous judgment of God and the destruction of all who hate Christ. However, some people curse God when they suffer. Some turn their backs on the church, and complain, murmur, blame others, question God and soon give up.

It is true that the Devil is a dirty fighter, a sneaky "sucker" puncher, whose tactics are evil, and his strategy diabolically clever; thus we saints are exhorted not to be ignorant of Satan's devices or evil designs (2 Corinthians 2:11). Satan is invisible and is a formidable foe indeed. But the Word of God tells us that our Lord is greater. There is no need for us to give up, surrender, or yield, for greater is He that is in us than he that is in the world (1 John 4:4).

And so I would encourage you. You are a member of the only army that has never lost a battle; a member of the only navy that maintains eternal vigilance and perfect surveillance over the seven seas; a member of God's marines who are always prepared; and a member of God's air force with angels encamped round about all who fear and love the Lord.

Lift up your heads and rejoice that you belong to a blood-bought armed services that is equipped (Ephesians 6:12-17), not entangled (2 Timothy 2:4), and that endures (2 Timothy 2:3).

November 20

. . . rightly dividing the word of truth. (2 Timothy 2:15)

God gave us the Bible to enlighten us. It is His Word to us, for us, to be memorized and stored in our hearts that we might not sin against Him (Psalm 119:11). It is good for our instruction, correction, discipline, edification and salvation. It must be rightly divided, correctly interpreted, spiritually read, honestly handled, and prayerfully considered.

The Bible is not an easy Book to understand. This is because it is the Word of God. And we are mortals. His thoughts and ways are far above our ways and thoughts. His Word is settled in Heaven, and we are earthbound creatures. His Word is truth; we are all liars. His Word is light, and we are born in darkness. Obviously there are difficulties for us when it comes to understanding the Bible.

Failure to rightly divide the Bible can lead to an unrealistic view of life. This is sad, because the God of the Bible desires that Christians properly understand the Bible so that they may enjoy life and live victoriously. The spiritual emphasis is upon the development of Christlikeness in spite of, or because of adverse circumstances.

Thank God for the indwelling Holy Spirit who makes possible for us to have peace within while others are at war; to *see* Christ in the midst of blindness; to enjoy spiritual wealth in the midst of material poverty; to be able to bless while others curse—this is our goal.

To step out in faith when others seek to walk by sight; to give out of our poverty to help others, while those who are well off close their fists and stop up their ears to the cry of the needy. To be consistent while facing a den of lions; to pray while facing a fiery furnace; to remain humble while exalted by Christ; to sing hymns while in prison, when others sing the blues though living in palaces; to enjoy things but not let things control us. Thank God for the Holy Spirit our Teacher as we learn to rightly divide (cut straight) the Bible.

November 21

But the Lord stood with me, and strengthened me.
(2 Timothy 4:17)

Paul Reggettz, 37 years old, a tall, thin, shy, heavily bespectacled man, lived near South Charleston, W. Va. On the morning of December 13, 1979, he had gone to work washing trucks, for he had dropped out of high school after the 11th grade. He had planned to go Christmas shopping with his wife and daughter, while his son was still in school.

When they did not show up at the appointed place, he went home to look for them. To his horror he discovered all three had been murdered. The police were called and Paul Reggettz immediately became a prime suspect. They cross-examined him for 14 hours, permitted him to make no phone calls and have no lawyer.

Finally, he broke down under the pressure and having had no sleep for two days, falsely admitted he was guilty. He spent the next 11 months in jail awaiting trial. The company he worked for sent him a notice of discharge while he was in jail; and all his wife's people believed he was guilty and turned against him too.

Reggettz said, "I felt like the whole world had turned against me. I was having nightmares and on more than one occasion, I almost took my life. I talked to Jesus then, and I said, 'Lord, you know I didn't do it, and you've got to help me.'" As the months passed, Reggettz sat in jail, reading his Bible and talking with the other prisoners.

Finally, a young man who formerly lived near the Reggettz family confessed to the killings. And Reggettz was freed, now with no family, no job and no home. He said, "The only thing that makes sense to these days is Jesus Christ. At least three times I almost gave up and just as I'd reach bottom, to the point where I'd decide how I was going to do it, the Lord would move on my heart . . . and as time went on He gave me the will to live again."

May Jesus Christ be praised!

November 22

But if he has wronged you or owes anything, put that on my account. (Philemon 18)

Paul is very tactful here. "If Onesimus did you wrong, Philemon, in any respect—I Paul want you to charge it to me." We are not sure exactly what occurred, whether monetary loss was involved through theft, embezzlement, mishandling of funds; or perhaps misrepresenting Philemon's reputation. This does not mean that Paul knew nothing definite about what Onesimus did, but that he graciously avoids speaking bluntly of any theft. This leaves it up to Philemon to claim what he considers right, or to refrain from claiming anything if he is so led.

Paul offered to be surety for Onesimus, "to meet every responsibility as to his past evil-doing" (Ironside). The apostle wanted the removal of anything from Philemon's mind that might hinder him from genuinely receiving Onesimus as a son of Paul and as a brother. "Whatever he did, you charge it to my account. Reckon his demerit to me."

Does it sound as if Paul says, "Philemon, you owe me one"? How wonderful to see here a picture of the Lord Jesus Christ, who of course, owed us nothing. But in love He came down, hung on the cross, and said, "Put your sins on Me. Charge them to My account." "Which account Lord, to *Discover*?" "No, I know where everything is already."

"Shall I charge it to *Master-Card*?" "No, you call me Master and Lord, and you say well; for so I am (John 13:13)." "Then to *American Express?*" "No, I died for the whole world, not just for America." "What about *Visa?*" "No, I don't need anybody's permission to go anywhere. I came all the way down from Heaven to Earth without a visa or passport. No, you charge it to Calvary! Put all your sins—past, present and future—put them on Me, and I will wash all of them away!" Rejoice today in knowing that the old account was settled long ago!

November 23

. . . upholding all things by the word of His power.
(Hebrews 1:3)

From time to time certain scientists predict that by such and
such a year the sun will be removed so many inches away
from the earth that all Baptists will no longer be God's
chosen people, but His frozen people. And others say that if
the sun comes closer there will be no longer any Primitive,
Missionary, Freewill or Seventh-Day Baptists, but we all
will be Tried-and-Fried Baptists. Those scientists point to the
highly regulated nature of the solar system in which we live,
although many see no personal God in the regulation.
Believers see Christ the Creator of the ages, by whom all
things were made; without Him was not anything made that
was made. It is inconceivable that the Creator of all things
should not likewise maintain or uphold what He created.

Suppose we had to pay the Lord for His maintenance
and preservation work, like those manufacturers who sell
their products to us and then send us notices for contracts:
"Pay us $34.99 a year and the item you recently purchased
from us will be protected by our convenient, comprehensive
warranty for one year. Provided you have not abused,
neglected, or otherwise mistreated the wonderful, efficient
machine you so wisely purchased from us."

If sinful man strives to maintain, preserve, sustain, what
of God? Well, if it were not for the Lord, man's feeble
efforts would fail. For you recognize that not all people
believe in upholding. Some believe in holding up. Not all
believe in building up. Some believe in tearing up; or is it
tearing *down*? So that selfishness is at the root of our
inability to preserve. However, in the process of decay and
disintegration, life goes on. World empires rise and fall. Who
is at the very center of it all? Who breathes life in all? In
whom do we move, live and have our being? Jesus Christ!
Through Him God's purpose for this world is achieved.

November 24

. . . upholding all things by the word of His power.
(Hebrews 1:3)

This opening sentence in the Book of Hebrews describes the glory of the Lord Jesus Christ. Surely this passage is good for the soul, for it tells us in a remarkable way who the Lord Jesus is. And everybody ought to know who Jesus Christ is! The verb rendered "upholding" means to carry, to bear, move by bearing, and thus to keep from falling. We learn that the Lord Jesus sustains, maintains, regulates, guides, propels and bears the universe. God the Son preserves the universe, and as the Upholder of all things He resists all disruptive forces.

This is because by Him all things consist, cohere or stick together (Colossians 1:17). Folks seek to break asunder what God put together and end up being broken in the process. This is because as the Upholder it is the Lord's job to bring all things to the desired goal or end He has purposed in His mind. And no man can successfully finally thwart God's plan. He is the One who is bearing up all things.

He preserves, governs, maintains and sustains the entire ecological system: the seasons, the air, animal and plant life, rising and setting of the sun, the orbits and distances of the planets, etc. Take for example the water or hydrologic cycle. Water leaves the earth by evaporation. Then the vapors form clouds, and the clouds condense into rain, snow or hail which fall back to earth (Isaiah 55:10).

Some of the water runs off the surface, forming into little brooks, then into rivers and finally into the ocean. Some of the water soaks into the soil and is absorbed by plant roots or soaks on through into the subsoil and porous rocks and may be stored up like a reservoir; and so the cycle continues. And who maintains the cycle? Who keeps this balance? Who sees to it that winter's icy grip is eventually released and the sap begins to rise? None other then the Lord Jesus Christ!

. . . upholding all things by the word of His power.
(Hebrews 1:3)

The message from this text echoes forth a strange-sounding truth. We are told that this upholding work of Christ is accomplished by the Word of His power. Do not picture some supernatural Hercules or a gigantic Atlas with the world as a global deadweight hoisted to his shoulder. The Lord Jesus does more than just keep us from sinking into oblivion or reversing orbits. His Word is powerful but the text says more than this.

Here is an omnipotent God who is pleased to express, manifest or reveal Himself by speaking. Through His word, His preaching, and His utterance power proceeds. His Word *is* the power to keep: "He spoke, and it was [done]; He commanded, and it stood fast" (Psalm 33:9). Hear the people at Capernaum say after Christ exorcised a demon, "What a word this is! For with authority and power He commands the unclean spirits, and they come out" (Luke 4:36).

When the Lord Jesus speaks something happens! He spoke peace to my soul one day. Did He speak to you too? And what thrills my heart is: He did not just get me started with a good push as a new creature on the Christian journey, but He is still my Upholder. He has sustained, maintained, preserved, spanked, chastised, defended, blessed, enabled, guarded, governed, watched over, protected, strengthened, and kept me. Has He done the same for you?

Praise His name He is coming back again for me. Is He coming for you too? For if I die before He comes, I will be with Him; and though my body lies sleeping in the grave, even there shall His voice, the Word of His power be heard and shall turn this corruptible body into incorruption. And if alive when He comes, I shall still hear His voice and in a moment, in the casting of a glance, I shall be changed from mortal to immortal, snatched up to the skies to seize the everlasting prize. Will you be there too?

November 26

Seeing then that we have a great High Priest who has passed through the heavens, Jesus the Son of God, let us hold fast our confession. (Hebrews 4:14)

Priest: Christ is a great High Priest, superior to all others. In service He surpasses the sons of Levi; in His Person and rank He is superior to Melchizedek. Merciful and faithful, called of God the Father; holy, harmless, undefiled, separate from sinners, made higher than the heavens, Christ is the perfect answer to man's inherent craving for a priest (Hebrews 2:17, 5:5, 7:26).

Look at the contrast: the high priest in the Tabernacle went in once a year, every year; Christ went in once for all. The high priest brought with him the blood of animals; Christ carried His own blood (Hebrews 9:14). The high priests of Israel died and were replaced by other high priests who likewise in time died; but Christ died once, rose from the grave, and lives forevermore.

Passage: He passed through the heavens. As the earthly high priest passed through the veil hanging there in the Tabernacle and entered the holiest place, so Christ entered not into the holy place made with hands, a mere copy of the true one, but into Heaven itself, now to appear in the presence of God for us (Hebrews 9:24).

Profession: Because we have such a great High Priest as Jesus Christ who has made this passage through the heavens, we ought to persevere. Through disobedience the Israelites in the wilderness fell short of that rest promised by God. The Lord wanted to see this rest fulfilled in Israel but the nation's disobedience disqualified them. However, God still desires that men share the joy and delight of His good and perfect work. This is the meaning of rest. That which Israel failed to gain is now available to us through Jesus Christ. What lies ahead for the believer is incomparable joy and delight, rest beyond man's comprehension.

November 27

Though He was a Son, yet He learned obedience by the things which He suffered. (Hebrews 5:8)

<u>His Sonship</u>: Even though He was God's Son, here was something He had to learn by experience. This is a remarkable fact. The Son of God was not exempt from the discipline He faced in completing the purpose for His coming. The author dares apply to the Son of God an idea that is really used when reference is made to undisciplined natures. Sonship did not, however, exempt Him from the school of obedience through suffering. And although He was the Son of God, yet He learned obedience through suffering.

<u>His Schooling</u>: "Learned" here is not the usual word found in the New Testament. It means to learn by use and practice; to accustom oneself to something; and to experience. This is not mere head knowledge of a formula in organic chemistry, or memorizing the multiplication table. Here is something He had to experience as the God-Man that He could not learn otherwise.

<u>His Suffering</u>: Because of the context some men would limit the suffering to that experienced in the Garden of Gethsemane. In Hebrews 5:7 are the words "prayers and supplications, with vehement cries and tears." However, the school of suffering is not thus limited. Gethsemane is included, but the school is not restricted to Gethsemane.

God the Son never had been separated from God the Father! The very thought was unthinkable, the idea boggling to the mind even after having been revealed to us. While sojourning here on earth He was destined to taste death for every man. Yes, He suffered. And I am glad that He did; for He demonstrated that it pays to be obedient. On the third day God the Father raised Him from the grave, and ever since mankind has been blessed because of what the Son suffered in the school of obedience.

November 28

. . . who have fled for refuge to lay hold of the hope set before us. (Hebrews 6:18)

Note that this hope, this expectation of good, is <u>Not Seen.</u> An anchor is a very fitting symbol of hope (Hebrews 6:19), and like an anchor, our hope is beneath the water and we cannot see it. "Hope that is seen is not hope; for why does one still hope for what he sees?" (Romans 8:24).

This hope is <u>Not Sin.</u> Such security, eternal and blessed, is not a license to sin. All Christians should live sanctified lives. It is not necessary to teach the possibility of losing salvation in order to motivate believers to clean living. The motivation for clean living is love, not fear; it is assurance, not doubt; and it is certainty, not uncertainty. You cannot lose that which you did not earn in the first place. Salvation is the gift of God.

This hope is <u>Not Self.</u> Our security as Christians is not found in us, but is entirely outside of us. Folks who believe they can lose their salvation give themselves too much credit. Our security is held fast by a risen, triumphant Jesus Christ, who went to Heaven to anchor our salvation to the immovable mercy seat of God.

Finally, note this is a <u>Set-Before-Us</u> hope. Thank God for the message set before us, and for the promise given. What God appoints, no man disappoints. What God promises, He keeps. What He swears to, takes place. This set-before-us hope is a very positive thing, an expression of the will of God. And we are to grasp firm hold of it, believe it, and know it is ours.

How firm a foundation, ye saints of the Lord,
Is laid for your faith in His excellent Word!
What more can He say than to you He hath said,
To you who for refuge to Jesus have fled?
(Rippon's Selection of Hymns, 1787)

November 29

Therefore, brethren, having boldness to enter the Holiest by
the blood of Jesus, by a new and living way which He con--
secrated for us, through the veil, that is, His flesh.
(Hebrews 10:19, 20)

You have the free right to come boldly into the very presence
of God. Go on in without hesitation, procrastination or fear;
and without holding back. Go on in, empty-handed. For the
text does not say *with* the blood of Jesus Christ, but *by* His
blood! There is no need to kill Him over again in some mass
or ritual. There is no sacrifice for us to take in.

Jesus paid it all, All to Him I owe;
Sin had left a crimson stain,
He washed it white as snow. (Elvina M. Hall)

Nothing in my hand I bring, Simply to thy cross I cling;
Naked, come to Thee for dress,
Helpless, look to Thee for grace;
Foul, I to the fountain fly, Wash me, Savior, or I die!
(Augustus M. Toplady)

By His blood, because of and in connection with His
blood the entrance is opened, never to be closed. Go on in
boldly to the throne of grace and obtain mercy, and find
grace to help in time of need. Go on in, and talk with Him,
for just a little talk with the Lord Jesus makes everything all
right. Go on in, and He will hide you in the secret place of
His presence from the pride of man (Psalm 31:20). Go on in
before His presence with thanksgiving (Psalm 95:2). Go on
in, for the upright shall dwell in His presence (Psalm
140:13). Go on in; for in His presence is fullness of joy and
at His right hand are pleasures forevermore (Psalm 16:11).
What a wonderful privilege the child of God has. Remember,
wherever you go today, you have access by faith into His
grace in which you stand (Romans 5:2). Go on in!

November 30

By faith we understand that the worlds were framed by the word of God, so that the things which are seen were not made of things which are visible. (Hebrews 11:3)

The doctrine of creation teaches the worlds were framed by the Word of God. He said, "Let there be!" and there was. Said the psalmist, "By the word of the Lord the heavens were made and all the host of them by the breath of His mouth. . . . For He spoke, and it was done; He commanded, and it stood fast" (Psalm 33:6, 9). He commanded, and they were created (Psalm 148.5).

We accept this by faith. We have to, for no man can find out the work that God makes from the beginning to the end; though he labor to seek the work under the sun, yet shall he not find it. Yea, further, though he attempts to know it, yet shall he not be able to find it (Ecclesiastes 3:11, 8:17).

When men sidestep the element of faith and proceed to construct their own solutions to the problem of creation, the best they can do is come up with a bunch of theories on evolution; and their hypotheses are worse than no solutions.

Look at it this way: If the Bible is mistaken in its science facts, how do I know it is accurate in what it has to say about the nature and character of God? Surely theology is much more important than science. Can the Bible be scientifically inaccurate, yet theologically dependable? Can the Bible be historically, geographically, chronologically, psychologically false, in error, and yet be right theologically?

I do not believe so. If wrong about what we see, how do we know it is right about what we do not and cannot see? The doctrine of creation teaches that life is not an accident. There are causes behind effects. Thus men need to ask themselves: "Why are we here? What are we doing here? What is life all about? What is the purpose in all of this?" Behind life is God. Failure to believe there is a Creator is destructive to the dignity of man, the very one whom God created!

December 1

It is impossible . . . (Hebrews 11:6)

To please God without faith (Hebrews 11:6): Seeing and believing is not good enough, for you cannot believe everything you see. Even when visible manifestations of His presence and power are given, men fail to believe or obey. Faith is taking God at His Word, regardless of what we see, hear, feel or what our condition may be. People who are experience-oriented, who rely upon their emotions to guide them through life evidently do not understand that self and feelings can lead them astray or that Satan can deceive them.

To love God without love of the brethren (1 John 4:20f): Our lives must not make a lie out of our lips. While we should be vocal in our praise of God, at the same time we should be practical in our expression of that love. God so loved that He gave. It was not just talk with Him. If we claim to love God, whom we cannot see, then we must not neglect those opportunities to love folks we see daily. Visible love for fellow Christian workers is proof of our love for God. Piety is productive. But if our claim to love God is false then false character is revealed. For love must express itself in action. If it is not expressed to fellow saints whom we see, how can we properly express it to God who is invisible?

To see the Lord without holiness (Hebrews 12:14): Holiness or sanctification must be seen in two ways: positional and conditional. When we accept the shed blood of Jesus Christ we are placed in His body. It is not something we feel; it is something God does to us and for us (1 Corinthians 12.13). He sets us apart, separates us unto Himself. And this act of setting apart is called sanctification or positional holiness. Through the eyes of Christ we are perfect. But thank Him also for conditional holiness, enabling those declared holy to also *live* the separated life. Praise Him today for making possible that which otherwise would be impossible.

336

December 2

For he who comes to God must believe that He is.
(Hebrews 11:6)

What a fantastic thing we see here! There is no attempt to prove God, whatever is meant by the word "prove." The Bible simply says, "Here He is! In the beginning God . . ." We are not exhorted to study in order to first understand God. We are not told first to search and find Him; nor are we commanded to reason out His existence and rationalize why there is a God. No! We are ordered first to believe. Believe!

The only presupposition for drawing near to God is faith. And then through faith we discover the truth, God is. Belief is a road to reality. Taking God at His Word is assurance that the Word is God. Once we get this matter of believing straightened out, then spiritual eyes are opened. And we are led to sing, "It was there by faith I received my sight, and now I am happy all the day."

Look at this matter negatively. You cannot prove God does NOT exist. Strange, isn't it, how we Christians are so often put on the defensive. Why should I be challenged to prove God exists? Why not confront the challengers to prove their contention that there is no God? And let them pay their dues for membership in the Society of Fools (Psalm 14:1). If there is no God, then there is no Heaven for His throne, no angels to sing His praises or watch over the heirs of salvation; no Devil who seeks to become God and to be worshiped by men as God.

In time the earth will run down, for there would be no one to sustain it, renew it, uphold it by the Word of His power, maintain the seasons, keep the planets in their orbits, preserve the ecology, and perpetuate life. If there is no God there is no Hell. Then who will judge men? Who will enforce the principle that whatever a man sows, that shall he also reap? No, my soul protests—God is! I know, because He met me one day through Jesus Christ.

December 3

For he who comes to God must believe that He is.
(Hebrews 11:6)

Someone has said, "On earth there are atheists plenty; in Hell there are not any." No God? What a waste of breath. Hear our great grandparents who lifted up their voices while under the cruel lash of slavery and sang with joy and hope: "I got a home ina dat Rock, don't you see!" Tell me, if there is no God, who created Adam and Eve? Who saved Noah from drowning in the Flood? Who delivered Lot from a burning Sodom and Gomorrah? Who blessed Job's latter end; who gave strength to Samson, and wisdom to Solomon?

If there is no God, who delivered the Hebrew boys from a fiery furnace, and who shut the jaws of hungry lions for Daniel? Who guided the stone from David's slingshot into Goliath's forehead; and who cast out demons, walked on water, cleansed lepers, and raised Lazarus from the dead? Who met Saul of Tarsus on the road to Damascus?

Who paid the penalty for my sins there on Calvary's mount? And why is it that the more man learns, the more he discovers that he doesn't know? No God? What opium have we smoked, what deception has enmeshed us, what delusion, mesmerism, chicanery, fraud, hypnosis, brain-washing or magic has been practiced upon us that we should pray, sing, be baptized, shout, take Communion, build beautiful edifices, preach, give, work, cry, attend, serve, fellowship and worship in our churches?

Faith is a road to truth and reality. God is. And His Word is my defense: "In the beginning God." Because I believe the Word, the things that happen in my life back up, corroborate, and authenticate what the Word teaches. God is! I admit then that I cannot prove God exists. But I am grateful that He has proven Himself to me. Every step of the way He has given me assurance of His existence. He walks with me and talks with me. And that's why I'm determined to go all the way! I want to see Him for myself. Do you?

December 4

Looking unto Jesus, the author and finisher of our faith, who for the joy that was set before Him endured the cross, despising the shame. (Hebrews 12:2)

It was not to the past that Christ looked, but to the future, the joy that was ahead. This was not mere stoicism, or that chewing-gum-popping arrogant air of sophistication; this was no "that's the way the cookie crumbles," or "that's the way the ball bounces" philosophy. There is no joy in such attitudes. Some folks put on a front and endure. But they murmur, complain, grumble, pout, wag their heads; they are sullen, uncooperative, hateful, chafing at the bits waiting for their day of payback. Their outside endurance disguises their inside turmoil.

I do not mean to play down the awfulness of the cross, or its shame. Rather, ignominy and brutality, and the experience of life becoming death in order that the dead might have life, were made bearable because of the encouragement and motivation of seeing by faith the joy that was ahead. What joy did Christ see? Was it immortality that follows physical mortality? Was it the joy of restored fellowship with the Father? Was it glory that comes after suffering? Was it kingship that follows humiliation? Was it the return to Heaven after a sojourn here on earth? What joy did Christ see? Was it exaltation after abasement?

Was it the joy of being seated at the right hand of the throne of God? Was it the birth and growth of the Church, His body, His bride? Was it the sending of the blessed Holy Spirit to dwell in believers? Was it the completion of the written Word that men might know the will of God? Surely He saw you and me washed in His blood and made whole. And now today, with a mind stayed on the risen Savior, and the joy of seeing Him face to face, of holding His nail-pierced hands, of walking and talking with Him—with such joyful anticipation, you too can make life's tedious journey a delight.

December 5

Come now, you who say . . . (James 4:13)

"What are you doing?" "We're planning to take a trip."
"When are you going?" "Today or tomorrow."
"Where are you going?" "To Atlantic City."
"Who is going?" "Why, we businessmen."
"How long will you be there?" "A year."
"What will you do there?" "What we please."
"What is your pleasure?" "To buy and to sell."
"What is your purpose?" "To make money, of course."
"What has God to say about all this?"
"God? Who is he? What business is he in?"

James describes the nature of presumption as the attempt to determine the future without God. Note the thoroughness of the plans of the presumptuous: when, who, how, where, what, how long and the purpose of their business; all are contained in the text showing the very heart of their pernicious lifestyle, the system of values by which they live.

Some people live audaciously. Presumption is part and parcel of their lifestyle. In short, they are arrogant, overly confident, excessively forward. They leave God out of their lives. It is to just such people that James, the half-brother of our Lord, made this brusque, vigorous appeal. The words he used were calculated to arrest attention: "Look here! Listen to me, just a moment!" Such is the insistence of the appeal.

God channels or directs the attention of those who would live presumptuously. He keeps tabs on us; He knows how we live and where we live. He hears all we say and sees all we do. And He knows what we think. Sensitive to neglect, He does not want to be left out of our lives. The reason for this is that God created us for His praise and glory. Failure to include Him in our plans strikes at the very heart of the meaning of life. To miss this purpose, to misinterpret life's goal is to live miserably a life of death.

December 6

Today or tomorrow we will go to such and such a city, spend a year there, buy and sell, and make a profit. (James 4:13)

James deals with businessmen, itinerant merchants doing a lucrative business throughout the then-known world. He does not say there is anything wrong with being in business or making a profit. However, some men have green eyes with dollar signs for eyeballs. They see everything with a price tag on it. Making money is an all-consuming passion, an obsession with them. It is not unusual for them to cheat, deceive and make merchandise of people (2 Peter 2:3). Their presumptuousness shows they are worldly.

On the other hand, Christians should be thrifty, not money-grubbers, gold-grabbers or silver-lovers, using all their time, energy and money just to make more money. Materialism leads men to ignore their own finiteness, limited knowledge, transitory stay here, and the uncertainties of life. They soon act as if they are God, tossing loaded dice and making the spots come up as they wish (Proverbs 16:33). In short, the love of things leads to presumption.

The man who seeks to leave God out of his plans is related to the foolish man who says in his heart, "There is no God" (Psalm 14:1). He relies upon his concepts of security to preserve the lifestyle, possessions and power that he has. Oh, that he would hear the voice of Christ pleading: "The future is in My hands. Drop your nets; break loose from your gang; never mind your peers. Follow Me! And I will guide you on the way from earth to Heaven."

Lead, kindly Light, amid th'encircling gloom,
Lead Thou me on;
The night is dark, and I am far from home;
Lead Thou me on:
Keep Thou my feet; I do not ask to see
The distant scene—one step enough for me.
(John H. Newman)

December 7

Instead you ought to say, "If the Lord wills, we shall live and do this or that." (James 4:15)

There are three wills in the world: the will of God, the will of Satan, and the will of man. What counts most in life is the will of God. All other wills count for death. James reminds us here of the very heart of presumptuousness: it despises, disdains, dishonors and disrespects the will of God.

We learned earlier (James 4:13) how businessmen made up their minds what to do, where to go, how long to stay there, and how much money to make (hopefully); everything was cut and dried, determined and decided, fixed and settled. Like the mind of the atheist, God was not in all their thoughts. They merely mouthed the words "Lord willing," or wrote "D. V." (*Deo Volente:* God willing), which mean nothing if there is not within the heart the sincere surrender of self to a Sovereign Savior.

Failure to seek God's will in our individual lives leads to disaster. Failure to do God's will in the church leads to a phony church, one that is powerless spiritually, without the ability to win souls, edify saints, shine in the darkness, witness against wickedness, preserve as salt, defeat the Devil, tell the truth, or spread the Good News of the shed blood of Jesus Christ our Lord.

For unbelievers who despise the will of God either through ignorance, delusion or deliberate disobedience, there can be only one result. Despise (look down the nose at) God and be despised by God. Disapprove of Him and be disapproved by Him. Despise Him and be left to the madness of man's will that manifests itself in misery. Or be sunk in the terrible will of Satan. Remember then: There are three wills in the world. But for the Christian what counts in life is the will of God. May His will be done in our lives today.

December 8

But now you boast in your arrogance. All such boasting is evil. (James 4:16)

One of the most important ingredients of presumption is hollow pretense, that boastfulness spelled out as acting smart when dumb; acting wise when a fool; pretending to be rich when poor; claiming to own what is not ours; and pretending to do what we cannot do.

All such acts tie in with the belief which some people have who believe that they can arrange the future when in reality the future is in God's hands alone. All such pretense is evil; and the presumption of protection actively wicked. The God of the Bible resents it.

He resisted the arrogant Pharaoh who said, "Who is the LORD, that I should obey his voice to let Israel go? I do not know the LORD, nor will I let Israel go" (Exodus 5:2). Jezebel swore to kill Elijah (1 Kings 19:2), but ended up trampled in the streets by horses and her flesh eaten by scavenging streets dogs (2 Kings 9:36).

Nebuchadnezzar boasted, "Is not this great Babylon, that I have built for a royal dwelling by my power and for the honor of my majesty?" (Daniel 4:30-34). God struck him with insanity for seven years. It is said that when Napoleon Bonaparte was all set to invade Russia, someone who had tried unsuccessfully to persuade Napoleon not to attempt the invasion, wrote him a note with this proverb in it: "Man proposes, but God disposes" (Proverbs 16:9).

Indignant, Napoleon answered, "I dispose as well as propose." God in heaven heard those words of pride, and as history records it, the invasion of Russia was the beginning of the end for Napoleon Bonaparte.

Keep in mind then the love of possessions, the attempts at protection, and the practice of pretension or boasting, all indicate the godlessness of presumption and the presumption of godlessness.

December 9

But now you boast in your arrogance. All such boasting is evil. (James 4:16)

We plan our affairs as if our own wills were supreme or there are no other wills in the world. This leads to boasting. Despising, regarding God's will with utter contempt leads to bragging. The word "boast" suggests here is one who makes more of himself than reality justifies; he promises what he cannot perform (Kittel). The apostle John called it the pride of life (1 John 2:16), the attitude of the worldly man who does not ask concerning God's will, but tries to make out that he can decide sovereignly his own destiny.

James reminds us that the man who acts as if he could dispose of the future is foolish. The future rests solely in the will of God. Man is too dumb, too ignorant, too weak, and too short-lived to decide the future. Only an omniscient God, who sees the beginning and the ending, who is Alpha and Omega, is able to plan far ahead and fulfill those plans.

Thank God our salvation was planned ages ago by the Lamb of God, Jesus Christ slain from the foundation of the world. We were chosen, elected by God before the world began. It was planned long time ago that in the fullness of time God the Son would be born of a Jewish virgin, Mary. And so He came.

And when the time was ripe, He died. He shed His blood according to schedule. According to a pre-planned program, He rose on the third day. He was seen at times during the forty days by believers. Then according to schedule He stepped aboard a cloud and ascended into heaven. When the time is ripe Jesus Christ is coming back again. May your theme today be: "Not my will, O Lord, but Your will be done."

December 10

. . . to an inheritance incorruptible and undefiled and that does not fade away, reserved in heaven for you. (1 Peter 1:4)

On coming back from Rocky Mount, North Carolina, I headed for Richmond, Virginia, and stopped and stopped and stopped along Route 95, trying to find a place to sleep overnight. I had to preach in Richmond the following morning, Sunday, and then proceed to Farmville, Virginia, to the nearby *Hol-Reba Bible Conference.* Well, every place was booked solid, or so I was told, even though the proprietors failed to put on their NO VACANCY lights (which I politely brought to their attention).

Finally, about 9:30 that evening I found a place where the manager let me have his room. The next day I preached in Richmond, and then headed for Prince Edward County. I never forgot the experience because at the church the folks shouted, several came forward for salvation, and after the offering was lifted, I received the grand sum of $20. I remember while later driving to Farmville saying, "Lord, thank You for finding a place for me to sleep last night!"

I learned the importance of having a reservation. Thank God we Christians have an inheritance reserved in Heaven. The word rendered "reserved" means also to keep or guard as a prisoner. Soldiers *watched* Christ hanging there on the cross (Matthew 27:36, 54).

Because the word is a perfect passive participle, literally, "having been reserved," it means the inheritance is the object of the action or effect of the verb. That is, the inheritance does not guard, keep or preserve itself. An outside force, the Lord, does the reserving. We are further reassured because the grammar indicates a present and continuous reservation and protection, suggesting an action in the past which has results right now. Expanded it means, "Having ever been and thus ever continuing to be preserved, reserved, guarded and kept in the heavens." What greater assurance could any one want?

December 11

Who are kept by the power of God through faith for salvation ready to be revealed in the last time. (1 Peter 1:5)

Sometimes folks leave their financial operations up to others, and they get scalped. Wills are lost or tampered with. Insurance policies disappear, signatures are forged. Bills are padded; jewelry stolen and funds are siphoned off. It becomes evident that someone should have guarded the guardians. Weak men, in love with the horses, and casino chipmunks in love with gambling defraud; and thieves break through and steal. Flimflammers trick the elderly.

Electronic swindlers and hackers cleverly manipulate and discombobulate computers; while pickpockets slit pants and pilfer purses, and sneaky punks snatch pocket-books. Fortunately, such characters cannot touch our inheritance. Heaven is too high for thieves to climb into. Astronauts have probed the heavens but have not yet gone as far as Elijah did some 2,800 years ago when he was swept up by a whirlwind into heaven (2 Kings 2:11). Many foes would rob us of our inheritance if they could, but they are powerless.

> *My Soul, be on thy guard, Ten thousand foes arise;*
> *The hosts of sin are pressing hard*
> *To draw thee from the skies.* (George Heath)

If evildoers cannot prevail here on earth, rob us of our inheritance, take away eternal life, chase away the Holy Spirit, prevent prayers from ascending, destroy the Bible or stop the preaching of the Gospel—if they cannot succeed in such nefarious endeavors here; and Satan and his demons cannot overcome the angels encamped round about us—they have no chance whatsoever of climbing up into Heaven and robbing us of our inheritance! Our God preserves our inheritance in glory, while watching over us on earth.

December 12

Rather let it be the hidden person of the heart, with the incorruptible beauty of a gentle and quiet spirit, which is very precious in the sight of God. (1 Peter 3:4)

It is nice to have a good reputation. Indeed, the Bible talks about our relationship with those outside the ark of safety (Colossians 4:5). It is also important to have good character. Personalities differ and we are impressed by certain types of personalities. But character is what you are on the inside all by yourself. True character shows itself under stress.

Anybody can act nice when things are going well; when there is money in the bank; bills are paid up; oil is in the tank and children are behaving. Some of us act splendid when we are in power, in the driver's seat, holding the leadership, or in positions of authority. But when adversities come, when we lose out, when illness strikes, things do not go our way, the balloon of pride is pricked—then what?

Well, the Bible says the truly beautiful woman is the one with a meek and quiet spirit. Such a one is precious, more valuable than rubies and diamonds, or silver and gold, of which my Father's coffers are full with riches untold. But such items of wealth are all corruptible.

What counts with God the Father is our growth in Christlikeness. Such growth should be the goal of life. What is meekness? It is an attitude of the character that bears with serenity the disturbances caused by others (Numbers 12:3).

What is quietness? It is that attribute of character that does not cause disturbance, or officiously meddle with the affairs of others. It is the description of one who does her own work and minds her own business. The Christian woman who is of a meek and quiet spirit is a beautiful person, a rare flower, a precious jewel, and prized by the God of the Bible.

December 13

Therefore let those who suffer according to the will of God commit their souls to Him in doing good, as to a faithful Creator. (1 Peter 4:19)

Without a Creator there would be no purpose in life or behind life. Our philosophy could easily become: Do before you get done, for when you die, you are done. How sad that sounds. To be alive without Jesus Christ is mere existence with no goal or aim. Folks without Christ are dead—alive physically, but dead spiritually.

Failure to believe there is a Creator is dumb, for surely we did not make ourselves (Beware of those "self-made" men!). If there is no Creator, then no one watches over us; no one is concerned and the blood shed at Calvary means nothing—God is not a faithful Creator; and Christ did not come to die for our sins—*if there is no Creator!*

But the record bears witness that God is Creator. Moses said, "Indeed heaven and the highest heavens belong to the LORD your God, also the earth with all that is in it" (Deuteronomy 10:14). Job wrote, "He stretches out the north over empty space; He hangs the earth on nothing" (26:7). David said, "When I consider Your heavens, the work of Your fingers, the moon and the stars, which You have ordained" (Psalm 8:3). Isaiah declared God created the stars by number and calls them all by name (40:26; Psalm 147.4).

Jeremiah said, "He has made the earth by His power" (10:12). John stated that by Christ "all things were made through Him, and without Him nothing was made that was made" (John 1:3). And Paul asserted God made "the world and everything in it" (Acts 17:24). Rest assured today, even as Simon Peter sought to strengthen the hearts of the persecuted believers of his day, if you believe God is Creator then you believe also that He sustains, provides for, takes care of, maintains, preserves, keeps, nourishes and watches over that which He created. We have a faithful Creator.

December 14

Casting all your care upon Him, for He cares for you.
(1 Peter 5:7)

Undoubtedly one of the keys to casting your cares on Christ is humility. A man who thinks he can make it in life without God is a man puffed up, egotistic, ignorant of the goodness of God. It takes a humble man or woman to relax and let go and let God, fully assured God is able to calm all alarms. And mind you, this text was written to Christians who at the time were bitterly persecuted.

Too often anxiety goads us to step out on our own. We push the panic button. We strike out. We attempt to solve our problems, to "take care of things." We reason, "Don't be a fool; don't let folks take advantage of you. Do before you get done!" And God says, "Let Me live My life in you; you be a fool for Christ." We rationalize, "God helps those who help themselves," but the Bible teaches, "God helps," period. We boast, "I'll get you if it's the last thing I do!" God says, "Vengeance is Mine, I will repay." Besides, it may well be the last thing *you* do!

We are to cast all our cares on Christ because He is able to make all things work together for our good. Do not just sing: "What a Friend we have in Jesus, All our sins and griefs to bear!" And do not just sing: "Take your burden to the Lord and leave it there"—**leave it there!**

Some of us have too many cares. We have concerns for our concerns and our worries even worry. We have given our cares a terribly high priority. Busy oiling the machinery, especially the big squeaks, we are not very useful doing exactly what God called us to do. Our production is pitiful because our priorities are poorly placed. And so the command comes: Roll all of our concerns on Christ. Why carry what our caring Christ commanded us to cast on Him?

December 15

To knowledge [add] self-control, to self-control [add] perseverance. (2 Peter 1:6)

For the sake of the goal he has in mind, the athlete striving towards that goal, desiring to fulfill his commission, refrains from all things that might offend or hamper (1 Corinthians 9:25). One year when Temple University played Syracruse University a brawl erupted. Five players were thrown out of the game—three from Temple, two from Syracruse; for ten minutes the basketball game was held up.

The senior tri-captain of the Temple team talked about the debacle: tension with the fans, people screaming, cursing, throwing beer, spitting at the players. Finally, unable to take any further taunting and verbal abuse, he jumped up and punched one of the fans. Later he said, "I'm embarrassed. I'd never do it again. That's all I've been hearing about from my peers, my parents. I'm afraid it could hurt my potential as a pro, that the scouts may think I lack self-control."

What God demands He supplies. Christians *can* exercise self-control in all areas of life because the power of the indwelling Holy Spirit is available. "He who is slow to anger is better than the mighty; and he who rules his spirit than he who takes a city" (Proverbs 16:32).

Is there significance in the fact that self-control is the last named in the list of the fruit of the Holy Spirit (Galatians 5:22-23)? Someone suggested self-control is the "summit of a Christian's spiritual walk". But how much credit are we to give the self in self-control? Do not misunderstand. God's Holy Spirit superintends the human spirit of every believer. We are not automatons, robots or mechanical creatures. We must not be lured into passivity to the point we make no effort to grow in Christlikeness. There is a will that desires to please God. And where there's a will, there's a way. All the credit for effective self-control goes to Jesus Christ (Philippians 2:13).

December 16

But if we walk in the light as He is in the light, we have fellowship with one another, and the blood of Jesus Christ His Son cleanses us from all sin. (1 John 1:7)

A paradox, a thing which seems contradictory, appears here. Walking in the light is to live the victorious life, where there is *no known unconfessed sin.* When the light reveals sin we are to judge it and put it away. "He who covers his sins will not prosper; but whoever confesses and forsakes them will have mercy" (Proverbs 28:13).

Do not argue with the light. Do not sit in judgment upon the Bible. And do not get angry with the preacher! Just walk in the light. Walking in the light makes available that constant cleansing effect of the blood of Christ. He is not dead; He is not hanging upon a cross; He is not buried in a tomb. Rather, He is alive forevermore! And the believer is cleansed once for all, saved for all eternity!

But there remains a right-now saving benefit. There is a daily cleansing or sanctifying of the conscience from guilt and moral dirt. By the blood of Christ we are able to walk well-pleasing to the Lord. When we were justified we were put in the light. When we were sanctified light was put in us.

Now we are to work out gradually that reckoned righteousness, assured that when we straighten up, when we walk in the light, and confess our sin, then sin's polluting effect is cleansed away. Look at it this way. It is like a big sum of money placed in the bank, and we are sent a monthly check on the interest.

So the blood of Christ saved us from Hell and the penalty of sin. But it also saves us every day from the power of sin. Look up then and see the sunshine of God's glory in the face of Jesus Christ. And it will cause you to enjoy fellowship with other saints because you enjoy fellowship with God Himself.

December 17

If we confess our sins, He is faithful and just to forgive us our sins and to cleanse us from all unrighteousness.
(1 John 1:9)

Response to a Requirement: Why confess our sins if we are Christians? Whether we understand or not, we should obey. Faith is taking God at His Word. Confession is an outward expression of an inner conviction.

Restore a Relationship: Sin has a present tense effect upon us. While our standing is secure, sin shakes our state; while our position is positive and permanent, our condition may be cracked. Because of sin we get out of fellowship with the Lord; by confessing we return in agreement with the Lord. Salvation is not affected by our sins; fellowship is. Just as Old Testament believers confessed and offered sacrifices in order to restore fellowship and prosperity with Jehovah, so we Christians confess our sins in the name of our Sacrifice, Jesus Christ the Lamb of God. The way to walk in the light is to continually confess and forsake sin (Proverbs 28:13), and enjoy the Lord's forgiveness and pardon.

Reason for Reverence: "But there is forgiveness with You, that You may be feared" (Psalm 130:4). Imagine! God forgives us so we may reverently obey Him. Here we learn something quite strange to our way of thinking: Gratitude for forgiveness produces reverence or fear of God. Respect for God is the product of the sense of forgiveness experienced when we confess (say the same thing about our sin that God says) our wrongdoing. It is a respect far greater than that engendered by threat of punishment.

The purpose of forgiveness is not to encourage us to sin, but to make us reverence God. His grace creates in us a desire not to grieve Him. All our sins—past, present and future have been forgiven! We are citizens of Heaven right now, with right-now available privileges. Rejoice that right-now forgiveness produces a right-now reverence for the Lord!

December 18

Beloved, let us love one another, for love is of God.
(1 John 4:7)

Christians are the people of God. We are people who love the Lord because He loved us first, and sent His only begotten Son to die on the cross for our sins. We Christians may express our love for Christ in many ways, but surely a primary way is to show our love for other believers. We are to "be kind to one another, tenderhearted, forgiving one another, even as God in Christ forgave you" (Eph 4:32).

As a second step, we demonstrate our love for unbelievers. In other words, the correct order is: Love God; love other Christians, and love non-Christians. Think about this order and see if it is good spiritual advice!

Whatever priority you may want to attach to the objects or recipients of love, you will agree the command to love other saints is often found in the Bible. For Christians to love Christians is to obey God. To love other saints is to wear the badge Christ gave His followers when He said, "By this all will know that you are My disciples, if you have love for one another" (John 13:35).

It is a new commandment because for the first time it is based upon that unique act of love in which the Incarnate God shed His blood at Calvary. For believers to love others who believe means that we have passed from death into life, and that we are not liars when we say, "I love God," or "We love God" (John 5:24; 1 John 4:20).

Keep in mind today these three reasons why Christians should love other Christians: Because:

(1) The *Source or Beginning of such love is God Himself.*
(2) Such love is a *Sign or Birthmark* from God.
(3) It means you are a good *Student of the Bible,* one who is not merely a reader or hearer, but a doer.

December 19

And everyone who loves is born of God and knows God.
(1 John 4:7)

The more you learn of God, the better you know Him, and the more you will love Him. The more you love Him the better you will act towards others who love Him too. Note the emphasis is not so much what you know *about* God, but knowing God. So we are not talking about facts, statistics, chapters and verses. Men can tote and quote and not know God. You can be a long-time church member and not know God. You can be a preacher and not know God.

This is a very real danger of tradition, formality, and religiousness (religiosity). To know God is to have Christ living in our heart. To know God is to be in tune with the will of the Creator. To know God is to be a good student of the Bible, growing in knowledge of His Person, character, mind, power, nature, goodness, grace, glory, mercy, loving-kindness, patience, faithfulness, steadfastness, holiness and truth.

It is to know the joy of salvation, the fruit of the Spirit, and the beatitudes he bestows. To know God is to have a clear conscience, clean hands, a pure heart, and a fixed and regulated mind. To know God is blessed assurance. It is to know His plans as revealed in the Bible and to rest assured He will do just what He said He would.

To know God is to become more like Jesus Christ. To know God is to obey His Word, to take Him at His Word. It is to love Him; and to love all that belongs to Him. To know God is to fellowship with Him; it is to love His Church; it is to appreciate His gifts. It is to walk with Him and talk with Him, whether we are in the hospital, or crushed by disappointment and ingratitude; or discouraged by feebleness and old age, or whatever! It is the ability to say, "Though He slay me, yet will I trust in Him."

December 20

And this is the testimony: that God has given us eternal life, and this life is in His Son. He who has the Son has life; he who does not have the Son of God does not have life. (1 John 5:11-12)

What is eternal life? The word translated *eternal* means age [unbroken], or pertaining to age [perpetuity]. The Jews divided time into the present age and the age to come. They saw the age to come as having no end. Thus the idea of eternal life or everlasting life is that life which is proper to the age to come. Since the coming age has no end, the life of that age is called eternal.

Eternal life is not just a future matter. It is also a present gift, as well as a promise for the future. Present tense verbs are used: He that *has* the Son *has* life. This indicates a present possession. You either have it right now or you do not have it right now. So that the emphasis of the song we sing is correct: "Get right with God, and do it now. Get right with God. He will show you how."

According to the record, eternal life is in Christ alone. Biblical Christianity is not broadminded. Rather, it is narrow and proclaims that the way to God is *only* through Jesus Christ. There is no other name under heaven given among men whereby we must be saved (Acts 4:12).

What is eternal life? It is being in good standing with God. It is the possibility of not dying physically, since those genuine Christians alive at Christ's coming will not taste death. Eternal life is more than mere existence; for frogs exist; but upon death they cease to exist.

Indeed, men in Hell will always exist. But they will not have eternal life. Such life is a partaking of the Divine nature. It is having the Holy Spirit living in you. It is to *know* God (John 17:3) intimately, personally. If you have Jesus Christ—believe in Him, love Him—you have eternal life right now!

December 21

That you may know that you have eternal life. (1 John 5:13)

Ignorance is the very opposite or antithesis of the emphasis of this text. The things John was moved to write are indeed factual, they are knowledge. I know there are those who would persuade you that you cannot know anything for certain now. They say such certainty is presumptuous.

But this text proves them wrong. God wants you to know, to be aware; He would not have you to be ignorant (Romans 1:13, 11:25; 1 Corinthians 10:1, 12:1; 2 Corinthians 1:8, 2:11; 1 Thessalonians 4:13; and 2 Peter 3:8).

Such awareness of what God has done, is doing, and shall do comes from the study of the Bible. While others wallow in ignorance, the believer should walk upright in knowledge. While others flounder in the sea of uncertainty, the Christian should move decisively in the arena of awareness. While others flit about aimlessly like chickens without heads, the Christian should rise up and soar like an eagle on wings of knowledge.

God wants us to know that the Bible was written to give us assurance. We can trust it; we can rely upon it, put our confidence in it, and believe it. To this end God gave us the Holy Spirit who lives in the bodies of all truly born again. "And by this we know that He abides in us, by the Spirit whom He has given us . . . By this we know that we abide in Him, and He in us, because He has given us of His Spirit" (1 John 3:24, 4:13).

Oh, doctors may probe, surgeons cut, technicians take X-rays and MRIs, and psychologists test and psychiatrists analyze and fail to see this personal, internal witness. Nevertheless, He is there. And He bears witness with our human spirits, He gives us assurance that we are the children of God (Romans 8:16). Thank God today that you know Him, and that you know you know.

December 22

That you may know . . . (1 John 5:13)

Have you heard it said, "What you don't know won't hurt you"? Well, the story is told of an 18-year old lad who dived from a sea wall to join a girl who was up to her neck in water. Minutes later he was taken out unconscious and paralyzed from the chest down. Police said the boy did not know the girl was sitting down in the water. So what you do not know *can* hurt you.

If you are ignorant of the fact that God's Word is truth, superstition can paralyze you. If you do not know God supplies the whole armor, your effectiveness as a soldier of Christ is hindered. If you do not know that God is no respecter of persons, racism can make you bitter. If you do not know Christ promised never to leave you, feelings of loneliness can depress you.

If you are not aware of the fact that all your sins have been forgiven, feelings of guilt can make you miserable. If you do not know that in Christ you are more than conquerors, defeat in small battles can make you think you have lost the war. If you do not know that God is a Burden-Bearer, worry will cripple you beneath its load.

If you are not aware that in Christ you are seated in heavenly places (Ephesians 1:3; 2:6), doctrinal error may lessen the joy of your salvation, as you confuse your state (condition) with your standing (position). If you do not know God makes all things work together for your good, adversities and set-backs can crush you down into the dirt, and make you a sad-sack-saint in the sanctuary!

However, we serve a God who wants us to know, to be aware. He has declared in His Word: "These things I have written to you who believe in the name of the Son of God, that you may *know* that you have eternal life." Thank the Lord today that our God does not want us to be ignorant.

December 23

Little children, keep yourselves from idols. Amen.
(1 John 5:21)

An ancient Arabian parable tells of a man who sent his four sons out into the world to get what learning they could. After four years they came home and he took them into the desert and showed them a strange sight. He asked the oldest son, "What is that?" "Why, the bones of a tiger," was the reply as the boy examined them. "And his age when he died was seven years and three months, and his length from the tip of his tail to the tip of his nose, was seven feet, nine inches," explained the son.

The father was greatly surprised that his son had learned so much and he turned to his second son and asked, "What can you do?" The second boy went to work and built up the skeleton of the tiger and set it on the desert sand.

Even more surprised, the father asked the third son what he could do. The third boy stuffed the tiger, covered it with skin, and put eyes in its head. "There is nothing more to be done," said the father. He wondered how he could test the fourth son who at that time spoke up and said, "Wait a minute."

He stood in front of the tiger, uttered some magic words, and sent a spark from the tip of his finger into the tip of the tiger's nose. The tiger rolled his eyes, life surged through its body, and then he opened his mouth, let out a mighty, terrifying roar, made a tremendous leap and ate up all of them!

How foolish for men to make that which destroys them. So it is with the gods they make. Rather than love the One and only True God who saves men from themselves, sin and Satan, they idolize their own gods. And they are devoured by them. Christian, guard yourself from idols!

December 24

Beloved, I pray that you may prosper in all things and be in health, just as your soul prospers. (3 John 2)

Is it well with your soul? I hope so, for it is dangerous to over-emphasize physical healing and material wealth. These days we are besieged by *Success Seers, Happiness Hucksters,* and *Prosperity Prophets.* However, the question remains: What shall it profit to be well off physically and materially, if we are mean and miserable, unscrupulous, and unwilling to submit to authority and reluctant to obey God's Word?

Those who push "blessing plans" and stress so-called "faith healing" ignore God's emphasis upon the spiritual; and disregard the Lord's priority which puts the spiritual first. "Conceive it, believe it, and achieve it" is a presumptuous and basically materialistic slogan. It is an attempt to remove God's prerogative to use illness in the lives of saints for His own glory and for the saints' higher good. Do not fall into that mentality that tries to make Heaven on this earth. Who knows what the materialists would do if our streets were paved with gold?

Whatever this symbolic language means, we won't find such streets and gates in Philadelphia. In God's Heaven only, not here on earth, shall all tears be wiped away, and there shall be no more death, neither sorrow, nor crying, neither shall there be any more pain; for the former things are passed away (Revelation 21:4). No matter how high our level of spirituality, or how victorious we are in Christian living, we may still be sick or poor, sick and poor, poor because of sickness, or just sick of being poor. Our poverty may not be from a lack of faith, but simply the permissive will of God.

What counts in life is God's will for our lives; and our attitude toward His will. If we believe in our heart that Jesus Christ shed His blood for our sins, then it *is* well with our soul. True prosperity and good success are ours!

December 25

Jesus Christ . . . who loved us and washed us from our sins in His own blood. (Revelation 1:5)

The God Who Loves Us: How wonderful it is to know this past great act of love at Calvary is still constant, continuing, present-tense, right-now love. For though saved, we saints often falter and stumble in disobedience, but the Lord still loves us. And it is this knowledge of His deep interest, concern, affection—indeed His love for us, that stirs our hearts and moves us to want to serve Him in a better way.

The God Who Loosed Us: The KJV reads, "Unto him that loves us, and washed us from our sins in his own blood." In Greek the word for *wash* is similar in sound and spelling to the word for *loose.* Only one letter makes the difference, so it is easy for someone copying the manuscript either to add or subtract a single letter.

However, *loosed* is preferable to *washed* here. So you will find it in many other Bible versions and translations. He set us free, released us, and loosed us from our sins. Of course, both renderings are true. Both make sense. And while the fact is God loves us, present tense, He also loosed us, past tense. While the loving goes on and on, the loosing was done once for all at the Cross of Calvary.

Note the loosing us from our sins was in connection with the blood of Jesus Christ. Only blood can loose or wash away sin; ritual, ceremony, education, hypnosis, meditation, medication, patriotism, politics, money, atomic energy, science, skin color, culture, etc. **cannot** eliminate sin. Without the shedding of blood there is no remission, no sending away, no forgiveness, and no loosing of sin.

The God Who Shall Lift Us: Perhaps today, we shall be changed and snatched (caught) up (1 Corinthians 15:51-52; 1 Thessalonians 4:16f). Even so, come, Lord Jesus!

December 26

Do not fear any of those things which you are about to suffer. (Revelation 2:10)

Why do the righteous suffer? Well, it certainly should not be for **crime.** The cross you bear is not for crimes you commit. Peter said, "But let none of you suffer as a murderer, a thief, an evildoer, or as a busybody in other people's matters" (1 Peter 4:15). Tribulation and cross-bearing are not the **common** sufferings of life which we have inherited. "Man who is born of woman is of few days and full of trouble . . . man is born to trouble, as the sparks fly upward" (Job 14:1; 5:7). Some saints try to make a bad cold, a broken leg, a smashed fender, or a snatched pocketbook the cross they bear. But such troubles are common to all, whether unbeliever or believer.

What concerns us here is that suffering which is associated with **Christ.** Bible tribulation is that oppression experienced because of our stand for the Lord Jesus. When we dare stand up for the truth, for righteousness, morality, holiness, or for the Word of God, and then get into trouble— this is Bible tribulation!

Why does God permit such tests? Is it to provide Him with an opportunity to show His grace? Is it to give the sufferer chance to obtain rewards or crowns? Is it to give the wicked time to repent? Would God then use our sufferings to win over the evildoer? Does tribulation strengthen other saints? (Has the Book of Job been a blessing to you)? Is it ours to suffer in order to purge our faith?

Think about such matters today, and hear again the exhortation Christ gave to the angel-messenger of the church in Smyrna: "Do not fear what you are about to suffer." Those words of comfort were calculated to strengthen the saints for what was ahead. Do not be afraid! We have his assurance: However long the tribulation, our ever-living Lord is able to help us. Through Him we are more than conquerors.

December 27

And you will have tribulation ten days. (Revelation 2:10)

What is the significance of the number ten here? There is the belief that ten distinct edicts were issued by Roman rulers demanding that Christians be sought out and killed. This series of ten persecutions began with Nero at the middle of the first century, and ended with Diocletian at the end of the third century.

But also see the number ten as meaning *complete*. Without denying the possibility of a literal ten, note that: Laban changed Jacob's wages ten times (Genesis 31:7); the Ten Commandments contain the whole cycle of God's moral requirements. The Israelites put Jehovah to the test ten times (Numbers 14:22).

The ten plagues in Egypt represented the entire round of judgment upon the gods and goddesses of that heathen land. Elkanah said to his barren wife, Hannah, "Am I not better to you than ten sons?" (1 Samuel 1:8). God made the sun dial go back ten degrees for Hezekiah (Isaiah 38:8). The Hebrew boys and Daniel were tested ten days; and the tithe signifies the whole property belongs to the Lord.

More could be said about the ten horns, the ten talents, the ten sons of Haman, the ten virgins, the ten lepers, etc. But ten certainly emphasizes the completeness of the trials; whatever the actual length of time, it would be sufficient, adequate to accomplish what the Lord desired. And so we take the number ten first of all as the exact measure of proving or testing necessary.

The saints suffering at Smyrna may well have been helped by the words of our Lord, "In the world you will have tribulation, but be of good cheer; I have overcome the world" (John 16:33). Knowledge of eventually overcoming all tribulation (literally, *pressure*) enables us to live victoriously.

December 28

And you hold fast to My name. (Revelation 2:13)

How do you hold fast to a name? What do you do? Do you mention it, adopt it, marry it or legalize it? Is it held fast by reciting it? Or using it as an "open sesame" formula? How about namedropping, an attempt to impress others that you know the big shots and the famous? Or is it by praise, forgery, or blasphemy? Just what is done to a name if you desire to "hold it fast"?

Study of the context helps us. Basically, the situation at Pergamos was not good. Persecution prevailed there; a man by the name of Antipas was killed. Perhaps he had been called before the Proconsul and ordered to burn incense and say, "Caesar is God!" and refusing to do so, he lost his life. The name Antipas means "against all", signifying perhaps this man stood alone against all of the enemies of Christ.

Singled out to be made an object lesson, he was put to death; but what an honor to be called by Jesus Christ, "my faithful martyr." Put to death by men, he went to live with God. Rejected by men, he was accepted by God. Put down by men he was picked up by God. Humiliated by sinners, he was exalted and honored by the Sinless One. And so this man, faithful in his witnessing was killed.

See then why the saints at Pergamos were commended for holding fast His name. There was a loyalty, a personal faith in the Lord Jesus Christ and all that this loyal faith represented. Holding fast His name is to firmly believe He is who He says He is, and never letting go your conviction concerning Him. No one holding fast the name of Jesus Christ can ever turn his or her back upon the Christian faith.

Take the name of Jesus with you,
Child of sorrow and of woe;
It will joy and comfort give you,
Take it, then, where'er you go. (Lydia Baxter)

December 29

These things says the Amen, the Faithful and True Witness, the Beginning of the creation of God. (Revelation 3:14)

The Amen: In each letter to each church the names given to Jesus Christ provide a solution to the problems of that particular church. Take, for example, the church at Laodicea, the last church age, the one in which we now live. Note the first name, *The Amen.* Taken from the Hebrew verb, *aman*, it means to support or confirm. By this name we learn He will uphold us in the midst of apostasy.

Where deceit, hypocrisy, pretension and phoniness prevail, in Him essential truth is expressed personally. So this title secures us in an age of insecurity. He is certainty in the midst of uncertainty; assurance where there is doubt. When men would make all things relative Christ stands as the eternal, true, immutable, and positive Absolute.

The Faithful and True Witness: How needed this name is in an age when perjury is so common. We tell lies without batting an eyelash; perhaps if we told the truth the eyelids might fall off. Christ, the Faithful and True Witness, strips away all phoniness in appearance, speech and deeds.

The Beginning of the Creation of God: The word rendered *beginning* means original source, first active cause, that by which anything begins to be, the origin. Christ is the Creator, out of Him came all things. Our present Church Age (Laodicea means *Laity-rights* or *People-rule*) emphasizing democratization, denies Christ is unchangeable (Amen), truly God's Witness; or that He is God the Creator! At such a time in Church History we do well to remember the Word is faithful, true, right, and by the Word all things were created. Hold high the blood-stained banner; and stand firm on the Lord Jesus Christ.

December 30

You are worthy, O Lord, to receive glory and honor and power; for You created all things, and by Your will they exist and were created. (Revelation 4:11)

See who speaks here. From whose lips come such words of praise for the Lord our God, Creator of heaven and earth? The scene is in Heaven; the speakers are the 24 elders whom we believe represent the Church. They are the redeemed, the glorified seated-in-Heaven believers of the Church age, crowned, and rejoicing in the Lord Jesus.

Paying homage to God enthroned, the 24 elders prostrate themselves before God and worship Him, casting down their crowns before Him. Crowns were worn by the victorious and by royalty. To take a crown off of your head and throw it down at the feet of another means you acknowledge loyalty to a superior being. In this case, the infinite supremacy of a Sovereign God who alone is Creator is denoted.

The elders declare by their act that they have no power, no honor and are without dignity of their own. All they have and all they are belong to God. We see why they say God is worthy to receive glory, honor and power!

Such praise directed to God as Creator is rarely heard today. The roles of Creator played by Jesus Christ and the Holy Spirit are often overlooked (John 1:3; Colossians 1:16; Job 26:13; Psalm 104:30; Genesis 1:1-2). Creatorship appears to be a forgotten doctrine. Surely the God of the Bible who created out of nothing, who spoke and the worlds came into existence, surely He is worthy of all power, majesty, splendor, praise, high esteem, honor, recognition, acknowledgment of glory, reverence, rule and dominion!

Upon the crystal pavement, down At Jesus' pierced feet, Joyful, I'll cast my golden crown, And His dear name repeat. (T. Shepherd)

December 31

Blessed are the dead who die in the Lord from now on.
(Revelation 14:13)

My two sisters died as young adults, having wasted away, afflicted by some paralyzing, undiagnosed disease. My older sister was named Beatrice. Only recently did I discover the dictionary pronunciation of her name is **Be' a trice,** not **Be at' trice.** I knew, however, that the name is Latin for *she who makes happy, she who blesses.* I recognize of course that it is the God of the Bible who blesses.

Having saved us through faith in the finished work of Christ, God stipulates conditions for further blessings [beatitudes]: faith, obedience, and service to others, confessions of sin, prayer, clean living, walking upright, and trusting God. Who is blessed? Those who walk not in the counsel of the ungodly, in whose spirit there is no guile, who turn not aside to lies, who consider the poor, dwell in God's house, whose strength is in God, and whom the Lord chastens. Who is blessed? The believer who observes justice, fears the Lord, delights in keeping God's commandments and His testimonies, and who seeks Him with a whole heart.

They that wait upon the Lord, and sow beside all waters are blessed. The believer who is poor in spirit; the mourners, the meek, those who hunger and thirst after righteousness; the merciful, the pure in heart, peace-makers, those hated and persecuted for Jesus' sake and who are reviled for Him.

Who is blessed? All who are not offended in Christ, who hear the Word of God and keep it; whose iniquities are forgiven, whose sins are covered, to whom the Lord will not reckon sin. They who endure temptations; who watch diligently for His coming; and who have part in the first resurrection are blessed. I realize this text refers to the Tribulation age, to those saints killed after the rapture of the Church. But I rejoice in its present application. And pray that you will be a blessing to others today.